Writing and Editing for Digital Media

Writing and Editing for Digital Media, 2nd edition, teaches students how to write effectively for digital spaces—whether crafting a story for a website, blogging, or using Twitter to cover a breaking news story or event. The lessons and exercises in each chapter help students to build a solid understanding of the ways in which digital communications have introduced opportunities for dynamic storytelling and multi-directional communication. *Writing and Editing for Digital Media* also addresses the graphical, multimedia, hypertextual, and interactive elements that come into play when writing for digital platforms and designing digital spaces. The book teaches students not only to create content, but also to become careful, creative managers of that content.

Based on Brian Carroll's extensive experience teaching the course, this revised and updated edition pays particular attention to opportunities presented by the growth of social media and mobile media. Chapters aim to:

▶ assist digital communicators in understanding the social networked, increasingly mobile, always-on, geomapped, personalized media ecosystem;

▶ help writers across multiple communication fields (journalism, marketing, PR, technical writing) make the transition from print to digital;

▶ teach communicators to approach storytelling from a multimedia, multi-modal, interactive perspective.

A companion website with exercises and assignments gives students the tools they need to put theory into practice.

Brian Carroll is Associate Professor of Communication and Director of the Honors Program at Berry College, and Adjunct Professor of Journalism in the School of Journalism and Mass Communication at the University of North Carolina at Chapel Hill. He is the author of *When to Stop the Cheering? The Black Press, the Black Community, and the Integration of Professional Baseball* (Routledge, 2006).

Writing and Editing for Digital Media

Second Edition

Brian Carroll

Routledge
Taylor & Francis Group

NEW YORK AND LONDON

First published 2014

by Routledge
711 Third Avenue, New York, NY 10017

and by Routledge
2 Park Square, Milton Park, Abingdon, Oxon OX14 4RN
First edition published 2010 by Routledge

Routledge is an imprint of the Taylor & Francis Group, an informa business

© 2014 Taylor & Francis

The right of Brian Carroll to be identified as author of this work has been asserted by him in accordance with sections 77 and 78 of the Copyright, Designs and Patents Act 1988.

Library of Congress Cataloging-in-Publication Data

Carroll, Brian, 1965–
    [Writing for digital media]
    Writing and editing for digital media / Brian Carroll. — Second edition.
       pages cm
    Revised and updated edition of: Writing for digital media. 2010.
    Includes bibliographical references and index.
    1. Online authorship.   2. Online journalism.   I. Title.
    PN171.O55C37   2014
    808.00285'4678—dc23   2013046150

ISBN: 978-0-415-72978-9 (hbk)
ISBN: 978-0-415-72979-6 (pbk)
ISBN: 978-1-315-85081-8 (ebk)

Typeset in Warnock Pro
by Apex CoVantage, LLC

Editor: Erica Wetter
Editorial Assistant: Simon Jacobs
Production Editor: Reanna Young
Copyeditor: Andrea Service
Proofreader: Hamish Ironside
Cover Designer: Gareth Toye

Contents

3   Editing for Digital Media: Strategies   57

PART TWO Practice

4   Writing for Digital Media II: Tools and Techniques   89

10 Digital Media and the Law   273

Introduction

As the first edition of *Writing for Digital Media* went to press in summer 2009, Apple unveiled its first iPad tablets. As this second edition goes to press, it is the Samsung Galaxy Gear "smart" watch that is grabbing the headlines. Technology's pace of change is breathless, and that makes a book on writing and editing for digital media a bit like chasing one's tail. The fast growth of social media, the proliferation and mass adoption of tablets, dramatic improvements in e-readers, responsive web design, and the replacement of desktop publishing by mobile as the dominant mode or platform for delivering content are just some of the bigger changes reshaping the digital landscape.

In revising *Writing for Digital Media*, this book is, in part, a response to the rise of social media and mobile media. But it continues to teach the basic skill sets of the digital writer and the digital editor, skill sets that transfer across most media. This second edition also broadens the intended audience beyond journalists and journalism students to include writers, editors, and producers of digital content across industry. The book does take an essentially journalistic approach, especially in terms of craft excellence; but the journalist's skill set is also the basic skill set of most communication professionals.

▶ PEDAGOGICAL GOALS

With these considerations in mind, the aims of this revised edition are to:

1. Help writers in journalism, marketing, public relations, technical writing, creative writing, and freelance writing, among other industries, to make the transition from print writing, or writing for flat surfaces, to digital writing, or writing in and for networked places and spaces.

2. Help digital communicators to better understand the implications of a communication world that is socially networked, increasingly mobile, always on, geomapped, and personalized.

3. Teach these communicators new skills, new tools, and even wholly new ways of approaching how to write, edit, and present digital content.

An important assumption of this book is the blurring of roles, responsibilities, and job titles in what is a digital age, one in which we all are consumers and producers, readers and publishers. The Internet has made it possible for anyone to publish his or her writing online almost instantaneously, and to reach the world with that writing. New rhetorical possibilities have brought with them both unprecedented challenges and opportunities. Thus, this book attempts to guide students and working professionals through this new landscape of digital media convergence, pointing them toward the best practices and techniques of writing and editing for digital audiences.

Understanding increasingly fragmented audiences and exploring how different media behave—their unique limits and possibilities—will help students to develop content that is ideally suited for digital formats and environments. With this book, students will analyze the technical and rhetorical possibilities of digital spaces and formats, including interactivity, hyperlinking, spatial orientation, non-linear storytelling, geolocation, and personalization.

▶ ON WRITING WELL

First and foremost, however, this book is about writing—clearly, precisely, accurately, with energy and voice, and for specific audiences. Fortunately, good writing is valued online and, yes, even on smartphones. And, unfortunately, it is still just as hard to find good writing on the web and in mobile media as it was and is in print. Though the premium on good writing has not changed, the process or activity of reading has, and dramatically so. People accessing information online and on the go via their phones are not so much reading as they are scanning, surfing, moving, and navigating. Digital writers, therefore, must be engineers of spaces and places in addition to being communicators with and through words.

Regardless of field or industry, irrespective of medium or media, at some level we all are storytellers. Throughout history humans have taught, learned, entertained, and communicated with stories, and this has held constant across media. Stories transmit information and transfer experience. This book, therefore, emphasizes digital storytelling and upholds the value of narrative, which also underlines the value of a journalistic approach to information gathering, writing, editing, and publishing online. Journalism, in other words, serves well the journalist and non-journalist alike, especially in digital environments, where the democracy of production and publishing are even threatening the relevance of such distinctions.

Building on a sound foundation of good writing, this book scaffolds on top new skills and sensitivities specific to digital spaces and places, which typically are also populated with graphical content, multimedia, and hypertextual, interactive elements. Learning how to achieve a careful, deliberate balance of these elements is therefore a primary goal.

Structurally, this book is divided into three parts. Part I, Foundations (Chapters 1 through 3), is devoted the fundamentals of writing and editing well, and to the stark differences between writing for flat surfaces (analog) and writing for digital spaces. Part II, Practice (Chapters 4 through 7), introduces students to the special skills and techniques needed to create content for digital environments and online publications. Part III, Contexts (Chapters 8 through 10), looks at specific digital contexts, including journalism, social media, and digital media law. Two appendices address the core values of digital journalism and what freelance writers can expect to be paid as free agents. In addition, a number of pedagogical features appear in each chapter to encourage students to further explore and build upon the lessons of the book:

▶ *chapter objectives* that establish the learning goals for each chapter;

▶ *chapter introductions* that concisely outline the major topics in the chapter and how they connect to chapter objectives;

▶ *chapter assignments* that ask students to apply the skills, critical perspectives, and best practices introduced in each chapter;

▶ *digital resources* that connect students to relevant websites and online resources where they can learn more about the topics discussed in each chapter.

By way of acknowledgments, the author would like to thank Louise Spieler, Rachel Lillis, and Maggie Hutaff at the School of Journalism and Mass Communication at the University of North Carolina at Chapel Hill; Erica Wetter and Simon Jacobs at Routledge; and the reviewers of the revision proposal. For help finding typos and other copy demons, the author would like to thank Diane Land and the students of JoMC 711, Writing for Digital Media, whose collective intelligence and wisdom of the crowds heavily influenced this work. Robert Stonaker assisted in preparing the manuscript and created some of the graphics. Josahandy Roman also created graphics for this book and assisted in securing copyright permissions. Andy Bechtel provided help with assignments. And Phil Buckley was an invaluable source for the section on search engine optimization in Chapter 3. The author would also like to thank Hisayo, Hannah, Sarah, and Mary Arden Carroll for their tolerance and forbearance.

PART ONE
Foundations

1

Writing for Digital Media

I sometimes think that writing is like driving sheep down a road. If there is any gate to the left or right, the readers will most certainly go into it.

C. S. Lewis

My goal as a writer is to make you hear, to make you feel – it is, before all, to make you see.

Joseph Conrad

If, for a while, the ruse of desire is calculable for the uses of discipline soon the repetition of guilt, justification, pseudo-scientific theories, superstition, spurious authorities, and classifications can be seen as the desperate effort to "normalize" formally the disturbance of a discourse of splitting that violates the rational, enlightened claims of its enunciatory modality.
Homi K. Bhabha, Professor of English, Harvard University, "Of Mimicry and Man"

CHAPTER OBJECTIVES

After studying this chapter, you will be able to:

▼

follow the basic rules of good writing;

▼

apply the fundamentals of grammar, style, and usage correctly;

▼

avoid common writing problems;

▼

determine the intended audience(s) and write specifically for that/those audience(s).

▶ INTRODUCTION

Whether a person is writing a news story, novel, letter to the editor, or advertising copy, the principles of good writing are the same. Different media place different burdens and responsibilities on writers, but the reason behind writing is always to communicate ideas in your head to an audience through words. Does Professor Homi K. Bhabha's sentence above clearly communicate his ideas? Can you understand what he means by efforts to normalize the disturbance of a discourse of splitting? This sentence was awarded second prize in an annual "Bad Writing Contest," because bad writing obfuscates and confuses; it promotes misunderstanding and perhaps even apathy. This chapter provides a foundation for good writing, including sections on writing's history, grammar, and orthography (spelling and punctuation). The chapter aims to help students identify weaknesses in their writing, then to offer help and resources to improve in those weak areas.

▶ THE MEDIUM IS THE MESSAGE: A BRIEF HISTORY OF WRITING

The writing tools of today are a far cry from the cave man's stone. Think about how the innovation of clay tablets, the first portable writing artifact, changed the written record of human history. Next, consider texting, snapchatting, mobile media, and the ways in which these and other digital technologies and tools are changing the way people communicate today. The tools that we use to communicate affect *how* and *what* we communicate. To better appreciate this truth, let's look to the beginning of writing for some timeless lessons on writing well.

In around 8500 BC, clay tokens were introduced to make and record transactions between people trading goods and services. This led to the emergence of a sort of alphabet. A clay cone, for example, represented a small measure of grain. A sphere represented a larger amount, and a cylinder signified the transaction of an animal. Only humans traffic in symbols, and these primitive symbols contributed to the genesis of writing by using abstract forms to communicate discrete human actions.

The alphabet we use today developed around 2000 BC when Jews in Egypt collected 27 hieroglyphs, assigning to each a sound of speech. This phonetic system evolved into the Phoenician alphabet that is called the "great-grandmother" of many Roman letters used today in roughly 100 languages worldwide (Sacks, 2003).

At about the same time, around 2000 BC, papyrus and parchment were introduced as early forms of paper. The Romans wrote on papyrus with reed pens fashioned from the hollow stems of marsh grasses. The reed pen would evolve into the quill pen around 700 AD. Though China had wood fiber paper in the second century AD, it would be the late 14th century and the arrival of Johannes Gutenberg before paper became widely used in Europe. So, what we think of as writing's primary utility—communication through language—proved a low priority for a long time, in part because literacy rates were so low. Until Gutenberg, there was not much for the average person to read beyond inscriptions on buildings and coins. When Gutenberg began printing books, scholars estimate that there were only about 30,000 books in all of Europe. Fast forward only 50 years and Europe could count between 10 million and 12 million volumes, which fueled increases in literacy. Democratization of knowledge brings with it advances in literacy.

In 286 BC, Ptolemy I launched an ambitious project to archive all human knowledge. His library in Alexandria, Egypt, housed hundreds of thousands of texts, though none survive today. Invaders burned the papyrus scrolls and parchment volumes as furnace fuel in 681 AD. So, some of history's lessons here should be obvious:

▶ Make a copy.

▶ Back up your data.

▶ Beware of invaders.

Although Korea was first to make multiple copies of a work, Gutenberg gets most of the credit in histories of printing. In 1436, he invented a printing press with movable, replaceable wood letters. How much Gutenberg knew of the movable type that had been first invented in 11th-century China is not known; it is possible he reinvented it. Regardless, these innovations combined to create the printing process and led to the subsequent proliferation of printing and printed material. They also led to a codification of spelling and grammar rules, though centuries would be required to agree on most of the final rules (and we are still arguing, of course).

New communication techniques and technologies rarely eliminate the ones that preceded them, as Henry-Jean Martin pointed out in his *The History and Power of Writing*. The new techniques and technologies redistribute labor, however, and they influence how we think. These early tools—pen and paper—facilitated written communication, which, like new communication technologies today, arrived amid great controversy. Plato and Socrates, for instance, argued in the fourth century BC against the use of writing altogether. Socrates favored learning through face-to-face conversation over anonymous, impersonal writing. Plato feared that writing would destroy memory. Why make the effort to remember or, more correctly, to memorize something when it is already written down? (Why memorize a phone number when you can store it in your smartphone?) In Plato's day, people could memorize tens of thousands of "lines" of poetry, a practice common into Shakespeare's day in the late 15th and early 16th centuries. Think for a moment: What have you memorized lately? Plato also believed that the writer's ideas would be misunderstood in written form. When communication is spoken, the speaker is present to correct misunderstanding, and the speaker has control over who gets to hear what. If you have ever had an email or Facebook wall post misunderstood—or read by the wrong person—these ancient concerns might still find a sympathetic ear today.

Another ancient Greek, Aristotle, became communication's great hero by defending writing against its early detractors. In perhaps one of the earliest versions of the "if you can't beat 'em, join 'em" argument, Aristotle argued that the best way to protect yourself and your ideas from the harmful effects of writing was to become a better writer yourself. Aristotle also saw the potential of writing as communication, as a means to truth and, therefore, a skill everyone should learn. He believed that with truth at stake, honesty and clarity were paramount in writing. These values are every bit as important and just as rare in the 21st century as they were in the fourth century.

Aristotle was also the first to articulate the notion of "audience," a concept that has been variously defined ever since. He instructed rhetoricians to consider the audience before deciding on the message (Vandenberg, 1995). This consideration more than any other distinguishes communication from expression for expression's sake, a distinction perhaps best understood by comparing visual communication to art, or journalism to literature.

Printing contributed to education in many ways, primarily by making it possible to produce multiple copies of the same text, allowing readers separated by time and space to refer to the same information. With the advent of the printing press, no longer were people primarily occupied by the task of preserving information in the form of fragile manuscripts that diminished with use.

The book changed the priorities of communication, and the book, like any communication technology, has attributes that define it:

▶ **Fixity.** The information contained in a given text is fixed by existing in many copies of the same static text.

▶ **Discreteness.** The text is experienced by itself, in isolation, separated from others. If there is a footnote in a book directing a reader to a reference or source material, the reader has to get that source, physically, by going to the library or filling out an interlibrary loan request, expending time and perhaps money.

▶ **Division of labor.** The author or creator and the reader or audience perform distinctly different tasks, and the gulf cannot be crossed. The book is written, published, distributed, and then bought or borrowed and read.

▶ **Primacy for creativity and originality.** The value set embodied by books does not include collaboration, community, or dialogue—values impossible in a medium that requires physical marks and symbols on physical (paper) surfaces.

▶ **Linearity.** Unless it is a reference book, the work is likely meant to be read from front to back, in sequence, one page at a time. After hundreds of years of familiarity with this linearity, non-linear forms have found it difficult to gain acceptance.

Compare and contrast the book's fixed attributes to web content, for which all writing and content development depends on a process of generating lines and lines of computer code. Webpages can be static, or writing on or for the web can be dynamic, increasing or decreasing in size, changing in font and color and presentation. Web "pages" aren't even pages; what you are actually viewing on screen is a picture of a page.

Web space is non-linear, with changing borders and boundaries. Unlike a book, the web is scalable and navigable, a space people move through rather than a series of pages read in a particular order. Online readers can easily subvert planned sequences of "reading" by accessing information in any order they wish. The web is also networked. Think about how the search function alone has changed use or consumption of documents compared to printed books, with search engines allowing a viewer to navigate directly to page 323 of a document and to begin reading there. Technology changes the way in which an artifact is used, read, stored, searched, altered, and controlled, and while these changes aren't necessarily progress, often they can be.

The idea that a technology is not inherently good or evil, that its virtues and liabilities evolve as its contexts change, is an important assumption that this book makes, one that underpins many of the book's other assumptions. It is not true that the technology of the book is somehow natural while digital spaces are somehow unnatural, though this is a commonly held view. Gutenberg's printing press was revolutionary as a technology; the Internet, too, as the product of hundreds of technologies, is also revolutionary.

▶ PRINCIPLES OF GOOD WRITING

When asked what he would do first if given rule over China, Confucius is believed to have said:

> To correct language. . . . If language is not correct, then what is said is not what is meant. If what is said is not what is meant, then what ought to be done remains undone. If this remains undone, morals and art will deteriorate. If morals and art deteriorate, justice will go astray. If justice goes astray, the people will stand about in helpless confusion. Therefore, there must be no arbitrariness in what is said. This matters about everything.

This section aims to help students better understand the principles of good writing. These principles are important no matter the medium and no matter the audience, and writing is a process of pre-writing, writing, editing, revising, editing again, revising again, and evaluating. Each of the principles that follow is paired with an exercise or two to demonstrate the instructional point being made. The exercises are designed to help you think like a writer.

Be Brief

> *I have made this letter longer than usual only because I have not had the time to make it shorter.*
>
> Blaise Pascal, 17th-century philosopher

Writing should be clear and concise. Readers need little reason not to read further, and this is especially and painfully true online and with smartphone-delivered information. Prune your prose.

EXERCISE 1.1

Here are some samples of cluttered writing. Rewrite the sentences to convey the same meaning, but with fewer words, perhaps using a sentence or phrase you have seen somewhere else.

Problem:

The essential question that must be answered, that cannot be avoided, is existential, which is, whether or not to even exist.

Solution:

To be or not to be, that is the question.

Now, try these:

▶ People should not succumb to a fear of anything except being fearful in the first place; and we should stick together on this so we can't be defeated.

▶ The male gender is so different from the female gender that it is almost as if the two genders are from completely different planets.

▶ There were two different footpaths in the forest, one that had been cleared by foot traffic and another that obviously fewer people had used. I decided to take the one that fewer people had used, and it really made a big difference.

EXERCISE 1.2

Hemingway once wrote a short story in six words. "For sale: baby shoes, never worn." He called it his best work.

The task in this exercise is to do as Hemingway did and write a short story in just six words. This will force you to be most judicious and deliberate in choosing your words. (This should be an easy, fun exercise for the more active Twitter users out there.)

Here are some examples, from *Wired* magazine's November 2006 issue:

▶ "Failed SAT. Lost scholarship. Invented rocket." (William Shatner)

▶ "Computer, did we bring batteries? Computer?" (Eileen Gunn)

▶ "Vacuum collision. Orbits diverge. Farewell, Love." (David Brin)

▶ "Gown removed carelessly. Head, less so." (Joss Whedon)

Be Precise

When I use a word it means exactly what I say, no more and no less.
Humpty Dumpty, from Lewis Carroll's *Through the Looking-Glass*

Strive to use exactly the word that your meaning requires, not one that is close or, worse, one that sounds close. A dictionary and thesaurus should never be far away (and online or with an app or two, they don't have to be). Here are a few examples:

▶ "A sense of trust was **induced**" >> No, trust is enabled or rewarded or encouraged, it is not induced.

▶ "Put into **affect**" >> No, put it into effect, though A might affect B.

▶ "She was **surrounded** by messages" >> Perhaps she was inundated with messages, or drowning in information, but surrounded by a ring of messages? Unlikely.

▶ "He was **anxious** to go to the game" >> He was probably eager, not anxious, unless he was playing in the game, in which case it is possible he was, indeed, anxious or worried.

▶ "He watched a **random** TV show" >> Perhaps he arbitrarily chose a show to watch, but it likely wasn't "random" at all; a broadcaster determined with great precision what to air and when. Random has a specific meaning, which is that each and every unit in or member of a population had an equal chance of being selected.

▶ "In **lieu** of this new information, we should . . ." >> No, in light of the new information . . . "in lieu of" means "in place of."

EXERCISE 1.3

Write a sentence for each of the words in the pairings of words below. The sentences should illustrate the differences in meaning or nuance in each pairing:

Example:

deduce: From the blood on the single glove, he deduced that the murderer was left-handed.

infer: By leaving her bloodstained glove on the table, she inferred her guilt.

▶ ambiguous

▶ ambivalent

▶ healthy

- ▶ healthful

- ▶ conscience

- ▶ conscious

- ▶ apprise

- ▶ appraise

- ▶ disinterested

- ▶ uninterested

- ▶ affect

- ▶ effect

Be Active

Just do it.

Old ad slogan for Nike

Though some passive voice is inevitable, too much yields writing that is boring and lifeless. Habitually writing in the passive is what we want to avoid. In the passive, which uses a form of the verb to be and a past participle, the subject is acted upon. An example:

- ▶ The ball was fielded by the baseball player (passive).

Inject energy into the sentence by flipping it structurally and making the player the subject doing the action:

- ▶ The baseball player fielded the ball (active).

You'll also notice that the active voice sentence is shorter and more readily understood.

EXERCISE 1.4

Rewrite the following two sentences to make them active and more descriptive.

First, here's an example:

Problem: I was tired, so I finished my work and went up to bed.

Solution: Exhausted and bleary-eyed, I somehow negotiated the winding staircase, spilling me into my bed. Work would have to wait for a fresh day.

▶ The labor leaders were frustrated by the latest offer which forced them to go through with the strike.

▶ She walked into the room without saying a word, sat down, and looked at me.

Be Imaginative

> *You have to try very hard not to imagine that the iron horse is a real creature. You hear it breathing when it rests, groaning when it has to leave, and yapping when it's under way . . . Along the track it jettisons its dung of burning coals and its urine of boiling water; . . . its breath passes over your head in beautiful clouds of white smoke which are torn to shreds on the track-side trees.*
>
> Novelist Victor Hugo, describing a train

Analogies, similes, and metaphors are like sutures and scalpels. In expert hands, they can be transformative. In the hands of quacks, however, somebody is going to get hurt. The reader can decide whether the surgery metaphor here is a good one or not. As Lakoff and Johnson argued, understanding experience in terms of objects allows people to pick out parts of their experience and treat them as "discrete entities" (1993, p35). Once a person has thus made his or her experiences concrete in some way, they can be referred to, compared, classified, quantified, and reasoned about. Metaphors are not merely language, therefore, but ways of understanding. Once expressed in language, metaphors begin to structure thoughts, attitudes, and even actions.

For the poet Maya Angelou, social changes have appeared "*as violent as electrical storms, while others creep slowly like sorghum syrup.*" For French novelist Colette, the skyscrapers of Paris resembled "*a grove of churches, a gothic bouquet, and remind us of that Catholic art that hurled its tapered arrow towards heaven, the steeple, stretching up in aspirations.*" Dorothy Parker, a riotously funny writer, once declared, "*His voice was as intimate as the rustle of sheets.*" (She also wrote that "*brevity is the soul of lingerie.*")

Visualize analogies and metaphors when writing them and see in your mind's eye the images they conjure. Are they apt and effective in conveying your intent? Are you mixing metaphors? Mixed metaphors are not only inaccurate; they distract the reader and discredit the writer. *"He smelled the jugular."* ESPN broadcaster Chris Berman actually said this in 2002 describing a playoff football game. (To hold a broadcaster to the standards of the written word is unfair, but it makes the point about how easily metaphors can go tragically awry.) It's also important to consider that because of cultural and language differences, global audiences will have great difficulty with metaphors and analogies. Great care should be exercised, using metaphors only where they *help* to communicate an idea and, conversely, do not *hinder* understanding or offend and alienate.

Berman's example points to another danger, which is that of clichés. It is easy to settle for a cliché, but in writing terms this is like arriving a day late and a dollar short, like taking candy from a baby, like picking some low-hanging fruit. And at the end of the day, when all is said and done, when the chickens have all come home to roost, laziness is perhaps the writer's greatest enemy.

So, avoid these clichés *like the plague*:

▶ last but not least;

▶ they gave 110 percent;

▶ he suffered an untimely death (think about this one for a minute);

▶ she was brutally raped (what could a "friendly" rape possibly be?);

▶ there were few and far between;

▶ just stick to the game plan;

▶ he fell off the wagon, on the wagon, or is circling the wagons.

EXERCISE 1.5

Think of some additional clichés, because the more the merrier. If you need inspiration, or a list of more clichés than you can shake a stick at, visit the American Copy Editors Society website, www2.copydesk.org/hold/words/cliches.htm

EXERCISE 1.6

Describe the Internet by using a different analogy in two sentences, each with a different emphasis in meaning. For attempts at this from the past, think information superhighway, cyberspace, or getting a Second Life.

Example: As an information superhighway, the Internet too often resembles a Los Angeles cloverleaf during rush hour.

Be Direct

> *I am hurt. A plague o' both your houses! I am sped.*
>
> Mercutio in Shakespeare's *Romeo and Juliet*

Shakespeare knew how to deliver a verbal punch with a stab of brevity. A short sentence, especially when paired with a long one, can provide energy and pop, as Ernest Hemingway shows here: "*He knew at least twenty good stories . . . and he had never written one. Why?*" For another example of this sort of rhetorical one–two punch, here's another master, the Reverend Dr. Martin Luther King, Jr.: "*This is our hope. This is the faith with which I return to the South to hew out of the mountain of despair a stone of hope.*"

In King's quote, the brief introductory sentence sets up the sentence of normal length that follows. In Hemingway's, the abrupt question, "Why?" adds emphasis to the character's flaw under examination. The short sentence (Hemingway's was one word) can also be used for transition. For Shakespeare, Mercutio's words are his last, like final, choking gasps for air.

Be Consistent

Failing to use parallel structure is one of the most common problems in writing. For example, if a list begins with a verb modified by an adverb, all of that list's items should follow that same structure. Verb tenses should not mysteriously change mid-sentence, nor should the singularity or plurality of subjects or objects being described or discussed vacillate or change in the sentence. Here are some examples:

Problem: One cannot think well, have love, fall asleep, if dinner was bad.

The solution: One cannot think well, love well, sleep well, if one has not dined well.

Problem: Jane likes to hunt and fishing.

The solution: Jane likes hunting and fishing.

EXERCISE 1.7

Rewrite the following sentences to correct problems with parallel structure.

▶ Delta Airlines promises a bounty of flights that are on time, have convenient connections and offer a well-balanced, in-flight meal.

▶ Heroes in movies are always wealthy, always get the girl, wear high fashion and usually arrive at the scene about two seconds after the bad guy has left.

▶ Telephones in movies are always knocked over after waking the character, never ring more than three times before getting answered, and get restored by frantically tapping on the cradle and shouting, "Hello? Hello?"

Be Aware

Even experienced writers can inadvertently fall into any number of common pitfalls. These include:

▶ **Stereotyping**—for example, "Journalists are cynical."

▶ **Generalizing**—for example, "Videogame players struggle with addiction." Every last one of them? This is a pitfall similar to stereotyping, and you can avoid it by being wary of words such as all, none, nobody, always, everything.

▶ **Plagiarizing**—of course, you wouldn't intentionally plagiarize; but it's easy to mistakenly commit this writer's sin by failing to cite a source or credit an idea to its originator.

▶ **Oversimplifying**—rarely is a choice either/or; rarely does a question or issue have only two sides. Attempt to represent as much of the spectrum of views or positions as is feasible.

▶ **Jumping to conclusions**—during summers in New York City, surveyors noted that sales of ice cream jumped. They also noted a spike in violent crime. Ice cream must cause violent crime, right?

- ▶ **Applying faulty logic or circular arguments**—using the Bible to justify one's Christian faith is an example of a circular argument, though citing the Bible is fine when explaining one's Christian faith.

- ▶ **Overusing pronouns and articles**—extremely common in writing, this problem is easy to catch. Look for mentions of "this," "these," "those," "he" or "she," "they" and "them," and perhaps the worst one of all—"it." Though the writer knows who or what is being referenced, the reader has no chance.

An Example of Good Writing

Alhough George Orwell wrote it nearly 70 years ago, his essay "Politics and the English Language" is as timely now as the day it was published, and in it you will find echoes of some of the themes of this chapter. Here are the most common problems in writing in 1946 as Orwell saw them:

- ▶ staleness of imagery;

- ▶ lack of precision or concreteness;

- ▶ use of dying (or dead) metaphors;

- ▶ use of "verbal false limbs" such as "render inoperative" or "militate against";

- ▶ pretentious diction (words like phenomenon, element, individual);

- ▶ use of meaningless words.

Orwell wrote that a scrupulous writer asks himself at least four questions in every sentence that he writes:

1 What am I trying to say?

2 What words will express it?

3 What image or idiom will make it clearer?

4 Is this image fresh enough to have an effect?

And he will probably ask himself two more:

1 Could I put it more briefly?

2 Have I said anything that is avoidably ugly?

In cautioning against "prefabricated phrases" and "humbug and vagueness generally," Orwell's essay provides writers with several points of advice:

▶ Never use a metaphor, simile, or other figure of speech that you are used to seeing in print.

▶ Never use a long word where a short one will do.

▶ If it is possible to cut a word out, always cut it out.

▶ Never use the passive where you can use the active.

▶ Never use a foreign phrase, a scientific word, or a jargon word if you can think of an everyday English equivalent.

To Orwell's last point, let's take a look at a concurring judicial opinion written by Supreme Court Justice Jackson in a First Amendment case from 1945, *Thomas v. Collins*. Revel in Jackson's directness, and appreciate how accessible his language is compared to most judicial opinions and legal documents generally, rife as they are with legal jargon. The court case had to do with the constitutionality of a Texas law requiring labor organizers to register with the state before soliciting memberships in a union. From page 323 of the decision:

As frequently is the case, this controversy is determined as soon as it is decided which of two well established, but at times overlapping, constitutional principles will be applied to it. The State of Texas stands on its well settled right reasonably to regulate the pursuit of a vocation, including—we may assume—the occupation of labor organizer. Thomas, on the other hand, stands on the equally clear proposition that Texas may not interfere with the right of any person peaceably and freely to address a lawful assemblage of workmen intent on considering labor grievances.

Though the one may shade into the other, a rough distinction always exists, I think, which is more shortly illustrated than explained. A state may forbid one without its license to practice law as a vocation, but I think it could not stop an unlicensed person from making a speech about the rights of man or the rights of labor, or any other kind of right, including recommending that his hearers organize to support his views. Likewise, the state may prohibit the pursuit of medicine as an occupation without its license, but I do not think it could make it a crime publicly or privately to speak urging persons to follow or reject any school of medical thought. So the state, to an extent not necessary now to determine, may regulate one who makes a business or a livelihood of soliciting funds or memberships for unions. But I do not think it can prohibit one, even if he is a salaried labor leader, from making an address to a public meeting of workmen, telling them their rights as he sees them and urging them to unite in general or to join a specific union.

This wider range of power over pursuit of a calling than over speechmaking is due to the different effects which the two have on interests which the state is empowered to protect. The modern state owes and attempts to perform a duty to protect the public from those who seek for one purpose or another to obtain its money. When one does so through the practice of a calling, the state may have an interest in shielding the public against the untrustworthy, the incompetent, or the irresponsible, or against unauthorized representation of agency. A usual method of performing this function is through a licensing system.

But it cannot be the duty, because it is not the right, of the state to protect the public against false doctrine. The very purpose of the First Amendment is to fore-close public authority from assuming a guardianship of the public mind through regulating the press, speech, and religion. In this field, every person must be his own watchman for truth, because the forefathers did not trust any government to separate the true from the false for us. *West Virginia State Board of Education v. Barnette*, 319 U. S. 624. Nor would I. Very many are the interests which the state may protect against the practice of an occupation, very few are those it may assume to protect against the practice of propagandizing by speech or press. These are thereby left great range of freedom.

This liberty was not protected because the forefathers expected its use would always be agreeable to those in authority, or that its exercise always would be wise, temperate, or useful to society. As I read their intentions, this liberty was protected because they knew of no other way by which free men could conduct representa-tive democracy.

Opinion available: http://supreme.justia.com/us/323/516/case.html.

The first thing you may notice is how Jackson is present with you in and through his writing. He is speaking to you, you right here, right now. He isn't "performing," trying to impress you with rhetorical flourishes and impressive legal diction. In addition, Jack-son's intellect, voice, and method of thinking are on vivid display. He first identifies what he sees as the core issue. He presents the facts. He identifies the principles by which he will decide. He decides. Then, he explains his decision in such a way that non-lawyers can understand him. In short, Jackson says what he means and means what he says.

▶ GETTING STARTED: PUTTING YOUR IDEAS IN WORDS

You now have a grounding in how writing has evolved, and why. You can gain inspiration from Pascal, Hemingway, Shakespeare, and Joyce. Finally, it is time to write. The steps that follow are designed to help you get started, and to start well.

A. Get the Idea: Determine Your Purpose

▶ **Freewrite:** write down anything and everything that comes to your mind. Clean it out. Rid your mind of mental "lint" so that you can focus on the writing task.

▶ **Brainstorm:** next, write down anything you think of related to the task, even if it seems irrelevant at the moment. There is no judgment in brainstorming, which, to use a sailing metaphor, can be akin to producing your own wind. As the Latin proverb goes, "If there is no wind, row!" The best way to get some ideas, at least one good idea, is to generate a bunch of ideas.

▶ **Write a purpose statement:** write down your thesis or purpose statement at the top of the page, then write under it all the ideas that flow from that thesis, including sources, questions to pursue, and things not to do.

▶ **Cluster:** this writing exercise is similar to brainstorming, but it is designed for visual learners and thinkers. To "cluster," put a main idea in the middle of the page, perhaps in a bubble or circle, then link to that bubble as many related ideas as you can, then ideas related to the related ideas, and so on. Your ideas should radiate out from a conceptual center, giving you a mind map to guide the writing.

B. Map It Out

The previous activities have helped you to establish your purpose. You're almost ready to write. First, think through this series of purpose-driven questions:

▶ What is my topic?

▶ What are my main point(s) or themes?

▶ Who is my primary audience? Do I have any secondary audiences?

▶ What is my goal in writing this?

▶ What sources will I use?

▶ How will I gather my information?

▶ What's my deadline?

A Word About Audience

Knowledge about who you are trying to serve should influence topic, tone, complexity, and presentation. To help you think through this all-important question, here are some prompts adapted from a worksheet developed by long-time literary agent Laurie Rozakis (1997):

1   How old are your readers?

2   What is their gender?

3   How much education do they have?

4   Are they mainly urban, rural, or suburban?

5   In which country were they born? How much is known about their culture and heritage?

6   What is their socio-economic status?

7   How much does the audience already know about the topic?

8   How do they feel about the topic? Will they be neutral, oppositional, or will this be more like preaching to the choir?

The answers to all of these questions might not yet be available. That's fine; the point at this early stage is to begin considering the readers* or users* as completely as possible before you begin writing or even gathering information.

BOX 1.1   *Interactors*

*We do not have a word for the people we are trying to serve in digital spaces. In the past, we have called them readers, users, consumers, and visitors, to list only a few. None of these terms adequately encompass the range of activities that people perform online, with their smartphones and with digital communication. A better term is desperately needed. They do more than read. They do more than "use" (and "users" has unfortunate drug-use connotations). What should we call the people who visit our blogs and websites, use our apps, interact with our content, and join the conversation via social media? This book suggests the term "interactors," and it uses this term throughout. "Interactor" better includes and allows for the multiplicity of activities our "readers" or users do in digital spaces. The term also hints at the various identities and personas people create and express in digital spaces, from LinkedIn to Facebook to Twitter and beyond.

C. Outlining and Storyboarding

Outlining helped to prepare this chapter, laying out a basic architecture for the presentation of its points. So, after you've answered some basic questions about purpose and audience, it's time to organize and lay out how the content will be presented. The metaphor here is new home construction. A blueprint (and other site maps and renderings) are used to organize the work, and it is especially useful when different pieces of the project are being done at different times by different people. For your writing, this blueprint can be changed, and it does not have to be elaborate, with Roman numerals and series of alphabetized lists. Even a visual map, using circles, for example, might do the trick.

Note: This is a good time to strongly recommend reverse-outlining, or outlining after the piece has been written, as well. So few writers do this, which is a shame, because it can reveal structural flaws, redundancies, awkward or ill-fitting sections, and perhaps a better order for the information.

Before getting to work, writing students are advised to buy or borrow a writing handbook like the one most of us used in English composition as first-year undergraduates. Examples include *The Everyday Writer* by Andrea A. Lunsford (my favorite); Longman's *Handbook for Writers and Readers*; *Rules for Writers*; or *When Words Collide*. Most every major publisher has one.

D. Revise It — Then Revise It Again

Ernest Hemingway famously said, "All first drafts are shit." Give yourself time to fail, to polish, to revise and perfect. The *only reason* for a first draft is to have something to work from and revise. Please Zen with this fact, and be tenacious! Editing and revising take patience and perseverance, but *all* good writing depends on it.

During this revision process, question hard the decisions you made writing the first draft. Reconsider, critique, and question the following:

▶ Your first paragraph. Even as simply an exercise, rewrite your first paragraph from an entirely different perspective, then sit back and see which beginning you like better. For that alternative beginning, try thinking sideways! Come at the subject from an entirely different angle.

▶ Your last paragraph. For the same reasons as were just mentioned, try rewriting your last paragraph. Is there a better way to bring closure and give your readers a soft, satisfying landing?

▶ The one or two sentences you absolutely love and simply could never tamper with or cut. Now delete them. That's right—cut them! Now ask yourself, "Is my writing stronger without my precious darlings previously there preening for attention?" The lesson here is to remove anything that is merely for effect, designed to impress, or to be admired as witty or clever. With this sort of language in mind, Hemingway described prose not as interior decoration but as architecture.

▶ Your adjectives. Look for redundancy and for empty descriptives, like "the long hallway," the "brilliant yellow sunflowers," or "the deep, blue ocean."

▶ Your adverbs. Often one good verb is superior to a verb–adverb combination. Example: "He ran briskly across the field." Try: "He sprinted in pursuit." While revising for adverbs, you might also reconsider your verb choices.

▶ Ambiguity, vagueness, generalities. If you are not quite sure what a passage means, your reader doesn't have a chance.

E. Myths

To serve you in improving as writers, it might help to explode a few myths. First, know that *writer's block does not exist.* It is a fiction, a fabrication, a myth, a crutch, and an excuse. Writing is a job, so we have to go to work. Imagine being a garbage collector: "Oh, I have garbage collector's block. I'm just not feeling it. I'll wait until I am inspired, until the muses of garbage collection have spoken, singing their siren songs into my ear." You may not feel inspired, but go to work anyway.

Writing is, or should be, "a rational, purposeful activity" that you can control, as Joan Acocella pointed out. She also noted that neither the French nor German languages even have a term for writer's block. So writing is not inspired by muses or magically, supernaturally guided by God. If there is no wind, start rowing. If you can't think of a beginning, start in the middle or the end. Establish habits. This book was written mostly in the mornings, 9 a.m. to noon, when energy was high and the day offered opportunity and possibility. The prolific author Anthony Trollope, writer of 49 novels, wrote 5:30 to 8:30 each morning. Ernest Hemingway wrote a workmanlike 9 to 5, at which time, of course, he began drinking . . . a lot.

Second, sometimes a first draft is all you need. No. Maybe for Mozart. We all want to write well right now, but don't expect too much from the first draft. In fact, expect very, very little. It is, after all, only the beginning. Allow yourself to fail.

Third, "I am a multi-tasker." No you're not. Well, you might be, but it's difficult to imagine Michelangelo painting the Sistine Chapel or chiseling David with an iPod pumping out Rihanna. Turn off all devices so you can write without distraction, disruption, or temptation. Most writers most of the time need uninterrupted peace and tranquility.

Fourth, writing is a chore. Yes, it was just written that it is a job, and that if there is no wind, start rowing. But writing is a tremendous privilege, a flowering of expression and even identity. So begin with a heart of gratitude. "Wow, I get to write! I get to maybe discover something about myself. I'm a writer." If it's a chore, the writing will reflect it. If it's a joy, the writing will reflect that, too.

F. A Writer's Checklist

Finally, read your writing one last time with the following in mind: a list that catalogs common writing problems the author has observed in students' writing over the years. This "top ten" list is the product of years of grading and editing undergraduate student writing:

1   Media is a plural term. Medium is singular. So media *are*; a medium, such as newspapers or broadcast television, *is*.

2   Avoid ethnocentric references such as "we" or "our" or "us" or "our country." They assume too much, and they communicate exclusivity. Many readers might not consider themselves members of any one person's "us" or "we" or "our." What of immigrants, green card aliens, international students? What does "us" even mean? Instead, be precise by using the proper noun for the population or group you mean.

3   Look for problems with singular–plural agreement, such as "The government is wrong when they tell us what to do." The government is an "it." People who work for governments are a "they." So, "the government is wrong when it tells us what to do." Another example: "A, B, and C are a predictor of future behavior." No, together they are predictors, because there are three of them. Example 3: "The surfer is able to read the article themselves."

4   Repeating an earlier warning: beware of imprecise, even reckless use of personal pronouns such as "they," "their," "them," and "it." Which "they" is being referenced, because most writing includes discussion of more than one group? Which "them"? What "it"? "Their" refers to ownership, but by whom? The writer knows to who or what the words refer because the sentences flowed from the writer's head. The reader, however, will be confused.

5   A related issue is imprecision with adjectives. "A lot" . . . "more and more" . . . "massive amounts" . . . "very detrimental" . . . "a great deal." None of these tell the reader much.

6   Do your part to prevent semicolon abuse. Semicolons, colons, commas, hyphens, and dashes each have their own specific purposes, and referring to a writer's handbook often is the quickest way to discern those purposes. The comma, for example, is "a small crooked point, which in writing followeth some branch of the sentence & in reading warneth us to rest there, & to help our breth a little" (Richard Mulcaster, writing in his 1582 volume, *The First Part of the Elementarie*). A common apostrophe problem confuses "its" and "it's." "It's" is a contraction for "it is." "Its" is possessive. Hyphens hold words together, like staples, whereas dashes separate. "Twin-engine plane" gets a hyphen; "twin-engine" is a compound adjective. "She was—if you can believe this—trying to jump out of the car." This sentence, by contrast, gets dashes to separate the parenthetical phrase or interruption in the thought. Because dashes have no agreed-upon rules, they are overused and can be a sign of laziness.

7   After beginning a quote, make sure you end it, somewhere, sometime. It is a common mistake to begin a quote but then to forget to add the close quotes, effectively putting the rest of the treatise into the quotation. This is the writing equivalent of flicking on your turn signal, turning, then leaving it blinking the rest of the way down the highway.

8   A related problem concerns orphan quotes. Quotes should all have parents, so be sure to identify this parentage, or who is saying the quoted words, in the text. Orphan quotes are quotations dropped into an article without identification of the speaker or writer or source.

9   Be careful of relying too much on quoted material. You are subletting your precious real estate to someone else. Too many quotations can transform your writing into a thin piece of string merely holding other people's work together, like a charm bracelet. The writer should be providing some pearls, as well, which means taking the time to integrate and weave the parts into a coherent, meaningful whole. Rarely is there benefit in merely grafting in quoted material just because it is on topic and seems worded more ably than the writer thinks he or she could accomplish.

10 Give your writing fresh eyes. Regardless of how short your writing piece is, even a single blog post or discussion board comment, step away and do something else. Go to the coffee shop. Go for a run. Then, refreshed and renewed, return to your writing to give it one more read. You will be amazed at the problems, possible misinterpretations, and opportunities for improvement you will quickly identify. This is also a good method for dealing with anger, or when something someone has written online inflames or enrages you.

CHAPTER ASSIGNMENTS

1 Generate a writing sample of 750 to 1,000 words, which will provide enough of your writing to spot strengths and weaknesses. The choice of subject is entirely yours, but here are some suggestions:

▶   your first vivid memory of writing;

▶   your best (or worst) experience with writing;

▶   a short travelogue about somewhere you have recently visited;

▶   a richly detailed description of your "brush with the stars";

▶   an opinion piece on some question or issue of the day.

Whatever you choose to write about, be sure to include in your presentation:

1   a headline that distills or summarizes the writing;

2   identification of your audience(s);

3   a one- or two-sentence abstract, which will help us to begin thinking about layers of meaning;

4   a list of key words a search engine might use to find this writing piece online, which will help us to begin thinking about search engine optimization;

5   a tweet of 140 characters or less to drive interactors to your story.

2 Once the writing pieces are finished, students should pair up for a writer's workshop. This exercise can be extremely valuable from both perspectives, that of being critiqued and that of (gently) critiquing. Some might be nervous or uncomfortable critiquing a classmate's work, especially early in a course, but don't fret. Just be civil and constructive, and demonstrate that you have or are (quickly) developing a thick skin. Writing improvement demands a great deal of constructive criticism and, therefore, an increasingly tough skin and short memory.

Workshop partners should have at their disposal a writing handbook and this textbook. Which writer's handbook does not matter; they cover the same general topics. Each student should use the handbook to analyze his or her own writing and that of his or her workshop partner(s).

Length: also in the area of 1,000 words, but this target is admittedly arbitrary. Feel free to establish a conversation about the writing, which can be used to ask clarifying questions. It's also recommended that workshop partners exchange multiple versions of the writing samples.

Online Resources

Elements of Style (original 1918 edition) by William Strunk, Jr. (www.bartleby.com/141)
A free edition of the classic guide to writing well.

"More Clichés Than You Can Shake a Stick At" (www2.copydesk.org/hold/words/cliches.htm)
A list of journalistic clichés compiled by Mimi Burkhardt for the American Copy Editors Society.

Purdue University's Online Writing Lab (http://owl.english.purdue.edu/)
Style guides, writing and teaching helps, and resources for grammar and writing mechanics.

Writing Sample Analyzer (http://bluecentauri.com/tools/writer/sample.php)
This online tool takes a sample of your writing and then calculates the number of sentences, words, and characters in your sample. From these basic statistics, it calculates the Flesch Reading Ease, Fog Scale Level, and Flesch-Kincaid Grade Level—three of the more common readability algorithms.

▶ REFERENCES

Joan Acocella, "Blocked," *The New Yorker*, June 14 (2004).

Jacques Barzun, *Simple & Direct* (New York, NY: Harper & Row, 1984).

Homi K. Bhabha, "Of Mimicry and Man: The Ambivalence of Colonial Discourse," in *The Location of Culture* (New York, NY: Routledge, 2004).

E. L. Callihan, *Grammar for Journalists* (Radnor, PA: Chilton Publishing, 1979).

John Dufresne, *The Lie That Tells A Truth* (New York, NY: Norton, 2003).

Elizabeth Eisenstein, *The Printing Press as an Agent of Change: Communications and Cultural Transformations in Early-Modern Europe* (Cambridge, UK: Cambridge University Press, 1980).

P. Elbow, "Revising with Feedback," in *Writing with Power* (New York, NY: Oxford University Press, 1981).

Michelle Esktritt, Kang Lee, and Merlin Donald, "The Influence of Symbolic Literacy on Memory: Testing Plato's Hypothesis," *Canadian Journal of Experimental Psychology*, March (2001).

Fred Fedler, John R. Bender, Lucinda Davenport, and Michael W. Drager, *Writing for the Media* (Oxford, UK: Oxford University Press, 2001).

Lauren Kessler and Duncan McDonald, *When Words Collide: A Journalist's Guide to Grammar and Style* (Belmont, CA: Wadsworth Publishing, 1984).

George Lakoff and Mark Johnson, *The Metaphors We Live By* (Chicago, IL: University of Chicago Press, 1993).

George P. Landow, *Hypertext 2.0* (Baltimore, MD: Johns Hopkins University Press, 1997).

Tamar Lewin, "Informal Style of Electronic Messages Is Showing Up in Schoolwork, Study Finds," *The New York Times*, April 25 (2008): A12.

Gunnar Liestol, Andrew Morrison, and Terje Rasmussen (eds.), *Digital Media Revisited* (Cambridge, MA: MIT Press, 2003).

Elizabeth McMahan and Robert Funk. *Here's How to Write Well* (Boston, MA: Allyn and Bacon, 1999).

Henry-Jean Martin, *The History and Power of Writing* (Chicago, IL: University of Chicago Press, 1994).

John Pavlik and Shawn McIntosh, "Convergence and Concentration in the Media Industries," in *Living in the Information Age*, Erik P. Bucy (ed.) (Belmont, CA: Wadsworth Publishing, 2005): 67–72.

Laurie Rozakis, *Complete Idiot's Guide to Creative Writing* (New York, NY: Alpha Books, 1997).

David Sacks, *Language Visible: Unraveling the Mystery of the Alphabet From A to Z* (New York, NY: Broadway Books, 2003).

Lynne Truss, *Eats, Shoots & Leaves* (New York, NY: Gotham Books, 2004).

Peter Vandenberg, "Coming to Terms," *English Journal*, April (1995).

Rick Williams and Julianne Newton, *Visual Communication: Integrating Media, Art, and Science* (New York, NY: Lawrence Erlbaum, 2007).

Gary Wolf, "The Great Library of Amazonia," *Wired*, December (2003): 215–221.

2

Comparing Digital and Analog Media

*Writers of hypertext . . . might be described as the design-
ers and builders of an information "space" to be explored
by their readers.*

Carolyn Dowling, author

*The Web is jam-packed with empty, incoherent, ill-orga-
nized, meaningless, repetitive pages. Gunk. Spam. Junk.
Crap. It gives the Web a bad name.*

Rachel McAlpine, web designer and author

▶ INTRODUCTION

This chapter takes a close look at how reading and writing for
digital spaces and places is fundamentally different than reading and writing for print surfaces, such as texts and, using the
metaphor used by word processing software, "documents." In
digital realms, interactors do not merely read content; they
interact with the content. Unlike print media, digital media are
spatial, not static, and typically networked: most digital spaces

facilitate and encourage interaction. Hypertext and the ways in which social media platforms are engineered make non-hierarchical, non-linear presentations possible, so that interacting in these digital spaces is more like entering a sort of matrix and moving around within it than it is like reading a book. Also important in this chapter is examining how credibility of information is established and communicated in digital spaces, and how these activities are different than for establishing and communicating credibility of information for print media.

▶ THE MORE THINGS CHANGE, THE MORE THINGS . . .

Before we get to the many fundamental changes digital media have wrought, let's consider what has remained constant. Think for moment about how much our understanding of how to structure information can be traced to how information is presented in books. In fundamental ways, writing for digital spaces is similar to writing for traditional print media. The fact that writing appears on a computer screen rather than a bound book does not diminish the priority on clarity, concision, accuracy, and completeness. Good writing is valued in digital content just as much as it is for any other type of content. It may seem like there is more poor writing in digital spaces because there simply is so much information being posted, published, and pushed out. Anyone with a computer and an Internet connection can publish to the web, so many do; anyone can Facebook, tweet and text. What has been produced for all media across time largely has been mediocre or worse. Perhaps 90 percent of what people write, regardless of medium, falls into these categories. For digital content, that 90 percent rule still holds true; but because there is, overall, exponentially so much more information, there really is more mediocrity, more gunk, spam, junk, and crap. Quality still counts and it is still rare.

Also unchanged by newer, digital media are many of the important roles of the writer, roles and responsibilities that include:

▶ **Communicator of a message:** how many websites, tweets, and blog posts fail to make a point, any point? The skilled digital writer conveys a message in provocative, clever, amusing, interesting, and profound ways regardless of the medium. By making choices and employing medium-specific tools and techniques, the skilled digital writer is also effective because of the medium, or media.

▶ **Organizer of information:** with so much information, never have the roles of organizer, guide, and curator been more important. Decisions must be made about what is most important and, in leaving information out, what is not important enough. Good digital writers help readers to prioritize and create order out of all the available information.

▶ **Interpreter:** the message has to be right for the medium, tailored to leverage the particular medium's strengths and to mitigate its weaknesses. There are particular kinds of freight each medium is especially suited to carry, and all sorts of freight each was not designed to deliver. Try to debate politics with, say, church bells or smoke signals. The skilled digital writer knows each medium's tradeoffs.

▶ BUT TIMES THEY ARE A-CHANGIN'

Of course, digital media have also brought major changes in the ways we interact with information and in the expectations interactors bring to these media. Mentioned in the Introduction are the matrix-like spatial environments that digital media allow, a contrast to the fairly predictable paths of readership for print media such as newspapers and books. Think about the words we use to describe information and how to get to it online, words such as *hypertext, hyperlinks,* and *cyberspace*—spatial terms that connote movement. On the web, we *visit* a site and *navigate* in and through it. To get where we want to go, we Google or key in an address, a Universal Resource *Locator.* These are ideas and terms that do not apply to flat, two-dimensional printed pages.

The implications for digital writers and editors are dramatic: We should consider ourselves architects of spaces and places, and authors and guides for interactors navigating through these often networked, socially mediated spaces. The luxury, or perhaps simplicity, of working with linear, sequential documents is a thing of the printed past. Another implication is the need in engineering these networked spaces, and editing within them, to anticipate the needs and wants of interactors and the many paths they may want to pursue. As a result, we also have to provide consistent, clear navigational aids throughout their journey to minimize if not eliminate disorientation.

To demonstrate the challenge this spatial orientation requires, imagine having a job interview in Chicago, somewhere in the John Hancock Center or Willis Tower downtown. Your cab deposits you at the front doors. After walking in, how will you find where you need to go? You'll likely ask the front desk, or consult a directory like those most office buildings display in their lobbies. With the floor and office designation in hand, you're next likely to step into an elevator. Because the path you took was predictable, well marked and basically linear, you'll likely also have a pretty good sense of how to get back to the lobby and out onto Michigan Avenue once the interview has concluded.

Now imagine receiving a *Matrix* movie-like phone call teleporting you from wherever you are sitting right now immediately and directly into that same office suite in one of Chicago's tallest skyscrapers. This type of flight would likely be a bit disorienting, and it would be really difficult to discern exactly where you ended up. Identifying the city itself would be a challenge, even if the office had windows. This is, of course, analogous to the ways in which interactors flit about from website to website, using search findings to navigate deep within a website, ignoring or simply unaware of its homepage. This direct flight is facilitated by, among other things, tweeted (and re-tweeted) hyperlinks, Google search findings, and Facebook "likes." Lost in this ease of movement is knowledge of how the site's other pages and content are interconnected, like the floors and offices of a skyscraper, and the comfort or ease of mind that comes with that knowledge. It's up to us as engineers of digital spaces to provide the navigation and contextual relationships in these spaces that minimize disorientation and discomfort.

For the web, it means that each page must stand on its own as a self-contained entity that does not require readers to navigate to it by following any sort of prescribed path. However, the page does live as one part of a networked world of similar or related content, a world that facilitates and even encourages teleporting to lots of other interesting spaces and places. Let's take a look at a couple of examples—two from journalism and one that is a sort of tour guide to Paris.

The first stop on our mini-tour is *The New York Times*'s "Snow Fall" (www.nytimes. com/projects/2012/snow-fall/), a Pulitzer Prize-winning multimedia story package about a tragic avalanche in the Pacific Northwest. (Unfortunately, the costs associated with licensing images associated with "Snow Fall" through the newspaper's third-party properties management vendor prohibit the inclusion here of screen grabs from the package.) The multi-chapter series seamlessly integrates opportunistic video, stunning photography, and sophisticated graphics in a way that for the user seems natural, as if God-ordained. "Snow Fall"'s immersive experience carries the user along its story arc in a way that naturally flows, without distraction and with minimal effort required on the part of the user. The elements are unveiled with a timing that contributes to this natural narrative flow, a quality that is very difficult to achieve online. The package's designers accomplished this by timing elements to configure just as a user scrolls to the end of a component part, re-contextualizing each individual element as the story progresses. And while there are surprises along the way, at no point does the narrative flow break down or fragment out. In short, as this textbook went to press, there was no better example of world-class visual design utterly in service to expert storytelling and the overall user experience. "Snow Fall" is an example of masterful digital storytelling, whether viewed on a computer or an iPad. Of course the project required six months and a development team of 16 people—not an inexpensive project, and not a model replicable on any sort of mass scale.

Second, consider the *Denver Post*'s multimedia storytelling project centered on Colorado resident Ian Fisher as he went from high school graduate to recruit to soldier. The series, "Ian Fisher: American Soldier" (www.denverpost.com/ci_14868562#ixzz2DYIHcuSf), published in September 2009, can be "read" or experienced in any number of sequences. The *Post* combines photography (for which it won a Pulitzer), video and text, leveraging the 27 months that photographer Craig Walker spent with Fisher to develop the stories. Though the content is organized by chapter, how an interactor navigates the package is, of course, up to him or her. It's important to note, also, that visual and textual quality is quite high; this was a project worth doing well.

Finally, let's appreciate how Bruno Latour achieves both narrative and a sequential networkedness with his multimedia tour guide website "Paris: Invisible City" (www.bruno-latour.fr/virtual/EN/index.html). Exploring the City of Lights "as routine," as a particular type of urban space, the site's content forms a sort of narrative puzzle that readers get to piece together in any order they choose. Though this approach would not work for all presentations online, it invites us to think through how to organize and layer information, and how to meet expectations of interactivity and control. The graphics are admittedly dated, but the approach to organizing the information and allowing multiple paths through it are worth our notice.

▶ TIMELINESS, IMMEDIACY, AND PROXIMITY

Thus, digital media have dramatically changed the reader's expectations. In addition to the relatively new dimension of space, these newer media have changed notions of timeliness. Roger Parker (1997) wrote that the digital media "permit you to immediately communicate great amounts of selective and updated information in color at remarkably low cost." This immediacy means content can be updated, added to, deleted, and refreshed at whatever frequency a publisher determines is valuable or cost-effective. Compare this with the months or even years required to publish a book. Information can be disseminated instantly, so it is, and to audiences that have become conditioned to receive immediate coverage of breaking news events. Major news organizations adopting live blogging and Twitter, Instagram, and Tumblr to provide coverage in real time are just a few examples of this paradigm shift. This has led to a higher tolerance for error, recognizing that breaking stories and immediacy in reporting are breeding grounds for rumor and hearsay. But because there is no end to the news cycle, readers have come to expect continuous updates on big breaking stories. As Kovach and Rosenstiel (2007, p15) reminded, people "crave news out of basic instinct . . . They need to know what is going on over the next hill, to be aware of events beyond their direct experience."

Proximity, too, has changed, or notions of it, with geographically based definitions of locality being replaced or at least supplemented with those that have more to do with affiliation, vocation, and areas of interest. Because digital delivery facilitates immediacy, audiences have grown accustomed to offerings and options in multimedia—photos, audio, video, games, graphics, and social media-enabled conversation. Audiences demand more because digital media can deliver more.

Parker's reference to "great amounts" underlines the nominal costs of digital publishing, costs that have little to do with how much is being published. For print media, printing costs increase proportionally with the amount being published. A related point from Parker's mention of "color" is the increasing sophistication of screen resolutions, including those for handheld devices and smartphones, as well as of color palettes and electronic ink that closely mimic the fidelity of color in print. And full color in digital spaces costs no more than black and white, a luxury print publishers do not have.

▶ READABILITY AND "SCAN-ABILITY"

Among the more important changes digital media have brought, for better and for worse, are those related to the activity we call "reading." Research shows that attention spans have diminished, and that people interacting with digital media aren't, in fact, reading as that activity has been traditionally understood. The web reader sits with hand on mouse scanning text on a monitor that is an uncomfortable distance away. Dale Dougherty proposed a "three-second rule": a website has approximately three seconds to download properly, present itself, and engage the viewer. Count off three seconds while staring at a webpage or mobile app that is loading, and you will probably agree. One-one thousand, two-one thousand, three . . . Time's up.

For the web, then, and even more so for the small screens of smartphones, digital writers have to quickly get to the point. Brevity is valued in all media, but it has to be a top priority for digital spaces. Think for a moment about those writing news for delivery to and on the tiny display screens on smartphones, for example. Rachel McAlpine, author of *Web Word Wizardry: A Guide to Writing for the Web and Intranet*, advised that to successfully write for the web, "You need to switch from 'think paper' mode to 'think Web' mode." Web users are "monsters of impatience," she observed, making a principal challenge of digital writers to hold a reader's attention, even for a few seconds. Like the television remote, the mouse button and a multiplicity of apps mean our content is always a click or scroll away from oblivion. If the experience of reading in digital spaces is fundamentally different, then our writing will have to change, as well, which is the focus of the next chapter.

Before we get to specific tools and techniques, consider a few more fundamental differences between digital and analog media. Unlike ink on paper, the 0s and 1s of the digital realm are ephemeral and manipulable. Digital media, therefore, can accommodate both the shopper (or surfer) and the hunter. Though tablets and e-readers are improving the digital reading experience, it is still uncommon for people to curl up by the fire with a computer to luxuriate in the prose of Sir Arthur Conan Doyle and *The Complete Adventures of Sherlock Holmes*. The typical interactor, whether on the web or on her smartphone, has an immediate need for specific information. With the exception, perhaps, of reference books, only digital media allow this premium on specificity and search. With this specificity, and thanks to the low to no costs of digital publishing, we have seen a boom in micropublishing, niche publishing, and narrowcasting. Content for small, targeted audiences is common, as the spectacular growth in blogging, apps, and music and video channels attests.

Although the desktop is diminishing in importance, with tablets and smartphones taking precedence, it is still important to remember that CRT (cathode ray tube) computer monitor screens make reading uncomfortable, especially compared to the tactilely pleasant experience of reading ink on paper. This discomfort is the primary reason interactors scan content rather than reading word for word. And scanners need cues and clues, signposts and highlights. Specifically, scanners need expertly written headlines, deckheads, subheads, hyperlinks, lists, and variation in typeface. The next chapter will walk you through these tools and techniques.

▶ CREDIBILITY

All three of the important roles of the digital writer described earlier in the chapter as communicator, organizer, and interpreter rely upon the writer's credibility. The ways in which credibility is established, maintained, and measured are changing for digital spaces as compared to traditional media. Given the preponderance of digital writers and publishers, in many ways source credibility has become an even bigger issue in the digital age than in previous eras, as the misinformation and unverified reports tweeted and broadcast after the bombings during the Boston Marathon in 2013 put on dramatic display.

In communication fields, credibility is one of the areas or topics of study originating with the ancient Greeks. Systematic empirical research, however, only began during the 1930s and 1940s, because of interest during wartime in learning how to persuade, developing propaganda, and harnessing the power of radio. One reason for such sustained interest by news media in credibility research is the long-term decline in newspaper readership, which has been causally connected to a diminishing of credibility over time.

Since the 1930s, there has been no widely agreed upon definition of credibility, as communication researcher Philip Meyer pointed out. Meyer surveyed credibility research in mass communication and developed an index for the two key dimensions of credibility that he identified in the literature: "believability" and "community affiliation" (1988, p588). Believability is based on the notion that news media present accurate, unbiased, and complete accounts of news and events. Community affiliation encompasses a news organization's efforts in unifying and leading the community it serves, efforts that require some degree of harmony in outlook or perspective. Meyer's two dimensions are important in suggesting that the public can disapprove of the way in which a media outlet or source covers a story but still believe what it says.

The rise of the Internet in the late 1990s and early 2000s fueled interest in research on credibility in online media. Surprisingly, many if not most of these newer studies suggest that those who do look online for their information deem what they find as more credible than that found in traditional print media. Increasing numbers of Americans access digital spaces and places for their information, and studies examining web credibility show that the more people go online, the more credible they evaluate the information they find there. In fact, the amount of time a person spends online might be the single best predictor of that person's perceptions of credibility for an online medium. The more users rely on blogs, for example, the higher their assessments of credibility, in spite of the fact that bias is recognized and even seen as a virtue by blog readers. Blog readers are "seeking out information to support their views and are likely to consider information they receive from blogs as highly credible," researchers Thomas J. Johnson and Barbara K. Kaye found (2004, pp631, 633).

▶ BIAS

That last point is worth further consideration. Research has shown that the credibility of blogs has much to do with bias—that is, the inclusion of the writer's perspective in the writing rather than its absence, as is encouraged and even required in most traditional news media following the model of journalistic objectivity. As one blogging journalist put it, "Veteran journalists know that the objectivity ethos is the 'big lie' of their profession . . . journalists are beholden to various points to view" (Zachary, 2006). Geneva Overholser, professor at the University of Missouri School of Journalism, told the authors of *blog!* that 2005 would be remembered as the year "when it finally became unmistakably clear that 'objectivity' has outlived its usefulness as an ethical touchstone of journalism" (cited in Kline and Burstein, 2005, p9). Acknowledging bias, then, is an important new dimension to credibility of information in a digital age.

▶ IDENTIFICATION

Identification is a foundational communication concept that helps us to understand how blogs, Twitter feeds, and other single-author digital media can generate trust among their readers. While theorists since the writings of Aristotle have focused singularly on the role of persuasion in public discourse, Kenneth Burke called into question traditional notions by introducing a theory grounded in identification. As Burke explained, "You persuade a man insofar as you talk his language by speech, gesture, tonality, order, image, attitude, idea, identifying your way with his" (cited in Foss et al., 1986, p158). Humans are uniquely individualized beings, according to Burke, but when their interests are joined, or one perceives or is persuaded to believe that they are joined, then identification occurs, a description that resonates at the individual level with Meyer's notion of community affiliation described previously. Burke added that one is "both joined and separate, at once a distinct substance and consubstantial with another," with consubstantiality rooted in the notion of a perceived "sameness" (Foss et al., 1986, p158). Burke, therefore, provides insight into the apparent resurgence of authenticity and genuineness as significant factors in establishing and communicating credibility.

Blogs, Twitter, Facebook, and Tumblr, to name just a few, are powerful new tools in building audience, even community within that audience, by offering more expression by individual voices, with all their flaws and because of their personality. The "everyday person" voice of many blogs, for example, encourages identification in ways the dispassionate, clinical, filtered voices of traditional media cannot. These voices provide a sense of presence with the reader in a way that traditional media's detachment, which is, in part, the result of allegiance to professional norms such as objectivity, actually prevents. Americans have also said that they want more interactivity, transparency, and accountability in their journalism (Journalism.org, 2006). With interactive media, the roles of sender and receiver are blurred, even interchangeable, making distinctions between the two less meaningful. Importantly for digital writers, this blurring and blending is being welcomed by online and mobile audiences.

▶ TRANSPARENCY

Digital writers should aim to adopt more of the principles and techniques of good blogging, including the considered cultivation of transparency. Blog readers respond to authors' willingness to disclose their personal politics and biases, their readiness to acknowledge error and to incorporate or consider new information, and the sharing of and pointing to original source materials that go into their posts.

In 2005, *The New York Times* seemed to awaken to the need for greater transparency. *Times* executive editor Bill Keller acknowledged that his newspaper could no longer argue "reflexively that our work speaks for itself . . . We need to be more assertive about explaining ourselves—our decisions, our methods, our values, how we operate" (*The New York Times*, July 4, 2005, C1, C4). Echoing Keller's sentiments, Richard Sambrook, director of the BBC World Service and Global News Division, said, "We don't own the news anymore. This is a fundamental realignment of the relationship between large media companies and the public" (*Durham Herald*, October 5, 2005).

Of course, allowing journalists (or public relations practitioners or marketers, for that matter) to acknowledge and even base comments on their biases, as well as to point to and otherwise reveal source materials, is to relinquish control, and institutions are reticent to yield control. In response to this reticence, New York University journalism professor Jay Rosen argued that the new values and priorities should allow individual journalists (or public relations practitioners or marketers) to themselves be involved in creating trust, to be at the point of the transaction of trust with the reader, rather than merely relying on the institutional trust of the publication, firm or brand. In doing so, this paradigm actually empowers individual digital writers because they can now add to the organization's reputational capital rather than merely spend it or ruin it, addressing at the individual level the key problem of eroding credibility.

▶ ACCOUNTABILITY

Accountability requires that individuals, companies, and organizations explain themselves, to be clearer with readers how they operate and why. In journalism, for example, a backlash against objectivity, and a general misunderstanding of even what it is, pushed editors and publishers on the defensive. At a Harvard conference on blogging, Rosen said that mainstream journalism is "dying," in part, because it has insisted on objectivity and, in the process, has "killed the human voice." Blogs, he argued, marked the return of "real human voices" and "real human conversations" (Rosen, 2005). Facebook, Twitter, and a host of social media platforms offer further evidence of the primacy in digital spaces of these conversations and of the interpersonal dimension to a lot of what is being done online. A big question for news organizations, public relations firms, and marketers, among others, then, is how to adhere to professional standards, such as ethical news gathering and balance in the overall presentation of perspectives, but at the same time communicate in "real human voices." For a public to hold an organization accountable, that public must first know to what standards the organization is holding itself.

▶ IMPROVING CREDIBILITY

Credibility studies suggest several elements that can give users confidence in a digital source and its content. Briefly, these include:

- ▶ easy-to-use, intuitive navigation;
- ▶ user-friendly design;
- ▶ high-quality graphics;
- ▶ good writing;
- ▶ full contact information;
- ▶ expertise in the subject area;
- ▶ links outside to other relevant sources and sites.

One of the goals of Stanford University's Persuasive Technology Lab (http://credibility. stanford.edu/) is to understand those design elements that have an impact upon credibility. The lab's web credibility project found that a broad range of design decisions ranging from visual elements to information architecture to the use of advertisements can powerfully influence whether visitors are likely to find a website credible. Like human communicators, websites benefit (or suffer) based upon their appearance. Among the project's many findings are these highlights:

▶ First impressions are important. People tend to determine the credibility of a website based upon how professional they think the site looks.

▶ Including an organization's name in the URL increases credibility.

▶ Designers should make sure there is a clear distinction between information and advertising. For the information, the source should be identified and the authors' credentials presented.

▶ Navigation should be intuitive.

▶ Everything should work, including links, downloads, graphics and multimedia.

▶ The company a site keeps matters. Links to, or affiliations with, other organizations, whether online or off, can have an impact on credibility.

Stanford itemized a multitude of factors that affect credibility. Each of these factors, which are presented in rank order of importance or potential impact, can be placed into one of the general guidelines just listed above.

A credible site:

1   has proven useful to you before;

2   is by or for an organization that is well respected;

3   provides a quick response to your questions;

4   lists the organization's physical address;

5   has been updated since your last visit;

6   gives a contact phone number;

7   appears professionally designed;

8   gives a contact email address;

9   is arranged in a way that makes sense to you;

10   provides comprehensive information that is attributed to a specific source.

For information-rich sites that present articles, credibility is based, in part, on:

▶ the authors' credentials;

▶ transparency about citations and references;

▶ the sites the articles link.

Dr. Francis Collins is Director of the National Institutes of Health. Dr. Arati Prabhakar is Director of the Defense Advanced Research Projects Agency

Follow new developments relating to the BRAIN Initiative and other advances in science and technology at the White House Office of Science and Technology Policy Blog and @whitehouseostp on Twitter.

FIGURE 2.1 Author credentials as listed at Whitehouse.gov.

Stanford's findings also recommend that sites:

▶ state their privacy policies;

▶ feature design appropriate to their subject matters;

▶ provide search;

▶ link to outside materials and sources;

▶ rank highly in search engine results; and

▶ recognize who has visited before.

FIGURE 2.2 eBay's site recognizes return visitors.

Generally, there are two website categories that typically have consistently low credibility, according to the Stanford lab's research: websites with commercial purposes and those that give the impression, real or imagined, that they have been produced by amateurs. People assign much less credibility to a site they know is trying to sell them something. More than one ad on a page, no matter whether or not the site is primarily commercial, can greatly decrease credibility. If a site is going to have ads, those ads should be for reputable products or organizations. The more reputable the ad, the more credibility it carries. Technical errors and less-than-frequent updates are typical problems for amateur sites, as are non-professional appearances and less adequate contact information.

Diminishing credibility for a site, in rank order from greatest to least, according to Stanford's research, are:

1   making it difficult to distinguish ads from content;

2   rarely updating with new content;

3   automating pop-up ads;

4   making it difficult to navigate;

5   linking to sites not perceived as credible;

6   leaving dead links;

7   making typographical errors;

8   using a domain name that does not match the company's name;

9   hosting by a third party;

10   having a commercial purpose.

▶ TOOLS AND TECHNOLOGY: THE MEDIUM IS THE MESSAGE

Neil Postman, author of *Amusing Ourselves to Death*, observed that a technology, any technology, is "to a medium as the brain is to the mind. Like a brain, a technology is a physical apparatus. Like the mind, a medium is a use to which a physical apparatus is put ... Only those who know nothing of the history of technology believe that technology is entirely neutral" (1985, p84).

Let's consider the various media and what they offer, beginning with television, to think about what Postman was describing and to build toward a better understanding of the capacities of digital media. The medium of television operates with or through its own rhetoric, one that is predicated on a few essential qualities. Because screens are typically small—and with smartphones increasingly so—TV emphasizes characters and set pieces rather than sweeping, epic dramas. For the big stories, we turn to motion pictures, which are shown in multi-speaker rooms with wall-size screens, sometimes in 3D. Because TV delivers moving images, its rhetoric is about experiencing something, and experiencing it right now. TV knows only one verb tense—the present. Even a documentary on World War II gives the viewer a present tense experience of the war, or tries to. TV's rhetoric is incapable of helping us process a great deal of information or to think rationally about complex topics. For this reason, TV must entertain. Even that WWII documentary must, above all else, amuse and entertain. Because TV is turned to for entertainment, it must ask very little of its audience. Even multi-part TV series allow viewers to drop in, in the middle of the series, and quickly figure out what is going on. Because many can view a program simultaneously in different geographic locations—and, when crises strikes, they often do—TV specializes in enabling a sort of societal communion or ritualized viewing. Think of the coverage on September 6, 1997, of Princess Diana's funeral, or perhaps the last episode of *Seinfeld*. In important ways, the rhetoric of the medium becomes part of the message itself.

So what? What does any of this have to do with us as digital writers and editors? We should think carefully about why we are deploying moving images, and whether **video** is the right medium for the content. What part of the story is the rhetoric of video best suited to deliver? The "Snow Fall" package from *The New York Times* described earlier in the chapter, for example, uses video clips of some of the tragedy's survivors to put the interactor and the survivor in the same room, in the present tense. It's powerful, and it enables an emotional connection between interactor and subject. Flash-driven animation, on the other hand, is used to explain visually and in motion the power and punch of avalanches, while the multimedia package's dazzling photography gives interactors poignant images to gaze at and to study.

Even during the last few years, improvements in capacities for streaming and showing video have vastly improved. Download times have decreased while resolution and fidelity have gone up. The currency of the realm is still brevity, however, and attention spans are punishingly short; videos of only a few minutes are the norm. YouTube, for example, discourages videos longer than ten minutes. In addition, YouTube provides short tutorials on producing and editing video (www.youtube. com/t/creators_corner), as does CNN for its "i-Report" citizen media micro-site (www.cnn.com/exchange/ireports/toolkit/index.html and www.cnn.com/exchange/ ireports/toolkit/tips.html#video1). CNN also gives tutorials on taking photography and on recording audio. Other tutorials for shooting and editing video include those from:

▶ University of California Berkeley's School of Journalism (http://journalism. berkeley.edu/multimedia/tutorials/vidcams/);

▶ ClNet (http://reviews.cnet.com/4520–6500_7–5510172–1.html?tag=txt).

Flash presentations can combine text and pictures, video and audio, interactive buttons, and animated charts and graphs. Flash employs vector graphics, which means Flash does not require a lot of bandwidth—much less than video. Flash is also widely misused, often employed merely as eye candy. Flash animation is best suited to explaining and breaking down complex processes and chains of events, as well as "how to" demonstrations. As if to prove this fundamental point, Flash's publisher, Adobe, uses Flash to demonstrate how to, among other activities, make a Flash movie. These "how to" Flash tutorials take something fairly complex and sequential, then break it down and make the discrete steps visible and repeatable. However, Flash requires a browser plug-in, and it doesn't play on the iPhone. While browser software often automatically updates users' browsers for the latest plug-ins, not all browsers are always up to date, and any time users are required to take action, like updating or downloading software, the potential audience shrinks because not everyone is willing or able to take that action.

Still images best tell some stories or parts of stories because they enable a lingering gaze and an emotional connection with the subject. Still images can rely on iconic

FIGURE 2.3 "The Migrant Woman": Florence Thompson.

messages implicit even in their composition, like the Madonna-and-child form seen in Dorothea Lange's "Migrant Woman" photograph taken in 1936, which is to underline photography's intrinsic relationship to memory. Only still images are described as metaphorically "burning" something into our minds, searing our memories. Most of our memories, after all, are images, because images, like memory, freeze time and preserve one slice of it for observation and reflection. To create and publish slideshows, with or without sound, there are an abundance of free and low-cost software programs, including Soundslides, Apple's iPhoto, Flickr, and Google's Picasa.

BOX 2.1   *Computer code: The building blocks of webpages*

Computer programming codes like HTML and CSS are the principal languages of the web. Although many web writers and editors aren't asked to build websites from scratch, they should be aware of how web-authoring code works and how it makes digital content manifest in a browser window. It's important to know, for example, that text on a computer screen isn't really text at all. Computer code assembles the tiny building blocks of pixels to form the letters we see on screen. Photos and graphics are also never part of a webpage, regardless of how they appear in the browser. The webpage and its constituent graphical parts are always separate files, coalescing in a download to appear as a singular entity. Webpages are coded or built to make it seem as if their images are knitted into their fabric.

The code languages most often used to create interactive or hypertextual content are HTML (hypertext markup language) and its progeny, XHTML (next-generation HTML), XML (extensible markup language), and CSS (cascading style sheets). XML is used especially for data-rich content and to enhance HTML by using attribute tags to categorize information. For example, an XML tag can tell other computers and search engines whether a certain piece of text is a phone number, a job application, an order form, an invoice, or whatever the coder writes into the language. Special search engines can then index documents in XML with great accuracy, regardless of the operating system or computer being used. Flash and actionscripting, JavaScript, Ajax, and Spry, as well as Fireworks all enable webpages to be dynamic and interactive. Web writers and editors do not necessarily need to become proficient in these web programming languages, nor do they necessarily need to know how to develop an app. But it certainly helps to be able to hand-code pages and to understand the capacities and limitations of these coding languages. Fortunately, most sites use authoring software programs, webpage templates, and content management systems to speed the process and better ensure consistency, taking a huge load off of digital writers and editors to become and remain conversant in a dizzying range of coding languages.

Most journalism websites use content management systems (CMSs), which are complex systems designed to automate most web publishing. These CMSs handle all sorts of digital content, from text files to audio, photo, and video, and they allow anyone within an organization to see all of the files and component parts. Also important to news organizations are application programming interfaces (APIs), which are programming tools that allow one site or program to interact with or otherwise accommodate other sites or programs. Facebook famously opened up its environment to third-party applications, while Apple allows anyone to develop and offer an application for and via its iPhone. Similarly, APIs allow third-party development and collaboration on or for news organizations, which are seeking to leverage the popularity of such sites as YouTube, Facebook, and reddit.com, to name just three examples. APIs give developers controlled access to the various websites and platforms.

To put those new to web design at ease, what follows are some basics about the primary coding languages, HTML and CSS. To see how this code generates what you see through your browser, you can go to almost any webpage, right click (PC) or control click (Mac), choose "view page source" (or its equivalent, depending on which browser you are using) and see the code. HTML uses tags, such as <body>, while CSS uses brackets and semantic style directions:

```
{
     background-color: #000000
}
```

This simple CSS command stipulates a page's background color as black, using the hexadecimal (or six-character alphanumeric code) for the color black (000000). CSS also supports semantic instructions:

```
{
     background-color: black
}
```

For web-based media environments, including blogs, extranets and intranets, learning at least the basics of HTML can aid design and streamline content development. HTML source codes are what make webpages behave or, when the code is faulty, what cause the pages to misbehave. In the code are instructions to browsers, including what to show and how to show it. In short, HTML does just what its name implies: it marks up language to allow browsers and, more importantly, those using browsers to interact with that language. This markup allows hyperlinks or references in the code to other sites, webpages, or other places within the same website or page (called anchors). This markup allows images to appear on or in the page.

To introduce HTML, here is a look at a few very basic tags (the commands appearing inside angle brackets < > that are used to build most webpages). After showing the tags, we will break down what they are and how they work:

```
<html>
<head>
<title>A primer on HTML source code</title>
<meta name = "description" content = "learning about
HTML">
</head>
<body bgcolor = "FFFFFF">
<h1><font: Georgia, Arial, sans serif>The basics of HTML
</h1><p>
```

We are learning about the basic tags used in generating webpages. These tags and content should always be in a simple text document, not in Word or WordPerfect. Once we are done, we can save the file, then open the document in a browser from our local hard drive:

```
</p>
</font>
</body>
</html>
```

Eight tags were used in the small sample above; two of them are essential. The <html> tag tells browsers they can read the code by signifying that the page is in HTML format. The </html> turns the HTML off, or closes the document. The <body> tag tells the browser what to display in the browser window. Most tags come in pairs: one to turn a feature or behavior on and one to turn it off again, much like light switches. The tag , for example, turns on boldface type. Adding a forward slash turns the behavior off again: . Failure to add the "off" tag would render whatever followed also in boldface, the functional equivalent to Grandpa forgetting to switch off his turn signal after making the turn. The tag </body>, then, ends the section viewable through the web browser.

The <head> tag indicates header information, such as the title of the webpage, the information that appears in the browser at the very top; it does not signify a headline. The <h1> tag turns on a heading, which is or can be like a headline, and specifies the size. The </h1>, then, would turn it off. The <body bgcolor> tag specifies a background color for the page, which in this case is white (#FFFFFF). Each of the web's 256 basic colors is assigned hexadecimal code, or six letter–number combination. For example, black is #000000 and brown is #CC6600.

Any tag with a "/" in it is called an "off" tag. An example: <p> starts a paragraph, while </p> turns the same feature off, ending the paragraph. The font is specified with a <font> tag, then turned off with </font>. Arial font would begin <font face = "Arial">. When the font changes, Arial would be turned off, </font face = "Arial">.

Metatags apply to the entire site. The term also comes from the fact that metatags provide data about data. Their content does not direct the browser and is not, therefore, displayed in a browser. These tags direct search engines in how to sort the site, its pages and content by providing key words, descriptions, and the like. They also cue other programmers by providing authorship information, copyright information, and general design notes. A common metatag sequence might look like this one, from the *Online Journalism Review* (www.ojr.org):

```
<meta name = "description" content = "News, commentary
and help for online publishers and bloggers, from the
USC Annenberg School for Communication.">
```

Here are a few more common tags used in XHTML:

Paragraph Break: <p> </p>

Line Break:
 (this XHTML tag comprises both the opening and closing tags; by adding the forward slash, the tag also "closes" or turns off the line break command)

```
Horizontal Rule: <hr> </hr>
<strong> something written in boldface </strong>
<em> something appearing in italics </em>
<a href = "http://www.cubanxgiants.com"> something hy-
perlinked to the CubanXGiants webpage </a>
```

Unordered list:

```
<ul>
<li> laptops
<li> desktop PCs
</ul>
```

Ordered list:

```
<ol>
<li> dolphins
<li> panthers
<li> jaguars
</ol>
```

Inserting anchors, which are used for internal page navigation, is easy. Anchors are internal hyperlinks, or links that take a reader to another part of the same webpage or to a specific section in another page of the same website. Here is what an anchored page would look like in code, inside a page of frequently asked questions (FAQs):

```
<a href = "#question1">Where do I find out more about
Crohn's?</a>
<a href = "#question2">Where does the support group
meet?</a>
```

Below, where the answers to the questions are presented, an anchor would be inserted just before each answer, a piece of code that is not visible in the browser. The anchor, which is signified by using the number sign (#) is merely a marker that enables the hyperlink—"question1"—to work, or to have a place to link. The two anchors for the two questions above would look something like this:

```
<a NAME = "question1"></a>Crohn's disease is a condition
that afflicts . . .
<a NAME = "question2"></a>The group meets in Rex
Hospital . . .
```

The <a NAME> refers to the name you gave the anchor in the hyperlink at the top of the page.

Perhaps the biggest difference between HTML and XHTML is that in the latter, all tags require a closing or off tag. In HTML, a command such as <p> to create a new paragraph does not require a closing tag: </p>. And this is intuitive. Creating a paragraph creates an extra line break, an execution that would not seem to require an "off" command or closing tag. It is a single operation. But XHTML is stricter, and one manifestation of this lower tolerance is the requirement that all tags, all executions, have opening and closing tags.

Another manifestation is the prohibition in XHTML on capital letters. That same paragraph tag in HTML could be either <p> or <P>. Not so in XHTML. Finally, XHTML varies by requiring quotation marks (single or double) for all attribute values. For example, in HTML, a tag reading <td rowspan = 3>, indicating a table with three rows, would be acceptable. In XHTML, the specification requires quotation marks: <td rowspan = "3">. Why do these differences matter? Eventually, XHTML will likely replace HTML and browsers will begin supporting HTML less and, therefore, will require XHTML to properly render webpages.

CSS is an incredibly powerful coding language that is used for two primary purposes: coding individual webpages with a more semantic or intuitive syntax than is used in HTML/XHTML; and creating "parent"-style sheets that can be applied to an infinite number of "children," or pages that refer to the style sheets for their attributes. In other words, CSS can be used merely to indicate (or declare) something simple, like the typeface on a webpage:

```
{
   font-family: Verdana, Arial, Helvetica
}
```

Or CSS can be used to generate entire style sheets that determine attributes for any page referring to that style sheet. A change made to the one style sheet, which is uploaded to the web along with all its children, will ripple out into all of those pages referring to the style sheet. For large sites, CSS saves an enormous amount of time, contributes to consistency, and prevents error. These are just some of the reasons why CSS has quickly been adopted by designers and supported by browsers and authoring programs.

HTML5, so named because it is the fifth revision of the HTML standard, has enabled an approach to desktop web and mobile web design that adjusts depending on the size of the device and screen of the user. Called "responsive design," this approach combines HTML5 and CSS to allow content to be refitted to almost any screen size automatically, with the use of a single CSS style sheet. Ever smaller screen sizes have presented monumental challenges to web designers. Responsive design makes it possible to accommodate even smartphone screens, while at the same time delivering the same content to big desktop monitors. A mobile-first approach stipulates that webpages be designed to be lean and modular, so that content can stack. By using media queries or element queries, which allow websites and browsers to "speak" to each other, web designers can have their sites ask a user's device the size of the screen being used. The answer can then trigger any number of versions of content. For example, if a media or element query reveals that a user is accessing a site from a Mac desktop, he or she might get a large high-resolution image. If the query determines that the user is accessing via a phone, the site will load only a small lower-res image, reconfiguring the content based on the size of the screen.

The challenges to responsive design are fairly significant. It requires far more time and effort than does traditional web design. And more testing has to be done to see what users get depending on the device they are using. In addition, advertising forms have to be kept very lean, lightweight, and simple. Rich visualization and large interstitial ads are largely not supported.

The goal in this box was merely to provide a taste of HTML and CSS, or just enough so that web writers and editors would not be intimidated by these authoring languages. The web design or HTML section of any local bookstore will have a dizzying depth and breadth of literature available on the topic. It is enough for now to learn what HTML tags are and how they operate in an HTTP (hypertext transfer protocol) environment such as the web. Many will prefer to hand-code because of the precision this control offers; others would rather save time in page-building by using web-authoring software packages, leaving more time for other tasks. But there are hundreds of websites designed to help you learn and use these coding languages.

The coding discussed in this chapter has largely to do with what is called front-end code, or the languages that build and design pages and sites. The primary front-end code languages are JavaScript, HTML, and CSS. On the server side, back-end coding languages are used to help send data to web applications, like those that populate news websites with news articles or weather sites with up-to-date weather conditions and forecasts. This code is meant to make it easier to manipulate data, render templates, and filter and sort data.

CHAPTER ASSIGNMENT

This chapter's assignment has two parts. First, revise your Chapter 1 writing sample based on the feedback and help you receive from your workshop partner(s) and the instructor.

Feel free to continue dialoging with your workshop partner(s) and/or the instructor during this revision process. Second, begin formatting the piece for online readership. The purpose here is merely to get started, so do not worry at all about how sophisticated your formatting is or about the limits of your knowledge of HTML or CSS. The important thing at this stage is to conceptualize how the information should be presented online.

A blogging software can be very helpful in this exercise, particularly since most offer an HTML or Code view, which will show you all of the code generated to create the web presentation.

Use this chapter to inform your formatting. You will need to know or experiment with some HTML, or have some familiarity with a web-authoring software package like Dreamweaver or Mozilla, both of which offer CSS support. Both Blogger.com and Word-Press also accept HTML coding, provided you first select the "Edit HTML" or "Code" view, rather than "Compose" or "Visual". If you use the shortcut buttons in your blog software, be sure to inspect or view the code to learn something of how the formatting is added.

Online Resources

Arts & Letters Daily (www.aldaily.com/)
A great example of a site for all writers and readers.

Living Internet (www.livinginternet.com)
A comprehensive site about all things Internet.

Purdue University Online Writing Lab (http://owl.english.purdue.edu)
Style guides, writing and teaching helps, and resources for grammar and writing mechanics.

Useit.com (www.nngroup.com/)
Jakob Nielsen's site for usability studies and a wealth of intelligence on design.

Additional Web Resources

For learning basic HTML/XHTML, including publishing to the Web:

▶ Dave's Site (www.davesite.com/webstation/html/);

▶ HTML Goodies (www.htmlgoodies.com/);

▶ HTML Guides/References from NASA (http://heasarc.gsfc.nasa.gov/docs/heasarc/Style_Guide/html.html);

▶ Lynda.com tutorials (http://lynda.com);

▶ Peachpit Press (www.peachpit.com/topics/topic.aspx?st=61442);

▶ Webmonkey (www.webmonkey.com).

▶ REFERENCES

American Society of Newspaper Editors, *Newspaper Credibility: Building Reader Trust* (Washington, DC: ASNE Credibility Committee and Minnesota Opinion Research, April 1985).

American Society of Newspaper Editors, *Newspaper Credibility: 206 Practical Approaches to Heighten Reader Trust* (Washington, DC: ASNE Credibility Committee, April 1986).

American Society of Newspaper Editors, *Journalism Values Handbook* (Washington, DC: ASNE Ethics and Values Committee and The Harwood Group, 1995).

American Society of Newspaper Editors, *Timeless Values: Staying True to Journalistic Principles in the Age of New Media* (Washington, DC: ASNE New Media and Values Committee and The Harwood Group, April 1995).

American Society of Newspaper Editors, *Journalism Values Institute: Insights on the Values* (Washington, DC: ASNE Ethics and Values Committee and The Harwood Group, 1996).

American Society of Newspaper Editors, *Examining Our Credibility* (Washington, DC: ASNE and Urban Associates, 1999).

R. Ambrester, "Identification Within: Kenneth Burke's View of the Unconscious," *Philosophy and Rhetoric* 7 (1974): 205–216.

American Society of Newspaper Editors, *The Newspaper Credibility Handbook* (Washington, DC: ASNE Journalism Credibility Project, 2001).

G. D. Baxter and P. M. Taylor, "Burke's Theory of Consubstantiality and Whitehead's Concept of Concrescence," *Communication Monographs* 45 (1978): 173–180.

William A. Benoit, "Comparing the Clinton and Dole Advertising Campaigns: Identification and Division in 1996 Presidential Television Spots," *Communication Research Reports* 17, no. 1: 39–48.

John Branch, "Snow Fall: The Avalanche at Tunnel Creek," *The New York Times*, December 19 (2012), www.nytimes.com/projects/2012/snow-fall/.

Brian Brooks and Jack Sissors, *The Art of Editing* (Boston, MA: Allyn & Bacon, 2001).

C. Bullis and B. W. Bach, "Are Mentor Relationships Helping Organizations? An Exploration of Developing Mentee–Mentor Organizational Identifications Using Turning Point Analysis," *Communication Quarterly* 37 (1989): 199–213.

R. H. Carpenter, "A Stylistic Basis of Burkeian Identification," *Today's Speech* 20 (1972): 19–24.

G. Cheney, "The Rhetoric of Identification and the Study of Organizational Communication," *Quarterly Journal of Speech* 69 (1983): 143–158.

G. Cheney and P. Tompkins, "Coming to Terms with Organizational Identification and Commitment," *Central States Speech Journal* 38 (1987): 1–15.

Jonathan Cohen, "Defining Identification: A Theoretical Look at the Identification of Audiences with Media Characters," *Mass Communication & Society* 4, no. 3 (2001): 245–264.

Bryan Crable, "Rhetoric, Anxiety, and Character Armor: Burke's Interactional Rhetoric of Identity 1," *Western Journal of Communication* 70, no. 1 (January 2006): 1–22.

Richard Craig, *Online Journalism* (Toronto, Ontario: Thomson, 2005).

D. Day, "Persuasion and the Concept of Identification," *Quarterly Journal of Speech,* 46 (1960): 270–273.

Dale Dougherty, "Don't Forget to Write," Webreview.com (archived at http://web.archive.org/web/20010414062442/www.webreview.com/1997/10_10/strategists/10_10_97_6.shtml).

Carolyn Dowling, *Writing and Learning with Computers* (Camberwell, Australia: Acer Press, 1999).

Andrew J. Flanigin and Miriam J. Metzger, "Perceptions of Internet Information Credibility," *Journalism & Mass Communication Quarterly* 77, no. 3 (2000): 515–539.

Sonja K. Foss, Karen A. Foss, and Robert Trapp, *Contemporary Perspectives on Rhetoric* (Prospect Heights, IL: Waveland Press, 1986).

Jennifer Greer, "Evaluating the Credibility of Online Information: A Test of Source and Advertising Influence," *Mass Communication & Society* 6 (2003): 11–28.

Jennifer Greer and Donica Mensing, "U.S. News Web Sites Better, But Small Papers Still Lag," *Newspaper Research Journal* 25, no. 2 (Spring 2004): 98–112.

Carl I. Hovland, Irving L. Janis, and Harold H. Kelley, *Communication and Persuasion: Psychological Studies of Opinion Change* (New Haven, CT: Yale University Press, 1953).

Katharine Jarmul, "Tips & Tools for Journalists Who Want to Learn Programming Skills," Poynter Institute, www.poynter.org/how-tos/digital-strategies/153925/tips-tools-for-journalists-who-want-to-learn-programming-skills/, accessed November 22, 2011.

Thomas J. Johnson and Barbara K. Kaye, "Cruising is Believing? Comparing Internet and Traditional Sources on Media Credibility Measures," *Journalism & Mass Communication Quarterly* 75 (1998): 325–340.

Thomas J. Johnson and Barbara K. Kaye, "Using is Believing: The Influence of Reliance on the Credibility of Online Political Information among Politically Interested Internet Users," *Journalism & Mass Communication Quarterly* 77 (2000): 865–879.

Thomas J. Johnson and Barbara K. Kaye, "Webelievability: A Path Model Examining How Convenience and Reliance Predict Online Credibility," *Journalism & Mass Communication Quarterly* 79 (2002): 619–642.

Thomas J. Johnson and Barbara K. Kaye, "Wag the Blog: How Reliance on Traditional Media and the Internet Influence Credibility Perceptions of Weblogs among Blog Users," *Journalism & Mass Communication Quarterly* 81, no. 3 (2004): 622–642.

Journalism.org, "The State of the News Media," Journalism.org (2006), accessed February 21, 2007.

John Kirk, "Kenneth Burke and Identification," *Quarterly Journal of Speech* 47, no. 4 (December 1961): 414–415.

David Kline and Dan Burstein, *blog! How the Newest Media Revolution Is Changing Politics, Business and Culture* (New York, NY: CDS Books, 2005).

Bill Kovach and Tom Rosenstiel, *Elements of Journalism* (New York, NY: Three Rivers Press, 2007).

Rachel McAlpine, *Web Word Wizardry: A Guide to Writing for the Web and Intranet* (Berkeley, CA: Ten Speed Press, 2001). McAlpine also has a companion website that is very good: Quality Web Content, www.webpagecontent.com.

J. C. McCroskey, "Scales for the Measurement of Ethos," *Speech Monographs* 33 (1966): 65–72.

J. C. McCroskey, "A Survey of Experimental Research on the Effects of Evidence in Persuasive Communication," *Speech Monographs* 55 (1969): 169–176.

John C. Meyer, "Humor as a Double-Edged Sword: Four Functions of Humor in Communication," *Communication Theory* 10, no. 3 (August 2000): 310–331.

Philip Meyer, "Defining and Measuring Credibility of Newspapers: Developing an Index," *Journalism Quarterly* 65 (1988): 567–574, 588.

John Morkes and Jakob Nielsen, "Concise, SCANNABLE, and Objective: How to Write for the Web" (1997), www.useit.com/papers/webwriting/writing.html.

Jakob Nielsen, "How Users Read on the Web," www.useit.com/alertbox/9710a.html.

Roger C. Parker, *Guide to Web Content and Design* (New York, NY: MIS Press, 1997).

Neil Postman, *Amusing Ourselves to Death: Public Discourse in the Age of Show Business* (New York, NY: Penguin, 1985).

Jay Rosen, "Bloggers vs. Journalists is Over," *PressThink*, January 21 (2005), http://journalism.nyu.edu/pubzone/weblogs/pressthink, accessed June 10, 2006.

Anthony Tedesco, "Adapt your Writing to the Web," *The Writer* 114, no. 5 (May 2001): 16.

P. K. Tompkins, J. Fisher, D. Infante, and E. Tompkins, "Kenneth Burke and the Inherent Characteristics of Formal Organizations: A Field Study," *Speech Monographs* (1975): 135–142.

Mark Wright, "Burkeian and Freudian Theories of Identification," *Communication Quarterly* 42, no. 3 (Summer 1994): 301–310.

G. Pascal Zachary, "A Journalism Manifesto," February 9, 2006, AlterNet, www.alternet.org/story/31775, accessed February 13, 2006.

3

Editing for Digital Media: Strategies

I revise a great deal. I know when something is right because bells begin ringing and lights flash.

E. B. White, novelist and poet

An editor should tell the author his writing is better than it is. Not a lot better, a little better.

T. S. Eliot, poet, playwright, and novelist

An editor doesn't count spelling errors and judge the writer accordingly; the editor is a reader, user advocate, and writing consultant.

Judith Tarutz, author of *Technical Editing*

▶ INTRODUCTION

The theory of Gestalt holds that the whole is different from, and usually more than, the mere mathematical addition of that whole's constituent parts. To ensure the quality of the whole, we have to inspect and evaluate all of the digital parts. Each and every element on a webpage, therefore, has to be scrutinized, from the page title at the top to the copyright notice at the bottom to the key words in the metatag. Graphics and illustrations, photo credit lines, headlines and subheads— everything should get a second (or third or fourth) look. The immediacy of digital might lead us to assume that editing for digital spaces means less attention to detail, or less time spent checking, rechecking, verifying, and vetting. In fact, the complexity of digital media means that there has never been more to get just right. This chapter covers these editorial roles and responsibilities, including some new to digital realms, such as search engine optimization.

▶ MULTI-TASKING, CROSS-TRAINING, AND SILO-BUSTING

Online publishing is not at all like editing for print, at least in terms of job responsibilities. In print, there are clear distinctions between roles and duties among writers, designers, editors, and copy editors. Media convergence has blurred and blended these roles and responsibilities. But the traditional skill set for writers and editors has never been more important. A world-class designer who can't write a declarative sentence is of little use. Digital newsrooms, marketing departments, and public relations teams are staffed with content producers and social media managers, not specifically writers or editors. At least for now. The job descriptions keep changing, making the most valuable employees those who are flexible and adaptable.

Because of their many job duties, digital editors and content producers typically are organized, self-directed, and versatile. They are ethical and persistent, and often they have a pretty good sense of humor and a rhino-thick skin. These attributes point to the very stark differences between the processes of writing and editing—though, of course, these activities are complementary and interdependent. Many of the editor's traits are required for the arduous processes of proofreading and copyediting, which require an eye for detail and a reservoir of patience. Editing is mostly about making choices and decisions—lots and lots of decisions. Editing well means being able to read at several different levels at the same time, from where commas should go to whether or not a navigation scheme is working to how topics and stories are trending across social media.

Ideally, an editor is involved in page or site development, even in the earliest stages of planning. As an advocate for readers, editors should influence, if not direct, information design and planning rather than merely fixing or correcting problems such as typographical errors later in the process. In fact, when and how editors are integrated into a website's or publication's design says a great deal about that site's or publication's estimation of editors' importance or value.

With these roles in mind, here are some of the responsibilities common to digital editors.

1   **Identify the audience and the purpose of your content.** The needs of your interactors should guide what you do and the decisions you make. Much more will be said on this in Chapter 6 when we focus on audience.

2   **Determine a scalable, sensible structure.** It's up to editors to develop a document and file structure that is suited to the content's purpose and that is obvious and easy to navigate. Sections and even individual pages have to be largely independent within that structure, however, because visitors often link directly to an individual page, often deep within your site or intranet. In other words, webpages should support non-sequential and incomplete reading; the content should be broken up into coherent, self-contained chunks that are understandable even if read out of sequence. However, though an interactor's path may be unpredictable, the structure of the documents and files should not be. Interactors need a clear sense of how the site and webpages are organized so they can easily, even unthinkingly, move through them. The goal, then, is to reduce if not eliminate disorientation.

An effective hypertext structure is organized according to a simple and meaningful pattern, one that anticipates interactors' needs. Such a structure features consistent visual design, such as the consistent placement of navigation links and the use of color and icons to identify different sections. Main structural divisions should be obvious, and typically the homepage or opening screen identifies these main structural divisions, functioning as a sort of table of contents. If this page establishes a consistent visual design, it successfully instructs interactors where to look for various types of information. Because interactors enter at points other than the homepage, each and every page should identify and link to the main structural divisions, as well.

3   **Edit the content.** Review and edit everything, including structure and navigation, links, writing style, style consistency, and visual design. Begin early and repeat throughout. Check colors, graphics, headlines, subheads, paragraph lengths, and consistency of all elements. You might edit content chunks in random order rather than in sequence to replicate the experience of many, if not most, interactors.

4   **Proofread and test usability.** Misspelled words are an embarrassment, and they detract from credibility, suggesting that multiple copyediting steps or stages should be in place. One stage or step, for example, could focus on consistency in visual design, another on testing links, and still another on naming conventions. Because the organization of a site is translated into file names according to certain conventions, this copyediting step is an important one, and it should include inspecting the naming

conventions for pages, folders, files, graphics—anything that is a separate file. And check pages in different browsers, using different monitors and connection speeds.

5 **Copyedit some more.** While it's true that good editors can read on different levels, looking for more than one type of error at the same time is difficult. When time allows, all editors should read multiple times, looking each time for different things. First, read for understanding. Does it make sense? Is it clear? Is the information complete? Are there big structural problems that will need attention before you can read for smaller-scale issues, mistakes, and weaknesses? Here are some of the other levels, or types of readings, editors should do:

▶ *For organization and focus.* Does each paragraph focus on a single idea? Are transitions clearly and simply made? Does the piece wander, or is it focused on the promised theme or topic? Is there a better organization?

▶ *For accuracy:* names, places, dates, titles, numbers. Facts have to be checked and, when they are counter-intuitive facts, corroborated. Are the facts consistent with each other? Do the numbers add up? If you're not sure, look it up. Is it Adolf Hitler or Adolph Hitler? If you are sure, why not look it up anyway? Is the Mendoza Line for batting averages in baseball .200? Is it .180? Look it up. (It's .200, even though the term comes from a lifetime .215 hitter, Mario Mendoza.)

▶ *For grammar, spelling and orthography, punctuation and style,* or the little demons covered in Chapter 1. This is basic copyediting.

▶ *For pacing, rhythm, and flow.* Is the language clear and precise? Does it flow? Is there too much jargon?

These kinds of copyediting tasks will require a few reliable sources, either in print or online, including:

▶ the stylebook(s) for your organization's adopted style (for most news organizations it is the Associated Press Stylebook);

▶ an all-purpose dictionary, and perhaps one specific to your field, industry, or area of specialty;

▶ a writing and usage handbook;

▶ a thesaurus;

▶ maps, an atlas, and a general information almanac;

▶ directories and perhaps biographical information, depending on topics and categories;

▶ an encyclopedia;

▶ archives of industry-specific publications.

6   **Write headlines**. Much more on this in the next chapter, but typically it is the online editor who writes the headlines. Because headlines online serve different purposes than do their print counterparts, they should be written differently. Primarily, this means that searchable key words should drive how headlines are written, because search engines "read" the headlines in order to create and rank their findings. In addition, headlines in digital spaces often are displayed out of context, in isolation, or as part of a list of articles, such as in a listing of findings for a search query, so they have to be written with this in mind. When scanning lists of stories, people frequently look only at the highlighted headlines, skipping summaries and other information. The headline, therefore, is all important.

7   **Test usability**. Test the tasks that readers will want to perform. Check that navigation is easy and intuitive. Evaluate reading comprehension.

This "Lucky 7" list indicates that online or digital editors wear a lot of different hats. Content developer, content strategist, producer, manager, managing editor, project manager, proofreader, usability expert, search engine optimizer, social media manager—a digital editor is a sort of superhero. Digital editors might also be tasked with producing multimedia, moderating discussion online, or going into the field to do the heavy lifting of original reporting. Media convergence has brought with it role convergence.

The list also dramatizes the many levels at which digital editors must engage with content, and the many types of error or missed opportunities for which he or she must look. A lack of resources, the pressures of immediacy and competition, and internal organizational dysfunction sometimes inhibit or even undercut many of these roles, of course; but in a healthy, productive work environment, they are valued.

▶ EDITING TECHNIQUES

You've heard the expression, "The devil is in the details," right? For editors, it's mostly about details, so there are a lot of places the devil can hide. To systematically check these hiding places, digital editors need routines, habits and systems of checks. For example, an editor responsible for editing a site's webpages might create a checklist for proofing and to make sure that errors are searched for in their usual hiding places, which include:

▶   bylines and datelines;

▶   headlines, deckheads, and subheads;

- ▶ photo credits and cutlines;

- ▶ hyperlinks and references to other articles, places, and sites;

- ▶ grammar and orthography (spelling, punctuation, and capitalization);

- ▶ quotations (checking for missing quote marks and proper punctuation);

- ▶ hyphenation and line breaks;

- ▶ line wraps (around photos, cutlines, pull quotes, etc.);

- ▶ metatags and descriptors;

- ▶ ALT tags for images (or the text that is displayed or read by computers for the blind);

- ▶ page titles, which are different from headlines, or the text that appears in the browser above the page;

- ▶ copyright and "last updated" text.

There are other hiding places, but this list provides a useful starting point. Other steps a digital editor might take include running a spell check, doing the math for any numbers that are presented, and looking for split infinitives and faulty em (—) dashes. Just as links should be checked, so too should phone numbers and addresses. If you are listing a phone number, someone should dial the number to make sure it's still working. If the site offers multimedia, someone should click to play any videos, slideshows, or audio to ensure everything functions as it should.

Many news organizations have a separate fact-checking phase for all copy, and this is a good idea. Routines should be in place, and someone should have the clear responsibility for applying a discipline of verification, someone who is therefore accountable for accuracy. In other words, fact-checking should be a standalone activity or function and not something that ends up blended or blurred (and probably lost) with other editing roles and functions. Established routines and a combination of methods and steps for editing give you the best chance at reducing, perhaps even eliminating, error.

Specific steps a digital editor can take include these below—all proven ways to vastly improve the copy:

- ▶ **Read once through quickly**. This gives you a sense of what the story is about and reveals the flow and arc of the narrative.

▶ **Read backwards.** This focuses the brain to engage at the word level as opposed to the sentence or paragraph level. Reading backwards forces you to read individual words, which is how you best see typos and spelling mistakes. Yes, it makes for a nonsensical reading, but that's one reason it works. Your brain isn't jumping ahead or assuming; it's merely encountering individual words.

▶ **Print a hard copy.** It might help to print out whatever it is you are editing on paper. Ink on paper is tactile, making it physiologically easier or more comfortable to read than pixels on screens.

▶ **Read it out loud.** You might feel a bit awkward or self-conscious at first, but reading out loud is perhaps the single most effective editing technique you can employ for several reasons. First, it slows you down. We speak more slowly than we read, so verbalizing what we're reading gives us more time to catch mistakes. Second, reading sentences helps us to identify problems with syntax and mechanics. We can hear the mistakes. Third, saying what we are reading allows us to hear the pacing of the writing, the rhythm and the flow. Problems in any of these three areas become immediately discernible when they are heard rather than merely being read. Finally, the method puts you in the seat of your reader, which is a good and right place to be.

▶ **Read to find holes in the story and to evaluate organization.** Think of the article as a building, with each paragraph serving as a floor or story. Is there a better order? If you moved the 13th floor to the 4th, would the story make more sense? If a floor disappeared entirely, would the building, in fact, be better off?

▶ **Cut it up and spread it out.** A professor now retired from the University of North Carolina, Colonel Don Shaw, would routinely take his journalism history students' writing into a conference room, laying out all of the pages, no matter how long. He would then note or mark transitions and changes in direction or theme. Next, he would physically cut up the paper with a pair of scissors, cutting at the marked breaks or transitions. In a step many of us found uncomfortable, he would ball up redundancies or tangents and toss them in the trashcan, rearranging what was left into a better, clearer order or progression. Often he would also ball up and throw away the first paragraph and the last one, an act of bravery we writers can rarely muster the courage to do. Whatever was left, Dr. Shaw would tape together, roll up, and hand back to the student author. Before exiting, the Colonel would say, barely audibly, "Now get to work." (Once you have a draft, he often reminded, you're ready to begin.) Try this yourself. It's an architectural-level editing that cannot be done well staring at a computer screen, and there is something visceral and exciting about physically cutting up and piecing back together.

▶ **Read it all again.** When you think you are finished, go get a cup of coffee. Go for a run. Walk the dog. Do something different. Then come back and give the piece one more read, especially the headline. A fresh reading is a prime opportunity to discover error. "What was I thinking?" is a common reaction even at this late stage of editing.

One Editor's Experience

To appreciate the multifaceted roles of digital editors, let's hear from one magazine editor at a large custom publishing company. In her description she identifies several steps or stages of editing at her company, steps any organization could implement. Her description also reveals many of the hiding places for error and carelessness:

When I proof a layout, I use "the ten steps to perfect proofing." These steps include checking:

▶ photo credits;

▶ folios (or four-page groupings of pages);

▶ throw lines (or "see p. x" lines) to other pages or sidebars;

▶ grammar and orthography in all display copy;

▶ byline name spelling and matching name in the biography;

▶ every single line for correct or best hyphenation;

▶ every line that wraps around a photo;

▶ photo cutlines;

▶ pull quotes, for matching body copy;

▶ consistency of spelling of all names;

▶ bad breaks, widows, and orphans.

On my publication, our copyeditor has a baseline list that she always checks, including running a spell check, cross-checking any mention of a page number, spacing around em dashes, city/state style, split infinitives, and checking that the table of contents entries match every layout. But she adds on items each issue based on recent experience. For instance, she is known as the "hyphenated adjective ninja." [Or is that "hyphenated-adjective ninja"?] Once a client complained about our splitting his company name over a line, so now she checks for that in the magazine, as well.

If a piece is intensive with service information, one round may be devoted only to phoning all numbers and testing every web link published. This may also be the time to check the spellings of proper names, places, and the like.

Most of our publications have a separate, fairly early fact-checking phase for all copy. Some editors' checklists for this simply state, 'check all facts.' I issue a two-page instruction memo that goes into much more detail.

And before all of this happens, the story undergoes content editing—from structure and length to identifying information to put higher in the story and smoothing out awkward language. The writer may have conducted additional reporting to fill information gaps. And another editor has written a headline, deck, and subheads.

By the time I'm looking at bluelines (the last phase before press time), I'm confident enough to have my checklist down to fewer than five items: looking at the display copy, quadruple checking the page numbers/folios, and reviewing the changes requested at the proof stage prior.

Another revising strategy: setting a word limit, or at least a target. I generally write long, particularly when I am quoting sources. Cutting a story down to the right length is an important part of my revising process. Why is this useful? Making a story shorter can't be done with only one method. I find it has to be a combination of line edits, substitutions of long phrases for short adjectives and removal of entire blocks of text.

This hints a bit at my pre-writing process. I have a rough outline of topics, and I work a lot of composing in my head, but I also let myself free-write at points, which then needs to be reined in.

This editor describes a process and a culture of editing and of careful attention to detail. She lays out a process of established routines shared by several people in her company.

The immediacy of online is forcing changes in these print-based processes, but not in the importance of and premium on a discipline of verification. The writer makes another critical point: no one method can substantially edit down a story or article or check that article for errors of fact or of writing. Both require multi-step processes.

▶ SEARCH ENGINE OPTIMIZATION AND USER EXPERIENCE

An important role many, if not most, digital editors are now responsible for is search engine optimization (SEO). Search engines algorithmically find and rank digital content using key words, looking especially in headlines and subheads, in tags typically listed at the beginning or end of the story, and in the HTML's metatags. When users type words or phrases into a search engine box, the computer tries to match those words with words it has found and recorded previously, and from that matching deliver a list of findings. And though search engines change their algorithms and, therefore, the ways they rank, basically they scan webpages to find repeated words and phrases. So, in terms of search, key words are the currency of the digital realm: you want your carefully determined key words to appear in the places the search engines are looking. Using popular key words will optimize even further the likelihood of your pages coming up in searches, and it is this process of determining and using these key words that is called search engine optimization. The better your key words, especially in your headlines, the higher your content will rank in search results.

So let's get started. Take a look at the article or piece that you are trying to optimize in terms of search. Think about what people might type into a search box to find the story for which you are writing a headline. After you've written the headline (and you'll get plenty of help with this in the next chapter), test out that headline by entering its key words into a search engine to see what comes up. You could also test by entering your entire headline into the search box. The findings will both gauge how "optimized" your headline is for likely searches for your subject, and it will turn up similar content from which you can glean key words to refine your own search engine optimization.

The next chapter will more comprehensively cover headline writing, but here now are some techniques that will improve your headlines for search success:

> ▶ **Be brief.** Google data show that headlines of about ten words work best. Shorter is better, and important key words should appear up front.

▶ **Be complete.** For example, if you were writing a headline for a story about the Boston Marathon bombings in 2013, you should use all of those key words: "Boston," "marathon," "bombing," and "2013." Some users may remember that it was in Boston but not when, and vice versa.

▶ **Be clear.** Will an interactor understand what the story is about by just reading the headline? She should, because this distillation and signaling are important tasks for any headline and roles absolutely crucial in digital spaces. Sometimes the headline is all that interactors will read. Given this punishing truth, it is amazing how few news organizations online get this right.

▶ **Be proactive.** Test your key words, and there are several ways to do this. You can use Google's auto-complete feature, which prompts additional words to complete a phrase. You can also test key words using Yahoo and Google SEO resources, such as www.google.com/trends and www.google.com/insights/search/#geo=US-FL-548&cmpt=geo.

Below were the most popular news stories trending on Google News on a summer day in 2013. Notice that none of the headlines are longer than ten words, and note the proper nouns they use (proper nouns make the best key words):

Zimmerman trial witness attempted to break up Zimmerman/Martin fight
USA TODAY

U.S. woman indicted in poison letter-to-Obama case
Ynetnews

Snowden's dad worries about son's ties to WikiLeaks
USA TODAY

Vatican clerics, two others arrested for corruption
Los Angeles Times

Heat wave settles in across the West
The Wall Street Journal

Common also to these headlines is that all are direct, clear, and straightforward in signaling the content. If a visitor is searching for the latest information on the big Christmas parade downtown, don't use the headline, "Yule procession to begin at 9 p.m." No one will ever find this story using even the best search jujitsu. While "Christmas Parade" might not be the most politically correct label to use in the headline, it is the clearest.

Google has made it clear that what counts the most is the content of the webpage itself. Presenting valuable information that has some density around a subject, and doing so in a straightforward manner, is rewarded by Google's algorithms. Keeping ads from cluttering that presentation is also rewarded by Google, so SEO is not an activity wholly divorced from maximizing the user experience (UX). Google uses machine learning to compare a page to a spectrum of similar pages ranging from dreadful to excellent, and it decides on this basis where that webpage page *looks* like it belongs. If you have less than eight seconds to engage a visitor once that person has landed on your webpage, it makes sense to be direct, clear, and useful.

Meaningful SEO takes time, and Google does not reward quick fixes. When implementing SEO practices, expect to be able to measure positive results in about six months. Improving SEO is more like planning out a city than putting out a fire, and it depends on great content consistently offered for a long time. You have to establish a track record. If you offer information that people need, if you present stories that make people feel something, they will share it with their friends and colleagues.

Meaningful SEO is also at least, in part, based on substance. From a pure SEO perspective, you need a minimum of 300 words, because articles shorter than this find it difficult getting indexed by Google. In Google's view, a piece that short cannot offer real value. Shorter articles may get more comments, but longer ones get shared more often.

Meaningful SEO avoids manipulative linking, or links created or cultivated merely to manipulate the system. The best links in terms of Google search come from sites that have authority, that are trusted by Google. Think nytimes.com, mayoclinic.com, and yale.edu. You can evaluate your own links using tools such as Moz.com's Open Site Explorer (www.opensiteexplorer.org/) and MajesticSEO (www.majesticseo.com/reports/site-explorer). You are still as good as the company you keep, so acquiring inbound links of the first rate is a powerful way to boost your page ranks in the search results. Keep in mind that Google is constantly tweaking its algorithms, making an estimated 500 to 600 changes per year based on thousands of tests. The fundamentals—user experience and satisfaction, meaningful content, quality inbound links—these are what will win the day.

The exception that perhaps proves many of these emergent "rules" is the hugely popular news blog Boing Boing (http://boingboing.net)—a sprawling site specializing in news and just interesting reads. In its presentations, it bucks conventional wisdom and breaks a lot of digital's "rules," or guidelines. For its hyperlinks, long phrases and sentences are common. The now passé "More at (insert URL here) site" kinds of referrals are also common at Boing Boing, which gets away with *how it links* perhaps because of *the integrity of its linking*: the content and usability of what it links to are consistently excellent. Boing Boing does a consistently good, even great, job linking to other content you might actually want to read (or view).

Boing Boing also gets away with its practices because it has built up trust among its interactors. When you click on a Boing Boing link, you know it's going to be a trustworthy site that is useful in some way. If the link points to a less-than-trustworthy site or source, Boing Boing lets you know why it's being linked. The Recording Industry Association of America, for example, is not a favorite of Boing Boing writers, but they link to it anyway when it adds to the presentation.

Another useful approach to linking can be found at A List of Things Thrown Five Minutes Ago (http://throwingthings.blogspot.com), a blog that integrates links into the text in ways that clearly signal to what the visitor is clicking, using phrases that avoid interrupting the narrative. Both Boing Boing and Throwing Things routinely link out; yet, in spite of the trends, these two blogs' interactors keep coming back. Great content, high trust, and an awareness that there is a lot of good, relevant content outside their sites add up to high readerships.

Still another model is that offered by Outbrain, a company that selects and highlights both a site's most-read headlines and top headlines from elsewhere on the web. At WRAL.com, the website of the TV station WRAL TV, based in Raleigh, NC, Outbrain runs a widget beneath WRAL news articles.

On the left side of the widget, Outbrain automatically feeds top headlines from WRAL.com; on the right, it lists top headlines from elsewhere on the web. Here's the interest-

More From WRAL.com
- Katie Beers' captor found dead at NY prison
- Man killed by remote control helicopter in NY park
- Birthday boy caught in Raleigh car break-ins
- 2 NC residents get prison for Medicaid fraud
- Entertainer Rolf Harris charged with sex crimes
- Hunchback King Richard III infected with worms

From Around the Web
- Is Your Website Due for an Audit? (BusinessNewsDaily)
- 7 Best Colleges for an Online Bachelor's Degree (Education Portal)
- 4 Examples of How Corporate America is Crushing Social Media (Scribit)
- More Employees "Going Rogue" On IT (Enterprise Social Network Blog)
- 10 Worst Teachers of 2013 (Parent Society)
- Why Laziness Is The Key To Customer Loyalty (Meet The Future of Retail)

FIGURE 3.1

ing part: It's Outbrain that pays WRAL to run the widget, not the other way around. Outbrain makes its money from other sites for the click-through traffic, and they run an algorithm on these headlines to see which ones generate the best click-through results. The "winners" are placed in the widget, delivering site traffic to Outbrain's paying clients. In other words, here is a business model built on good headline writing. It is the headlines that make this work. Though a different business model than SEO, it is based on the same principles as SEO. And like much of SEO, the Outbrain model blurs the line between human and machine readers in determining the most shareable or potentially viral content. Humans write WRAL.com's headlines; Outbrain's widget then ranks and displays them as a result of a complex algorithm that attempts to maximize cost per click revenue.

Commercially Sponsored Search Results

In late summer 2013, the Federal Trade Commission's consumer protection staff sent out letters (www.ftc.gov/os/2013/06/130625searchenginegeneralletter.pdf) to search engine companies instructing them to better distinguish between commercially sponsored results (third-party ads) and non-sponsored (or "natural") results to avoid consumer deception. The distinction, according to the FTC's letter, must be "clear and prominent" when evaluated from the perspective of consumers, taking into consideration how the results appear when using various browsers, apps, devices, etc. As the FTC's announcement noted, paid search results have become less distinguishable as advertising. Failing to clearly and prominently distinguish advertising from natural search results could be determined by the FTC to be a deceptive practice. To prevent this, the FTC recommends visual cues, labels or other techniques to effectively distinguish advertisements.

Some search companies have been doing the opposite. The shading in the top ad boxes, or boxes for paid ads at the very top of a search page, has lightened, making it more difficult for consumers to recognize them as distinct from natural search results. In addition, some search engines' results that integrate or offer specialized search options as part of the service—for example, by allowing users to refine their search to categories such as news or local businesses—are, in reality, another way of presenting paid ads. The FTC's efforts to combat the resulting confusion is good for content producers in clearly and transparently labeling and identifying what they publish, because, as the FTC posted, readers "expect that natural search results are included and ranked based on relevance to a search query, not based on payment from a third party. Including or ranking a search result in whole or in part based on payment is a form of advertising."

For its part, Google is fighting search finding manipulation specific to links and key words in press releases (https://support.google.com/webmasters/answer/66356?hl=en). Excerpting from Google's guidelines: "Any links intended to manipulate PageRank or a site's ranking in Google search results may be considered part of a link scheme and a violation of Google's Webmaster Guidelines. This includes any behavior that manipulates links to your site or outgoing links from your site." Thus, repeated words raise a red flag for Google's search monitors. Multiple postings of the same release similarly promise greater scrutiny from Google, which might see this common public relations practice as an "unnatural" boost to the popularity of a piece of content. According to Google, press release publishers must "create unique, relevant content that can naturally gain popularity in the Internet community."

Public relations practitioners are faced with a difficult dilemma, therefore. Including hyperlinks is good practice, and it helps journalists writing stories that use the press release. But these links could now be penalized by Google in its search findings for being "unnatural" in their promotion of a website. The same might apply to feature articles, columns, and posts, depending on a range of variables Google does not completely disclose. The simplest advice in this matter is to stick to the basics and conspicuously avoid attempting to game Google's or any other search engine's algorithms. Google has long been upfront about what it's looking for from site owners and publishers: Great original content that serves the best interests of their sites' visitors. This imperative valorizes good writing, and it rewards honesty and straightforwardness.

▶ MULTIMEDIA STORYTELLING

Determining key words, then, is an important role common among digital writers and editors. Because, as a delivery channel, the Internet can handle text, photo, video, and sound with equal ease—they all are 0s and 1s, after all—digital editors are also determining the best or most appropriate media through which to tell the stories. Before digital distribution, TV stations showed video, newspapers printed articles and photos, and radio broadcast music and talk. Via the web and mobile, anyone can do all three, allowing the story to drive the media choices rather than the medium, determining the kinds of stories that are pursued and produced. It is this convergence as much as any other that has changed media industries in the past 20 years. Thus, knowing the capacities and limitations of different publishing environments can inform important choices even in conceptualizing stories. Further down the production line, digital editors should be able to create simple webpages and have a basic understanding of HTML and CSS, to better understand the capacities of hypertextual environments.

To again use the Boston bombings of 2013, remember that TV provided breathless coverage of the chase for the pair of suspected bombers, placing talking heads in prominent locations in greater Boston to provide live standups and to punctuate what was entirely visual coverage. Meanwhile, newspapers did what they do best, providing narratives of the fast-changing events and doing the heavy lifting of explanation, such as how the bombs were likely made, how they were detonated and did their damage, and what law enforcement was doing to apprehend the culprits. On the web and powered by mobile, news organizations could do it all. So they did, providing:

▶ Twitter feeds of breaking news and updates of what police were discovering and how the city was dealing with the aftermath of the bombings;

▶ interactive maps of the marathon route, showing the locations of the bombs and of traffic closures subsequent to the attacks;

▶ Video, podcasts, and photo slideshows;

▶ links out to resources, such as Boston's mass transit system for information on disruptions in service and when service would be restored;

▶ a narrative with sidebars guiding readers through the major developments and explaining their significance;

▶ fact-checking, revising earlier reports and correcting mistakes, which were numerous.

Editors could choose the medium best suited to a particular angle or element of the story, rather than being restricted to one medium. And editors weren't limited to the kinds of stories they could tell through or by their primary medium. "If it bleeds, it leads," is a rather well-known aphorism from TV news, explaining how news gets on television.

Editors could (or should) ensure that whatever they pursue with their coverage, it adds something and serves the reader or viewer. Local TV news, by contrast, shows an inordinate number of live camera shots because they have invested heavily in the equipment to do it. Whether a story merits a live reporter on the scene or not, often TV news will go live simply because it can. This nonsensical approach to informing a democracy isn't necessary online.

Poynter Institute's Eyetrack studies reveal that successful multimedia presentations are typically:

▶ short;

▶ interactive;

▶ personal (or local or hyperlocal); and

▶ navigable (the better the interface, the better the experience).

Mapmaking

When thinking about multimedia, one of the easier layers of information to add to a story or story package is an interactive map. With digital mapmaking applications, many of them free and simple to use, digital editors can leverage the growing abundance of geomapped information about our globe. For a public increasingly armed with smartphones and an array of geomapped applications, a public that increasingly expects customized, localized information, interactive maps are standard fare.

The geomapped data are coming from efforts such as Google Earth and Google Streetview, which are comprehensively charting the surface of our globe with incredible

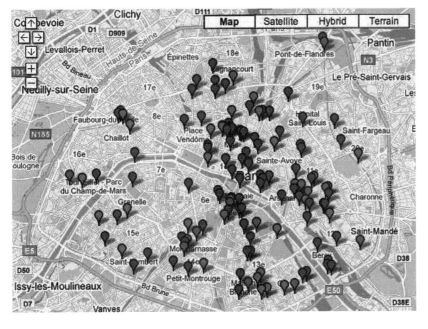

FIGURE 3.2 A Google map of coffee shops with Wi-Fi in Paris. When clicked, each marker reveals additional information, such as café name, location, and hours.

granularity. Google offers this data freely to web and mobile app developers. Fortunately for all digital editors, the multiplicity of inexpensive, even free tools available online have fairly short learning curves. More importantly, a smartly developed interactive map can offer interactors a high density of information in a small space.

Some common uses of maps include plotting routes; showing directions; signifying key locations of something, such as Wi-Fi spots or public transportation; and layering spreadsheet data such as crime or traffic data. Most of the online tools also offer the capacity to annotate your maps, allowing you to add clickable regions, points or icons, as well as images, sound, and even video.

Most digital mapmaking applications generate the necessary HTML code needed to add the map to another webpage, code that can simply be dropped into a webpage's coding for full interactivity. For example, the code below was generated by Zeemaps. com, a snatch of HTML that inserts a frame with a map of Paris showing the location of the Palais Garnier opera house:

```
<iframe frameborder = 0 style = 'width:200px;height:300px';
src = http://www.zeemaps.com/widget?group=618923 ></iframe>
```

The code, generated automatically by Zeemaps.com, sizes the map at 200 pixels wide by 300 pixels high, and once in a webpage, the code will pull the map data from Zeemaps. com using a unique URL, www.zeemaps.com/widget?group=618923.

To create mashup maps, or maps that combine different types of information, such as crime statistics, school rankings, weather and climate conditions, etc., there is a great deal of information available without cost, such as data from the Government Printing Office (http://gpo.gov) and the U.S. Census Bureau (http://census. gov). You can also solicit data from your interactors, which engages and involves them while at the same time leveraging what they know or can gather—the wisdom of the crowds.

Ideally, an interactive map will allow zooming and rotation for a sort of magic carpet ride. In terms of the amount of information your map conveys, though, be judicious. As with most everything in digital spaces, less is more; maps too cluttered and encumbered with information risk being ignored. For example, maps that show significant, easily recognizable landmarks or tourist attractions are effective because they quickly orient users and avoid overwhelming with too much information.

For a model of what a map can do when combined with a dataset, take a peek at a *New York Times* map powered by Google showing major crimes in New York City from 2003 to 2011. The data represented came from police reports, news accounts, court records, and original reporting, and the map shows changes over time (http://projects.nytimes.com/crime/homicides/map). The dots of various colors represent the locations of major crimes. The blue dots, for example, represent homicide locations. Clicking on a dot pulls up information about the homicide, including when it occurred, the name and a description of the victim(s) and of the perpetrator, a motive, and the weapon used. This data can be categorized and represented using a range of variables, including day and time, race/ethnicity of the victim, race/ethnicity of the perpetrator, sex of either victim or perpetrator, age, weapon, or New York City borough in which the crime(s) occurred.

Smartly combining information from several credible sources produces a robust interactive data map that layers or cascades information with interaction with its users. For example, at the top of the *Times*'s map is a timeline that can be used to show how many murders occurred each year, hiding the ones that occurred in other years, and a box into which a reader can enter a location or address to check if any homicides occurred there. This is possible because this map's developers layered the data to reveal important patterns and trends.

To help journalists and journalism students develop map-based presentations like the homicide map, the Knight Digital Media Center has developed a series of tutorials (http://multimedia.journalism.berkeley.edu/tutorials/cat/maps).

If you are ready to get started, you might first try one or two of these mapmaking applications online:

▶ **Bing Maps** (www.bing.com/maps/) generates maps that can be embedded in a webpage and that can include point A to point B directions. Free.

▶ **Google Maps** (http://maps.google.com/) offers the same features as Bing Maps. Free.

▶ **MapQuest** (www.mapquest.com/) offers the same features as Google Maps. Free.

▶ **Yahoo Maps** (http://maps.yahoo.com/) offers the same features as Bing Maps. Free.

▶ **Zee Maps** (www.zeemaps.com/) powered by Google, allows users to make custom maps. Free for basic maps, or users can pay to place more markers, including markers with advanced features, such as links to email, websites, audio, or video. Also enables map-makers to highlight a region of the map using a particular color, or to save as a .pdf or .jpg file.

Content Management Systems

How an editor does his or her job is influenced, if not dictated, by the publishing environment that editor must work within. During the last decade, the movement has been away from pure HTML environments and toward content management systems that combine coding languages with pre-fab templates and shells. Content management systems (CMSs) constrict what editors and web developers can do; but with the use of templates they also make updating and adding content fairly routine and much, much simpler than writing code.

A CMS is essentially a sophisticated software system that automates many of the processes or functions of updating, moving, and archiving copy and content. A CMS also helps digital publications to achieve and maintain a consistency in look while updating content from any number of sources both within the organization and from without. CMS software makes it easier to publish, and it erases the need for writers and editors to learn or to know more than a little HTML, CSS or JavaScript—though, of course, for troubleshooting and customizing, it's good to be comfortable with these languages. A good content management system makes it fairly simple for almost anyone to learn how to upload content to the publication's site and to format that content using simple tags or by clicking a few buttons on a dashboard.

CMS software packages also automate how a site interfaces with databases. For example, if an online newspaper wants to allow site visitors to search and view its database of real estate listings, a CMS can be built to provide a drop-down menu or sequence of drop-down menus enabling that database to be searched by price or location, or any other data field, and to do so without leaving the CMS environment. A CMS might also be used to automatically feed a homepage with updated content, and a common utility of this function is populating a page with breaking news headlines that link out to whole stories published, also automatically, on interior pages. In short, a good CMS can perform many of the functions of print editors, freeing up human resources for the more important tasks, such as fact-checking and copyediting.

With the fast growth of mobile, CMS tools are emerging for smartphones and tablets, as well. A company called MobileCMS, for example, offers a mobile app CMS that generates RSS (really simple syndication) feeds and manages updating of photography and video. But the MobileCMS app, like the vast majority of apps, has very limited and standard functionality. This aspect of digital publishing is still nascent, and because of competing platforms (Apple's IOS, Android, etc.), each with its own specs and standards, development is slow going and fairly expensive relative to HTML development.

For the brave willing to develop an app, try AppMkr, which is inexpensive and provides a relatively easy tool with which to learn the basic characteristics of the app development environment. If its end products aren't sophisticated enough for a final app to offer your audience, AppMkr can be used to prototype in order to pitch an app concept inside the organization, perhaps, or to show a third-party developer what your organization wants.

▶ MAKING THE TRANSITION

"Ink-stained wretches," as veteran print writers and reporters are sometimes called, have had difficulty making the transition from analog to digital. It takes time to learn new tools, technologies, and routines, even to discern what changes need to be made and what are merely passing fads. For many professional print writers, the big leap to digital has produced a sort of crisis, both at a personal level ("Do I still have what it takes?") and at an organizational level as analog companies get left behind or find their business models obsolete. The jobs that allow writers to focus only on writing, to work only with words, are vanishing. Necessary today are communication professionals with many skills and aptitudes. Even Clark Kent (a.k.a. Superman) ditched *The Daily Planet* in October 2012 to start his own blog, after all.

"I was taught to believe you could use words to change the course of rivers—that even the darkest secrets would fall under the harsh light of the sun," Kent told his newspaper colleagues. "But facts have been replaced by opinions. Information has been replaced by entertainment. Reporters have become stenographers. I can't be the only one who's sick of what passes for the news today."

Who could blame Kent? The proportion of Americans who read news on a printed page is declining, according to the Pew Research Center for the People & the Press, which in 2012 reported that just 23 percent of those surveyed said they read a print newspaper the previous day. This figure represents an 18 percentage point decrease over the past decade.

Digital editors don't have to be superheroes, though it might feel that way at times. But, at a minimum, digital writers and editors need to know how:

   ▶ to capitalize on the new rhetorical capabilities of digital in terms of presentation;

▶ those presentations can be monetized to pay the bills;

▶ to choose the media most appropriate for the story, and then to effectively utilize those media;

▶ to work with others as a team, and to share their work as a whole and not as separate or disparate pieces.

This doesn't mean that every digital writer or editor has to know how to win awards with their video *and* their photography, *and* how to code a website from the ground up, *and* how to manage social media to best promote the content, *and*, oh, by the way, still write powerful prose. But, today's digital communicators do need to take advantage of the new tools for presentation and for distribution, and to embrace convergence, just as Superman did.

▶ HELP FOR FREELANCERS

Since the first edition of this book was published, a number of students, most of them working professionals, have asked for help to succeed in the fluid, fast-changing world of freelancing. The days of working for one company for 30 years are long gone, and most new jobs in communication are with small start-ups. Change is rapid, frequent, and inevitable. Many traditional media professionals are finding themselves freelancing to make ends meet and to soften the blow of layoffs and business shutdowns. Help is here.

As anyone who has tried to freelance full time well knows, freelancing is a punishing business for all but an elite few. Your academic degree(s) don't matter all that much, even if they are journalism degrees, and you can lose that key contact at a publishing house, magazine, or website in an instant. Legions of prolific, tireless, talented writers are out there shaking the publishing trees, so the life of a freelancer is a relentlessly challenging one. The best way to survive—in fact, the only way to survive—is to write interesting, compelling, clear, accurate, deeply reported stories, and to do it on deadline to spec. And this is to simply get in the game.

To get someone interested in publishing or running your story, you have to pitch it, and this, too, requires skill and industry. Once you've identified a potential publication, you should read it. Become familiar with its presentation, its sensitivities and style, and, most importantly, its audience. Learn the types of stories that publication likes to run. Once you've edited your story to fit that publication's style of writing, find out whom to send it to. Search the publication's masthead or online staff listing. Email and/or reach out via social networks such as LinkedIn or Facebook. (And you absolutely must spell the name and title of the person you are contacting accurately; a misspelling here and your story will never get read.)

In a cover letter or message, (very) briefly introduce yourself, with just a little about your background. The key words here are "briefly" and "just a little." Autobiographies and breathless listings of academic honors are door-closers. The editor doesn't care, at least not yet. Then quickly get to your pitch. What is your story about? Why is it a good story? Why is it a good story to run now? Why would the publication's audience be interested in it? Finally, include all of your contact information. Make it easy for the editor to contact you.

Just as you learned when searching for a job, follow-up is important, but don't overdo it. Editors are busy, and with all of the layoffs resulting from the diminishing of print, they are as busy and overworked as never before. Give them grace. Follow up once or twice, but no more than that. Give editors a week or so to respond. If two follow-ups or two weeks roll by without response, it's probably time to move on. If you do find interest, be flexible. Rarely—almost never—does a story get published just as it was submitted. Some rewriting is likely, a lot is possible, and sometimes all an editor is interested in is the basic story idea or concept.

Your story might be accepted on spec, which means you can write or rewrite the story and, if the publication likes and runs it, you get paid. If the publication rejects the piece written on spec, you can take it elsewhere, but you don't get payment unless a "kill fee" was negotiated upfront. (A kill fee is typically a fraction of the amount that would have been due upon publication, and it compensates at least some for the effort required to put it together, even though it was "killed.") Writing on spec is a way for both the publication and the writer to try each other out.

Here's a sample cover message for an article submission, to give freelancers some help starting out:

Dear Ed Etoor,
I'm Ryder Leonard, a veteran sports journalist who has published in a number of national and regional newspapers, magazines, and websites. I've written an

in-depth feature on Derek Jeter's recovery and rehabilitation after shattering his ankle in Major League Baseball's playoffs last October, a feature written after several interviews with the Yankee shortstop and future hall of famer. I have attached that story to this email. I also have several images for which I own the copyright, if you are interested in running those, as well. If you're interested in running the story, please let me know. I can be reached at . . . .

Another method is to offer yourself as an expert on a topic, with the hope or aim of being contacted for stories on that topic. Here is a form of press release announcing a person's expertise and availability:

Sports training expert and CEO of BodyImpact.com, Gerry Toome (headshot and bio below) is available to take the mystery out of personal training by offering tried-and-true tips and tricks. Toome is available to provide insight and answer questions on sports training, fitness, and fitness programs.

If you are interested in setting up an interview with Toome to discuss these topics, or to see one of Toome's many columns written on these topics, please contact him at. . . .

Bio: Sports training expert Gerry Toome is an industry leader in helping people maximize their physical potential. In addition to serving as both CEO and key expert for Body Impact, Gerry frequently speaks to college athletics departments, teams, and youth athletics organizations throughout the country.

CHAPTER ASSIGNMENTS

1 Generate a map using any web-based mapmaking software, such as Google Maps (http://maps.google.com/) or Map Builder (www.mapbuilder.net/). Use Chapel Hill, NC, as your locality (zip code: 27514). The map you will build will show site visitors where in the city there are Wi-Fi hotspots for wireless Internet access.

Plot the following data on your map, label the map "Wireless Access Points in Chapel Hill," then publish the map to any blog or webpage:

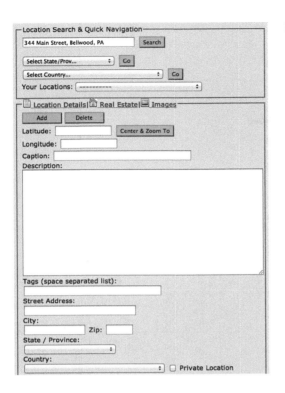

FIGURE 3.3 Mapbuilder's map-making interface.

101 East Weaver Street
27510

100 Europa Drive
27517

103 E Franklin Street
27514

141 Chatham Downs Drive
27514

213 West Franklin Street
27516

910 Raleigh Road
27514

1748 Fordham Blvd

27514

409 W Franklin Street

27516

116 West Barbee Chapel Road

27517

201 South Estes Drive

27514

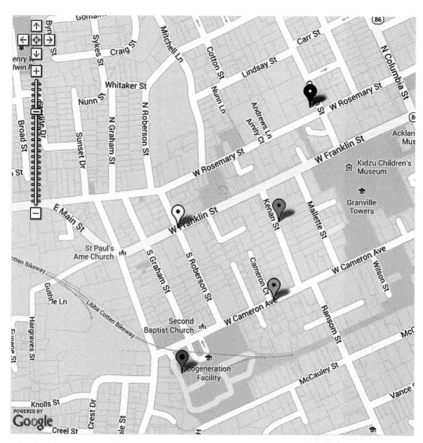

FIGURE 3.4 Example of the beginnings of a Chapel Hill Wi-Fi identifying map.

2 Create and infographic: There are many free and low-cost tools online with which to create infographics, which can bring data to life for interactors. In this exercise, you will take freely available census data found at http://census.gov and create a simple graphic to visually communicate that information in a digital environment. Here's how:

(a). Go to http://census.gov. Off the top-line navigation, choose "Data." Next, choose "QuickFacts." Use the graphical map to select your state. From the second-layer navigation line, choose or click "More STATE data sets." Next, from "Population Estimates," select "Estimates for all counties" (Excel). This will give you an Excel spreadsheet that you can download and pull from to make an infographic.

(b). Next, go to http://infogr.am. You will have to register, but the service is free. Of the options, choose "New Infographic." From the Excel spreadsheet at census.gov, select three years' worth of data for the counties you wish to highlight. Copy and paste into your new infographic. Experiment with the labels, and with getting the rows and columns to align correctly with the data from which you are pulling.

(c). Empowered and emboldened? Experiment further with your infographic by adding a map, a photo, or even a video.

3 Editing and layering: First, find a long (3,000 words or more) feature online. (If you need a suggestion, try *Esquire*'s painful-to-read-online article "The man who killed bin Laden is screwed": www.esquire.com/features/man-who-shot-osama-bin-laden-0313.) Second, remake and edit the feature article into something more conducive for digital presentation. Use the guidelines discussed in this chapter to facilitate scanning and to make the piece interactive. More specifically:

▶ Look for elements or key words to hyperlink. Be sure to indicate what you would link to, what would happen when clicked (a new tab, a new browser window, etc.), and why that's the best decision.

▶ Break the article up into text "chunks" or subdivisions that will encourage readership. Do this by adding subheads and even sub-subheads, by looking for places to convert text into lists, and by restricting each paragraph to one idea.

▶ Look for content to pull out and make its own entity, like a "how-to" box or "best of" list. This shortens the main story and helps the reader more readily use what's pulled out of the main.

▶ Finally, brainstorm suggestions on how to improve the content even further to make it a more useful digital experience. For example, produce a video to accompany the text? A Flash presentation? Interactive graphics? But be specific, detailing the content for any of these, spelling out exactly what should be developed and how it would be experienced online.

4 Fact-checking: This exercise is designed to help you evaluate sources and to think through the fact-checking process. The following is a list of facts that you, as the copyeditor of a news website, need to confirm. Sources for the information can be found on the Internet. Be sure to write the answer and the URL for each question, and remember that a URL is not a source, but rather the online address of a source.

▶ Your newspaper is doing a story on the registrar of the University of North Carolina at Wilmington. Find that person's name and confirm the name and its spelling. List your source and its URL. Corroborate that source by finding a second source verifying the information.

▶ You are doing a story celebrating the establishment of the First Amendment. What is the exact wording of that amendment? List your source and corroborate by finding a second credible source with the same exact wording.

▶ You are doing a story on a new airline servicing the international airport in Atlanta, GA. The airline will be based out of the international concourse of that airport. What is the proper name of the airport? Which of its concourses is the one devoted to international flights? Identify your source and corroborate.

▶ The blog you write and edit for is working on a feature on alternative weeklies. You need to find and confirm the name of the editor-in-chief of the *Metro Pulse* in Knoxville, TN. Corroborate what you find with a second source.

▶ According to the Georgia Bureau of Investigation, what is the most common violent crime in the state of Georgia, and is it rising or falling?

▶ What is the most recent population figure for Floyd County, GA? How does this number compare to the total for or in year 2000? Be careful: there is also a Floyd County in Iowa.

▶ Your blog is doing a story on Pulitzer Prize-winning fiction. You need to confirm the 1995 recipient of that award and the name of that author's book.

▶ You are editing a financials story for Bloomberg News. You need to know how many employees are working for Atlanta-based Coca-Cola Enterprises. Be careful, there are several companies and divisions with the name "Coca-Cola." Find out the name of the company's highest-ranking female executive (name and title). What were the company's most recent annual total revenues (called "operating revenues") for the most recent fiscal year? (Note: the fiscal and calendar years are not always the same.) How much was the company's profit (or loss) for that year? Be careful with how you present the answers. Often they are reported with thousands assumed (US$000s), meaning that you have to add three zeroes to correctly answer the question. Provide your source(s) for your answers and rely only on credible sources, such as the Securities and Exchange Commission or Lexis Nexis Academic Universe database.

▶ According to court documents, what did the U.S. Supreme Court decide in the case *Hosty v. Carter*, No. 05–377, 546 U.S. 1169; 126 S. Ct. 1330? This is a kind of a trick question, so be careful to get precisely what the Supreme Court determined. Make sure you understand your own answer. Provide your source(s) for this answer, and do not rely on news accounts.

▶ How do modest amounts of coffee intake affect a person's risk of renal cancer, according to the *International Journal of Cancer* (published November 15, 2007, vol 121, no 10: 2246–2253)? The article, "Intakes of *coffee*, tea, milk, soda and juice and renal cell *cancer* in a pooled analysis of 13 prospective studies," was co-authored by about 28 people (J. E. Lee et al.). Make sure your answer is in layman's terms.

▶ REFERENCES

Irene Hammerich and Claire Harrison, *Developing Online Content: The Principles of Writing and Editing for the Web* (New York, NY: John Wiley & Sons, 2002).

Steven Levy, "Can an Algorithm Write a Better News Story than a Human Reporter?," *Wired*, April 12 (2012), www.wired.com/gadgetlab/2012/04/can-an-algorithm-write-a-better-news-story-than-a-human-reporter/.

Eduardo Lorea, "Improving Accuracy: Creating a Newsroom System," Poynter Institute, March 10 (2008).

Patrick Lynch and Sarah Horton, *Web Style Guide 2* (New Haven, CN: Yale University Press, 2001), www.webstyleguide.com.

Jakob Nielsen, *Designing Web Usability* (Indianapolis, IN: New Riders, 2000).

Roger C. Parker, *Guide to Web Content and Design* (New York, NY: MIS Press, 1997).

Jonathan Price and Lisa Price, *Hot Text: Web Writing that Works* (Indianapolis, IN: New Riders, 2002).

Carolyn Rude and Angela Eaton, *Technical Editing*, fifth edition (Harlow, UK: Longman, 2011).

Catherine E. Sholchet, "Clark Kent Quits Newspaper Job in Latest Superman Comic," CNN.com, October 24 (2012), http://edition.cnn.com/2012/10/24/showbiz/superman-quits-job.

Alysson Troffer, "Editing Online Documents: Strategies and Tips" (August 1999).

PART TWO
Practice

4

Writing for Digital Media II: Tools and Techniques

Everything that is needless gives Offense.
Benjamin Franklin

We must abandon conceptual systems founded upon ideas of center, margin, hierarchy, and linearity, and replace them with ones of multilinearity, nodes, links, and networks.
George Landow, educator and author of *Hypertext 2.0*

Each of us literally chooses, by his way of attending to things, what sort of universe he shall appear to himself to inhabit.
William James, psychologist

CHAPTER OBJECTIVES

After studying this chapter, you will be able to:

▼

write effective headlines, deckheads, subheads, and lists;

▼

organize content in layers to facilitate deep drilldowns;

▼

expertly hyperlink to organize information, facilitate navigation, and make proximous related information;

▼

convert large wads of text into digital-friendly chunks and packets.

▶ INTRODUCTION

In the last chapter we explored the differences between digital and analog media, and the implications of these differences for the way we write and edit. Now it's time to get practical. This chapter introduces you to specific digital tools and techniques that leverage the capacities of digital environments, including layering, or arraying content to permit drilling, skipping, surfing and scanning; chunking; headline writing; hyperlinking; and using lists. We will cover how to convert big, intimidating text blocks into smaller, more varied digital content. Finally, this chapter covers the more important lessons learned studying web and iPad tablet users.

▶ LAYERS

Layering is a response to the well-documented fact that interactors do not read. They just don't. Instead, they surf and scan, scroll and skip, hurtling through digital spaces searching for something they need, or for something that might grab their attention. One early web usability study by Jakob Nielsen showed that perhaps more than three-fourths of web users merely scan any page they download. Nielsen found that only 16 percent reported reading word for word, and that was for the early web. With the proliferation of smartphones, apps, and social media, these percentages have not gone up. With these low readership statistics in mind, Nielsen recommended several web-page characteristics to enhance "scan-ability," attributes that apply also to most other digital environments:

- ▶ highlighted key words;
- ▶ hyperlinks;
- ▶ typeface variations;
- ▶ variation in color;
- ▶ subheads;
- ▶ bulleted lists, just like this one;
- ▶ paragraphs with one idea each;
- ▶ information presented in inverted pyramid style (with most important up top);
- ▶ perhaps above all, brevity (Nielsen controversially recommended half the total word count or less for webpages than for printed texts).

Rather than creating a story or an article, digital writers and editors should present story packages that link and array related content, and that organize information in such a way that even a speeding surfer can quickly—emphasis on *quickly*—determine what to attend to (and what not to). Readers can delve into these packages as deeply as they wish, and they can access the content in the order they want. The goal, then, is to create visually appealing experiences that maximize the advantages or capacities of the medium (or media) and minimize their limitations. One of digital media's chief capacities is allowing the layering and juxtaposing of information and even disparate media, such as photography and video.

An example: Your team just won the championship. You saw it live, but you want to luxuriate in the afterglow of the win by reading, watching, looking, and conversing. So you visit your team's (or school's or newspaper's) website or mobile app to read the immediate game write-ups. Layered just under the game summary is a menu of video highlights. To the side are box scores or scoring summaries. In the "related content" section, there is a photo slide show of some of the game's more memorable images, links to the post-game press conferences, and, of course, ways to buy championship t-shirts and hats. Layered at the bottom are what fans (and foes) are saying about the big game, comment that includes channels for Twitter, Facebook, Instagram, and other social media platforms. An hour has just whizzed by, but it doesn't matter. The experience is what you were after, and the expert layering and combinations of media are what enabled that experience.

So, the information or content layers at our disposal include, among other possibilities:

▶ headlines, subheads, and sub-subheads;

▶ one-sentence teasers and lead-ins;

▶ brief summary paragraphs or abstracts;

▶ visuals, photos, and information graphics;

▶ audio and video clips;

▶ related stories, interviews, timelines, and statistical charts;

▶ maps;

▶ discussion, chat, and ways to share the content;

▶ related links.

"Snow Fall" from *The New York Times* was highlighted in the previous chapter as an expert example of digital storytelling that very intentionally combines media to tell pieces of a larger story, and that uses media in ways that make the most sense for the different aspects of the story. Another expert example is "The Chauncey Bailey Project," located at www.chaunceybaileyproject.org/ and the result of a collaboration among San Francisco Bay area journalists, media organizations, and university journalism departments.

FIGURE 4.1 A model for collaboration: The Chauncey Bailey Project.

"The Chauncey Bailey Project" blends media that work together to tell a rich, complicated story, as well as to provide the necessary historical, social, cultural, and personal contexts of and for that story. No one medium could carry the freight of this story, and no one medium is an afterthought. Video achieves intimacy and immediacy, bringing interactors into the medium's "present." An interactive timeline supplies historical context and a sense of the sequence and chronology of events. Text provides the narrative, as well as the very complex interrelationships between actors in this drama, which centers on the case of a journalist gunned down in Oakland in August 2007.

One of the significant differences between the two multimedia story packages is user interaction and control. Developed for the web, "The Chauncey Bailey Project" is a mosaic of elements that each can be clicked at any time, with the textual narrative providing the skeleton and the supplementary media pieces offering drill-downs and additional information. "Snow Fall," on the other hand, is meant to be experienced in a narrative flow, with supplemental media appearing when the package's developers determined they would be most useful, when the narrative suggested deepening the telling of the story through other media. "Snow Fall," a much more recent digital artifact, is therefore more intuitive and more suited to readership on tablets and smartphones. But both are excellent models for multi-modal digital storytelling. And both leverage many of digital's capacities, such as:

▶ *No limits on space.* If printed on paper, both would be much more substantial than either a newspaper or a magazine could accommodate.

▶ *Navigation.* Interactors can easily move, surf and scan either package, making the distance between any two elements or even media inconsequential.

▶ *Hypertextuality.* Both hyperlink abundantly but judiciously, allowing readers to access background and related information throughout.

▶ *Multimedia*, or multiple channels of information, are featured, as well as multiple ways of experiencing the same story.

▶ *24 x 7 availability and accessibility.*

▶ The opportunity exists to *update, correct, revise, and expand* at any time.

▶ *Digital distribution.* No trees were killed to produce or publish either, no trucks had to roll, and no unused copies had to be thrown into the landfill.

▶ *Conversation* is encouraged (and metrics on that conversation, such as hit counts, email referrals, trackbacks, Facebook likes, tweets and re-tweets).

▶ *Portability.* With Wi-Fi and mobile phone connectivity nearly ubiquitous, these packages can be enjoyed in airport waiting areas, at home with a cup of coffee, or even on a treadmill at the gym.

But neither package was easy or inexpensive to produce. The costs, both direct and indirect, were high. Among the questions the development teams for both had to consider were:

▶ *Spatial relationships and interconnectedness.* It is more difficult to build a space than to lay out a newspaper or record a broadcast news segment. Consider how difficult it can sometimes be to navigate even a brochure or road atlas, then consider how complicated it was to map out the individual pieces of these projects and how they all fit together.

▶ *Technical questions*, such as the varying specifications and standards for browsers, computers, tablets, colors, text sizes and type.

> ▶ *Bandwidth and download times.* By comparison, how long does it take for a photo in a newspaper or magazine to download?

> ▶ *The competition for attention and time.* With three seconds or less to load and engage, there is primacy on making that first impression.

▶ WHAT INTERACTORS DO

It's also important to know something about how your audience wants to use or interact with your content, desires, and habits that vary depending on the device, medium, or machine that audience's members are using. In a study by the Poynter Institute (www. poynter.org/extra/Eyetrack/previous.html), researchers tracked web users' eye movements, particularly those of people who read newspapers online. Here is a sampling of what the Eyetrack researchers found (several of the findings are counter-intuitive):

> ▶ Interactors' eyes most often fixate in the upper left quadrant of a webpage first, before hovering, then moving left to right. The "F" pattern of readership is well established in describing how and how much time and attention are dedicated to webpage content, generally, with attention concentrated along the top and down the left side, with some attention left to right at a second level of the page.

> ▶ Dominant headlines most often draw the eye upon entering the webpage, not photographs, especially when placed in the upper left quadrant of the page. In contrast to print, online photos are not ideal entry points. So, text rules on computer screens, at least generally, both in terms of when it is viewed and in how much time is spent interacting with it.

> ▶ Though headlines prove better entry points than do photos or graphics, surprisingly smaller headlines are more closely read than are the larger, which are merely scanned; the larger headlines can be perceived as graphical elements as opposed to text. The Poynter study shows that smaller type encourages focused viewing, while larger type promotes scanning.

> ▶ To return to headlines, when a headline is bold and in the same size as the deckhead, both are read, as opposed to scanned or skipped. When the headline is larger, however, and the deckhead text is on a separate line, readers skip the deck.

> ▶ Navigation placed at the top of the homepage performed best, and by a wide margin, outperforming navigation on either side of the page or placed at the bottom.

▶ Shorter paragraphs are more highly read than long ones by a factor of two. One-column formats are more highly read than those with more than one column of text, which is a change from print newspaper readership. And summary descriptions, or abstracts, are well received. Boldface summary descriptions are read 95 percent of the time.

▶ By contrast, static advertisements typically are ignored. Those graphical ads that are attended to get only a half second to 1.5 seconds of the reader's attention. Text ads, however, garner nearly 7 seconds of attention, underlining text's primacy online.

▶ Mug shots (or head shots) are ignored. The average size of photos on news sites is 230 pixels wide and 230 deep, which, surprisingly, is not the golden rectangle with a 3:2 ratio for which print traditionally strives. These small, boxy photos online are attended to by 70 percent of visitors, who like clean, clear photos with human faces.

▶ The most read typefaces online include Arial, Courier, Georgia, and Verdana, none of which are a surprise. Verdana, for example, was developed for Microsoft by typeface master Matthew Carter, and sans serif fonts generally render better in pixilated environments.

"The Chauncey Bailey Project" was developed with the web primarily in mind, while the developers of "Snow Fall" designed specifically for the iPad. Poynter's Eyetrack research has also looked at iPad use, revealing the very different ways in which the tablet's users interact with content, and hinting at some principles that could apply to smartphone use, as well. Not surprisingly, "touch" is all important. According to the Eyetrack study's findings:

▶ iPad users are either closely involved with the screen while reading, keeping nearly constant contact by touching, tapping, pinching, and swiping to adjust their views, or they arrange a full screen of text before sitting back to read.

▶ Active users, which represented 61 percent of the study's sample population, are, not surprisingly, highly focused, reading a line or two of text before swiping to move the text much like a teleprompter.

▶ Many text stories are read completely, which is a comfort to digital writers and editors; however, an average of about 1.5 minutes were spent on the first story selected by the study's participants.

▶ People not finishing a story read for an average of about 78 seconds, which suggests that at about that point in the text, digital editors should insert some visual element to keep the reader in the story package.

▶ An average of 18 items are viewed before the first selection to read is made. The high number means some headlines or images are seen multiple times before a choice is made.

▶ Importantly, participants preferred holding the tablet in horizontal or landscape position, with 70 percent preferring it to the vertical or portrait position. This preference has to do with the screen dimension for watching video.

▶ iPad users tend to enter a screen through a dominant element, often a photograph, with faces in photographs and videos attracting a lot of attention.

▶ Importantly for navigation design, iPad users preferred using a browser to navigate between stories, even where navigation was designed into the publication. About 65 percent of the participants used a browser's back button rather than the publication's navigation design. Not surprisingly, then, people default to what they know.

▶ EXTRA! EXTRA! GET YOUR GOOD HEADLINES HERE!

Poynter's Eyetrack findings make it abundantly clear: Headlines are crucially important. Good headlines engage and stir interest, and because digital readers skim, surf, scroll, and scan, often a good headline can slow the reader and mark the way. Good headlines help the reader to quickly discern what the story is about, allowing that reader to decide whether to pause, to read further, or to keep moving.

If an article or story is longer than 350 words, digital writers and editors should employ subheads to guide readers through the story. Both headlines and subheads should be brief, straightforward, active and useful, adding a layer of information rather than merely repeating something said somewhere else. To maximize consistency in style and substance, digital writers should consider headlines and subheads in sets or groups, distinct from the text. Editors, in particular, should write and review headlines for a story package as a set or group; the same should be done for subheads.

Across media, print and online, headlines serve several functions. In *The Art of Editing*, Brian S. Brooks and Jack Z. Sissors give headlines at least six tasks. Well-written headlines will:

▶ attract the reader's attention;

▶ summarize the content;

▶ organize the content and give it visual identity;

▶ help the reader to index that content;

▶ depict mood and tone, or attitude and personality;

▶ provide typographic relief.

For digital spaces, we might add to this list that headlines feed and inform the search engine algorithms and are, therefore, an important part of any search engine optimization strategy; headlines include key words users likely will employ to find the story. Of course, headlines also help readers to determine what *not to read*, and this is every bit as important as helping readers decide what to focus on.

To the first point made by Brooks and Sissors, good headlines attract attention to content that otherwise may be ignored. In attracting attention, however, resist the sometimes seemingly overwhelming temptation to be clever. (Most attempts at "clever" fall short, achieving, at best, only "cute.") First and foremost, headlines should inform; if they also entertain and amuse, if the tone of the story allows it—all the better. But humor is tricky for several reasons, including the very different comedic tastes of your audience's members and the fact that your potential audience is global. Concision, clarity, and accuracy should not be sacrificed for personality. For the same reasons, carefully consider abbreviations, slang, idioms, colloquialisms, and puns. A reference or pun that might make your headline seem clever to you may be lost on a global audience. Lurking in the semantic brush is sexual innuendo, as well, so headlines and subheads should be descriptive in tone and aim to convey useful information about the text. Remember that a primary reason interactors need the various heading types is simply to navigate the webpage or digital space, to get the meaning of the content. Though the "just the facts" style won't win prizes for originality, it will help readers to make intelligent decisions about whether to stop or keep moving. A sidebar menu from *The New Yorker* magazine website (www.newyorker.com) illustrates many of these points, and that menu would be displayed here but copyright considerations prevent it.

The department header, "The Talk of the Town," is on the top line and in larger type, establishing a hierarchy of information. Sub-departments are set off with smaller red subheads, "Comment," "Here to There Dept.," etc. And individual stories are stacked on the right with clear, easy-to-read headline–deck combinations. The headlines here mostly are label heads, or headlines with no verb that typically focus on a theme or mood. The deckhead, then, performs most of the functions of a typical headline, sum-marizing and distilling, and drawing the reader in. (A deckhead is a small headline under the main headline that provides a next-layer level of information about the story. Deckheads are also called drop heads.) The headlines as a group are similar in style and substance, and as a set provide clear navigation. And this layout would work well online, on tablets, and for smartphones.

Keep It Simple, Stupid (The KISS Method)

When the actor Heath Ledger died in January 2008, the online version of *The Sydney Morning Herald* in Australia posted the following headline: "Heath Ledger dies." Compare this to the headline that ran on the website of the *Herald*'s competition, *The Age*: "Dead in bed." Cute? Clever? You be the judge, but remember that search engines get a vote, too, and they overwhelmingly voted for "Heath Ledger dies." Direct, perhaps even a little dull, it generated all of the traffic because it includes the necessary key words, and only the necessary key words. Search engine optimization is a multi-billion dollar business that is driving how content is being found or left on the sidelines. (More coming on SEO in Chapter 6.)

So, how to write good headlines? Key words help here, as well. There are two basic steps to composing a headline:

▶ Determine what to highlight.

▶ Decide how to phrase it given the limitations on space.

To determine what to highlight, Brooks and Sissors recommend "the keyword method." Select the key words that convey the meaning of the content, like "Heath Ledger" and "dies" or "dead." Think about how the content might be indexed in a book or found by Google. In other words, WWGD (what would Google do)? Online headlines should be intuitive, not cryptic, vague, or misleading. Simply by reading a headline the reader should be able to grasp what the story's about, as he or she readily can with "Heath Ledger dies."

To come up with these headlines, here's an easy exercise. Copy the text of the article. Visit wordle.net and click "Create your own wordle." Paste in the text to generate a graphical illustration of the words in that article rendered to correspond to frequency of use of the word in the article with size. Figure 4.2 shows a wordle of the text of this chapter up to this point.

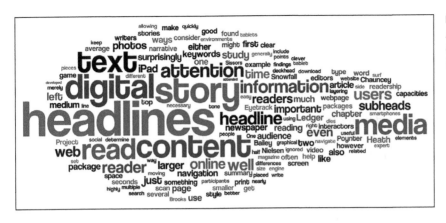

FIGURE 4.2
A wordle for this chapter, generated by wordle.net.

This simple exercise quickly reveals a handful of key words that can be used to drive headline and subhead composition, not to mention metatags, headers, and webpage titles. Using these specific key words in a well-crafted headline will provide the reader with sufficient information and incentive to decide whether to read the story. But be specific in a way that the second Heath Ledger headline was not. The headlines "Panel re-visits damage plan" or "Congress passes bill" fail to say what their respective stories are about with any meaningful degree of specificity.

With these principles in mind, let's shift now to specific rules for writing headlines, rules that take a little getting used to and that sometimes bend or break the rules of grammar and style. For example:

▶ **Use present tense.**
"Heath Ledger dies"
Ledger was dead when the headline was written and published, but headlines about events in the recent past are written in the present tense. This gives readers a sense of immediacy and drama, and it underlines that the news is, in fact, new.

▶ **Omit articles.**
Both to shorten headlines and to contribute to a "no nonsense" style, articles such as *A*, *An*, and *The*, especially when starting the headline, are simply omitted.
"~~The~~ Yankee pitcher to miss ~~a~~ start this weekend"

▶ **Omit present-tense forms of the verb *to be*.**
The verbs *is* and *are* can be assumed, so leave them out unless they really are needed for clarity.
"Lebron James named most valuable player"
Assumed in this headline is the *to be* verb *is*.

▶ **Replace *will* with *to*.**
If immediate past stories are presented in the present tense, what about the future? Stories about events in the future tense use *to* in place of *will*, mostly because it shortens the headline.
"Sales tax to increase in June"

▶ **Replace *and* with a comma or semicolon.**
"Tar Heels demolish Duke, advance to title game"
Use a semicolon if the elements joined by *and* are independent clauses with different subjects.
"Astros finish in last place; the manager's contract was not renewed"

▶ **Use numerals rather than spelling out numbers to save space**
"120 killed in landslide in Myanmar"

▶ **Omit end punctuation.**
Don't punctuate your headlines with periods, and exclamation points are annoying and perhaps sensationalistic. Question marks are recommended, but only when the headline is, in fact, a question.

▶ **Attribution is important, even in a headline.**
If you are quoting someone, and likely it will be a partial quote, you need to attribute the source. Your friends in these instances are the colon and the dash. The colon for providing the source first:
"Obama: Healthcare law will prevail"
The dash for providing the source last:
"Airlines to keep jacking up fares—experts"

▶ **Use single quote marks.**
When quoting in a headline, use single quotes.
"Tea Party candidate a 'dirty, rotten scoundrel,' rival candidate claims"

What works best for print might not work as well in digital spaces, and vice versa. In other words, headlines should be written with the medium in mind, and different media likely will warrant different headlines for the same story. Again, the "Heath Ledger dies" case study is useful. "Dead in bed" might work in print, where the headline can be accompanied by a photo of the actor to immediately identify just who it is who was found dead in his bed, as well as a deckhead with another layer of information. This context is more difficult to immediately provide in the smaller digital spaces, particularly the punishingly small smartphone displays. Compare the amount of information, for example, that can be displayed in a single smartphone screen with that on a page in the newspaper.

Prominent and abundant use of headlines would be expected at a newspaper site, like *The New York Times*, which employs some of the industry's most capable editors to write the headlines, editors who typically accomplish most and sometimes all of Brooks and Sissors's purposes in a single headline.

To visualize this, go to www.nytimes.com/. The *Times* headlines enable readers to scan, skim, and drill down. The headline gives a snapshot of the story, while the deckhead underneath provides the logical next layer of information. For many interactors, this will be all they need, so off they go. For others, this is a natural drilldown into the story itself and the accompanying Q&A nestled underneath. As sets, the headlines, deckheads, and department headers provide structure and organization to the page—in this case, hierarchically according to news value.

Another useful tool to break up the text, offer a measure of visual relief, and provide another entry point into the story is to incorporate what are called "pullout quotes." Magnifying a particularly colorful, provocative, or summative quote can draw attention, and it can stimulate interest in the story. Figure 4.3 shows a pullout quote from *Pacific Standard* magazine online that has been offset, magnified, and presented in blue type to contrast with the article at right from which it came.

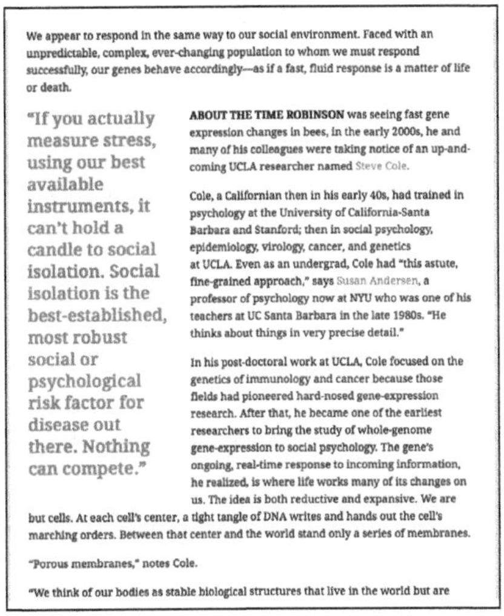

We appear to respond in the same way to our social environment. Faced with an unpredictable, complex, ever-changing population to whom we must respond successfully, our genes behave accordingly—as if a fast, fluid response is a matter of life or death.

"If you actually measure stress, using our best available instruments, it can't hold a candle to social isolation. Social isolation is the best-established, most robust social or psychological risk factor for disease out there. Nothing can compete."

ABOUT THE TIME ROBINSON was seeing fast gene expression changes in bees, in the early 2000s, he and many of his colleagues were taking notice of an up-and-coming UCLA researcher named Steve Cole.

Cole, a Californian then in his early 40s, had trained in psychology at the University of California-Santa Barbara and Stanford; then in social psychology, epidemiology, virology, cancer, and genetics at UCLA. Even as an undergrad, Cole had "this astute, fine-grained approach," says Susan Andersen, a professor of psychology now at NYU who was one of his teachers at UC Santa Barbara in the late 1980s. "He thinks about things in very precise detail."

In his post-doctoral work at UCLA, Cole focused on the genetics of immunology and cancer because those fields had pioneered hard-nosed gene-expression research. After that, he became one of the earliest researchers to bring the study of whole-genome gene-expression to social psychology. The gene's ongoing, real-time response to incoming information, he realized, is where life works many of its changes on us. The idea is both reductive and expansive. We are but cells. At each cell's center, a tight tangle of DNA writes and hands out the cell's marching orders. Between that center and the world stand only a series of membranes.

"Porous membranes," notes Cole.

"We think of our bodies as stable biological structures that live in the world but are

FIGURE 4.3 A pullout quote from a page at *Pacific Standard* magazine online, which also uses boldface lead-ins to break up the text and keep readers moving through its articles.

BOX 4.1   *A Word About Typography*

The type choices we make for print often do not work as well online. When printed on paper, type can handle ornamentation, serifs, ascenders and descenders, and embellishments. Online, however, fewer typefaces read or render well, though improving resolutions and increasingly sophisticated display technologies, such as electronic ink, are erasing the gap. Computer monitors have trouble displaying fonts with serifs—the curved embellishments on letters—because monitors use tiny squares

FIGURE 4.4

called pixels to build each letter (or anything else, for that matter). Therefore, every letter's "curve" on screen is really a collection of tiny squares that actually follow a tiny jagged line, not a truly smooth curve. Magnify a letter in a serif typeface to 400 percent or so to see the pixels.

Sans serif fonts like Gotham, Helvetica, and Neutra perform better in these pixilated environments because they have straight lines and fewer embellishments.

Perhaps the most famous of sans serif types is Helvetica. Note the lack of ornamentation and how one letter flows into the next for a wonderful push and pull within the type:

Aa Bb Cc Dd Ee.

Compare Helvetica's clean look, which makes it ideal for online use, with a highly ornamented serif typeface such as:

Snell Roundhand

Snell Roundhand's ascenders and descenders would pixilate at even a relatively small size online, and it would be more difficult to read than any sans serif font, regardless of medium. Italics also can be ineffective in digital spaces, and for the same reasons.

HTML code poses other challenges for type online because it has many rules controlling line spacing, hyphenation, column and table cell widths, and line leading. The web uses far more defaults and lowest common-denominator rules than does print or tablet readers. Because monitor sizes vary from user to user, web designers cannot lock in dimensions for display in the same way that print designers can. Design specifications will simply change from browser to browser, giving web designers another significant challenge or barrier. Not only will webpages look different on monitors of different sizes, they may also display differently depending upon the browser the interactor is using.

Typeface choices can also add to or subtract from your credibility, or, more accurately, from interactors' perceptions of your credibility. For example, when CERN announced that its researchers could confirm the existence of "the God particle," the Higgs boson, at least one CERN scientist very oddly chose Comic Sans MS for his PowerPoint presentation on his group's findings. (CERN is the European Organization for Nuclear Research, a Geneva-based laboratory for particle physics.) This typeface choice elicited ridicule and worse. As one scientist warned CERN, "Every time you use Comic Sans on a PowerPoint, God kills Schrödinger's cat. Please think of the cat" (Morris 2012). This typeface kerfuffle inspired *New York Times* writer Errol Morris to conduct an experiment on the relationship between typeface and credibility.

Morris not surprisingly found that typeface does matter. Comic Sans inspires contempt, while Baskerville boosts credibility. The aesthetic appearance of words and letters does affect how the information they are carrying is perceived. Comic Sans, which was developed for presenting text in comic books, is too informal or casual in appearance to carry the intellectual freight of one of the more important recent scientific discoveries. Baskerville, on the other hand, "is a little bit more tuxedo," according to psychologist David Dunning, who helped Morris with the experiment. "Baskerville has a tad more starchiness."

Here is CERN's announcement, first in Comic Sans, then in Baskerville:

> At the Moriond Conference today, the ATLAS and CMS collaborations at CERN's Large Hadron Collider (LHC) presented preliminary new results that further elucidate the particle discovered last year. Having analysed two and a half times more data than was available for the discovery announcement in July, they find that the new particle is looking more and more like a Higgs boson, the particle linked to the mechanism that gives mass to elementary particles.

> At the Moriond Conference today, the ATLAS and CMS collaborations at CERN's Large Hadron Collider (LHC) presented preliminary new results that further elucidate the particle discovered last year. Having analysed two and a half times more data than was available for the discovery announcement in July, they find that the new particle is looking more and more like a Higgs boson, the particle linked to the mechanism that gives mass to elementary particles.

In short, then, interactors will perceive the same information differently purely based on its aesthetic appearance, on how it looks. Typeface matters.

Making a List and Checking It Twice

Another excellent tool for breaking up text blocks, facilitating scanning, and distilling, layering, and emphasizing information is the list, which comes in two varieties: ordered and unordered. Ordered lists are numbered; unordered lists are not. Sequential lists, step-by-step process, and "how to" forms of content are ideal for ordered list-making. For example, here is a list instructing a young ballplayer how to throw a curveball:

1   **Holding the ball:** Grip the ball between your thumb and middle finger, placing your middle finger along the bottom seam of the ball and your thumb along the back seam. The curves of the seams should be close to your palm, with one on top and one on bottom. Don't use your **index finger** to help the grip. Use that finger to point where you want the ball to go.

2   **Throwing the ball:** Your dominant foot should be on the pitching rubber in a parallel position. Lift your opposite knee and rotate your hips forward as you throw the ball. Your elbow should be level with or above your arm, bent at a 90-degree angle.

3   **Releasing the ball:** Keep your palm facing inward. Release as your arm extends and you step forward with the opposite foot. As your arm comes down from the throw, it should be headed toward your opposite hip.

4   **Practicing the pitch**. The spinning action of the throw is achieved by the hand moving as if it is turning a doorknob or snapping your fingers as the ball is released.

The ordered list above judiciously uses **boldface** to lift the text ever so slightly off the page, which slows a reader just enough to command attention. To use a roadway metaphor, boldface serves as a sort of speed bump, and like speed bumps, boldface can become annoying rather quickly, so digital writers and editors should show restraint.

Another type of digital reading speed bump is the teaser, or a short burst of text that arrests attention or asks a question, like this one from a health magazine online:

READ MORE: Can Coffee Intake Reduce Cancer Risk?

The bolded "READ MORE" slows a reader just enough to give the hyperlinked headline a chance.

Unordered lists are for information that doesn't need to be presented in any particular order, such as lists of criteria, benefits, and requirements. For example, here's a list of the benefits of renting a room at the Happy Days Motel:

▶ Free in-room Wi-Fi

▶ Hot breakfast every morning

▶ Cable TV

▶ Indoor and outdoor pools

▶ Wake-up service

Because good lists can be quickly read or scanned, there is less need for punctuation, as in the unordered list above.

For both ordered and unordered lists, there are established guidelines for creating good ones:

▶ **Take time to set it up.** Lists shouldn't come out of thin air, so take the time to set up the list. Signal to the reader what she is about to see.

▶ **Be opportunistic.** Look for "how to" articles that include step-by-step instructions, chronologies or timelines, quantities, and, among other things, strings of names and places.

▶ **Present all list items consistently.** Bulleted items should be roughly equivalent in length, structure, phrasing, spacing, punctuation, cap style and typeface. If you start one list item with a boldfaced imperative, begin all list items with boldfaced imperatives.

▶ **Be similar in grammatical structure and syntax.** If you use a verb to start the first item, for example, use verbs to start all of the items. If you use a complete sentence in one, use complete sentences in all.

▶ **Keep it brief.** When possible, make sure the list is no longer than six to eight items. Longer lists risk losing the reader's interest. Think about subdividing longer lists and consolidating shorter ones.

▶ **Consider the order.** Is the sequence important? If it is, go with an ordered or numbered list. If all of the list items are of equal importance, an unordered list makes more sense.

▶ **Avoid overusing lists.** Too many erode any one's effectiveness or impact.

List-making is also a valuable tool in transforming wordy paragraphs into something that is easily scanned and that makes the information in that paragraph easier to interact with, as this before-and-after example demonstrates.

First, the "before":

> Tokyo is filled with internationally recognized attractions that draw large crowds of people every year without fail. During the first six months of 2014, some of the most popular places were the Imperial Palace (1.2 million visitors), Tokyo Disneyland (1.1 million), Ueno Park Zoo (678,000), Toshugu Shrine (386,598), Tokyo Science Museum (360,000), and Yasukuni Shrine (228,446).

This wad of words can easily be edited to become a rapidly read list, one that links to the individual sites mentioned:

> In the first six months of 2014, six of the most-visited places in Tokyo were:
>
> ▶ Imperial Palace
> ▶ Tokyo Disneyland
> ▶ Ueno Park Zoo
> ▶ Toshugu Shrine
> ▶ Tokyo Science Museum
> ▶ Yasukuni Shrine

▶ HYPERTEXT

Of the arrows in the digital writer's quiver, none is more powerful than the hyperlink, the most common form of hypertext. In Chapter 1, we discussed the process of printing, the "technology" of the book, and how books have shaped our understandings of composition, publication, and readership. Hypertext, or computer-coded text capable of taking the reader somewhere else—anywhere else—with the click of a mouse or touch of an icon, has changed these traditional understandings. *Hyper*, from the Greek root meaning "beyond" or "over," refers to being taken beyond a webpage or website to some other source, page, or site, potentially making any two sites or sources proximous. Hyperlinks remove the separation between text and sources, without requiring more ink or space, and they build trust by allowing readers to see what was used to put a story together.

Because links change the direction of the reader's experience in or through a page or document, as opposed to the linear activity of reading strongly suggested by books, a new rhetorical style is needed for digital spaces, one that recognizes non-linearity and the spatial relationships possible in digital spaces. This new rhetorical style must acknowledge that the interactor, not the author or producer, dictates the order in which the information is read or accessed in their use of navigational hyperlinks, which take visitors to other pages or sections within a site, and content hyperlinks, which take visitors to other sources of information. Hyperlinking should be viewed as the quickest way to get a reader to the most relevant information that reader might be interested in.

A useful metaphor for appreciating the changes hypertext have brought might be homebuilding. You would likely enter a new home through a front door, into a foyer, seeing from that vantage point several rooms and doors. A good floor plan, especially an open floor plan, would give you a sense of what to expect behind each door and how to navigate through the house. One of the mistakes inexperienced digital writers make is to assume that everyone enters a site through its homepage. Writers may assume that the visitors know the context of all the other pages on the site, having carefully constructed this digital space to be intuitive. But search engine findings, Facebook "likes," tweeted URLs, and the like are more often than not giving interactors entry to specific information directly, with no thought to front doors or even first floors, metaphorically. Each and every webpage should be designed and written with this consideration in mind, and each webpage should be able to stand on its own as independent, self-contained content that does not require readers to access it by following any particular sequence.

For the same reasons, each and every page of a site should prominently display a link or route back to the homepage, indicating how the individual page or document relates or belongs to the whole of the larger site. Hyperlinks provide jumping off points within these spaces. No other medium allows a reader to jump so easily to another story, another source, even another subject altogether. We should link to related content to allow the reader to further pursue the subject rather than simply moving on to the next story. One of the best sites at doing this, at creating a sort of connective tissue of related information and at allowing readers to scan as little or as much as they want on any particular topic, is Wikipedia. The crowd-sourced online encyclopedia layers information and links to logical and intuitive next-level sites and artifacts. The "Florence Cathedral" entry in Wikipedia, for example, for the Duomo in Florence, Italy, demonstrates effective layering, with a "contents" list, hyperlinked terms, and, at the bottom, a list of other resources.

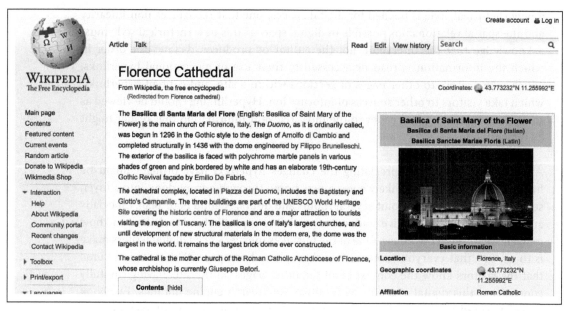

FIGURE 4.5

To What Should We Link?

Digital writers and editors should carefully consider how, when, and where to link. Before linking to another site, ask what the reward for following that link will be for the reader. This consideration will prevent gratuitous linking, or over-linking. The main reasons you might link to another article or site or source are to:

▶ direct attention;

▶ attribute information (citing and referring to sources and source documents, such as court cases, research studies, transcripts, public records, court opinions, etc.);

▶ provide context for your article (referring to related articles, next-layer sources, definitions, and explanations, much as Wikipedia does);

▶ entice and reward readers with something more, with additional layers or dimension to the story, such as related or archival stories;

▶ offer interactivity and allow for personalized texts.

If you have written term papers or research articles with footnotes or endnotes, you have a window on the kinds of information to which you might link. The information offered in footnotes is ideal for hyperlinks, which make other information immediately accessible and proximous. To access resources footnoted in print, you would have visit a library or courthouse. In digital environments, these resources are a click or touch away. The once solitary main text now can have a potentially infinite number of next-door neighbors.

How To Hyperlink

With the popular web more than 20 years old, conventions have developed to guide hyperlinking. These include:

▶ **Size.** Hyperlinks should be the same type size as the main body text.

▶ **Differentiation.** Once almost always underlined, hyperlinks today can be any color and underlined or not. But they should stand out one way or another— boldfaced or underlined, appearing in an alternating but consistent color.

▶ **Intuitiveness.** Readers should be able to predict with high fidelity what they will find by clicking or touching, enabling them to decide whether to visit now, later, or not at all.

▶ **Clarity.** The links should be explicit about the type of content to which they lead, and they should be consistent in appearance.

▶ **Goodwill.** Linking to a product or a site selling something will likely be punished; no one likes false or misleading advertising.

A convention that has evolved stipulates that hyperlinks should not appear merely as labels or pointers to content, they should be regarded as content themselves, much as headlines are. "Click here" is the equivalent to a headline in print that states, "Important story below." Such a pointer fails to provide enough helpful information; it merely points to content. So, for hyperlinking:

Bad: For more information on the Boeing 777, click here.

Good: The company has more than a dozen Boeing 777s in its fleet.

Bad: The commission's report is available by clicking here.

Better: The commission's report is available at www.report.com.

Best: Read the commission's report.

Let's look at another example of good hyperlinking, from an undergraduate student's blog:

> The news media, including journalists, editors and executives, largely agree that
> the core principles of journalism are getting the facts right, getting both sides of

the story and not publishing rumors. According to the <u>Pew Research Center for the People and the Press</u>, journalists increasingly agree with public criticism of their profession and the quality of their work. About half of news media executives and journalists rank *lack of credibility* with the public as a major reason for declining audiences. In 1989, only one-third of the press said this. Americans' evaluations of the news media's credibility have declined since the mid-1980s.

<u>The poll</u> was conducted in coordination with the <u>Committee of Concerned Journalists</u> from November 20, 1998 to February 11, 1999. Lack of credibility is the single issue most often cited by the news media as the most important problem facing journalism today.

This short post offers some lessons on how to hyperlink effectively. Her links:

▶ take readers to the supporting evidence and primary source material in such a way that neither the links nor the sources interrupt the flow of main body of text;

▶ help readers to predict where the link will take them;

▶ are brief, only a few words each—long, hyperlinked phrases are difficult to read, and likely will not get read;

▶ appear in a contrasting color, in this case the very conventional web-friendly blue, and they are underlined (the growth of blogs and the increased style capacities of CSS relative to HTML have fueled a move away from underlining and from blue link text to a range of contrasting colors).

The specific text and link color choices are not that important, provided they are legible; but consistency and repetition are important. If one hyperlink is deep green, all of the hyperlinks should be in deep green. If the first hyperlink is magenta, use magenta for all of the links. Because they typically are a different color, links are similar to bold-faced words in how they slow the reader, if ever so subconsciously. An example, coincidentally from the homepage of the Association of Lighthouse Keepers (www.alk.org.uk/), demonstrates this function as a guidepost (or lighthouse!) in surfing and scanning:

The **Association of Lighthouse Keepers** was formed in 1988 by a group of serving and **retired keepers**, with the aim of maintaining contact between its members and enthusiasts throughout the world who share an interest in **lighthouses** and other **coastal** and **inland** aids to **navigation**. Our aims are to forge links with other **lighthouse associations**, to act as an information exchange, to expand our growing **archive** on lighthouse-related material, and in the long term, to establish a museum/study centre to promote the growing interest in **pharology**.

Readers likely will scan the boldfaced words to discern the purpose of the site and its basic organization. A scanning eye can only pick up two or three words at a time, so the verbiage uses no long phrases in its hyperlinked text.

In summary, ask the following questions when developing hyperlinks and presenting them in digital spaces:

▶ How can I assure and orient readers when they first arrive on or at the page?

▶ How can I help them to read efficiently and with pleasure?

▶ How can I help readers to retrace the steps they have taken in their reading paths, or to return to any one step or level in any one of those paths?

▶ How can I describe or signal the destinations for the links in the document?

New Tab? New Window? Same Window?

There is considerable debate about whether hyperlinks should open in new windows, new tabs, or within the same browser window, and whether they should link to outside sites or keep the interactor within the same environment. If linked material opens up in a new, separate window, the original window and story are still there, so the reader can resume reading the main narrative after accessing the sidebar or background information. But new windows can quickly clutter up a desktop, which, of course, readers do not appreciate. Linking to content to open up within the same browser window leaves the linking page behind, and few interactors return to sites and pages from which they have surfed away. Links that open up a new tab on the same browser seem like a good compromise between the extremes, one that leaves the original story in one tab but that also provides access to sidebar information under a new tab within the same browser window. Nothing gets left behind, and clutter is kept to a minimum.

The hyperlinking ethos has changed dramatically in the past few years, from one resistant to jettisoning readers from a company's or organization's site to a philosophy that acknowledges that readers want, even demand, this kind of universal access. News organizations now link even to competitors, making them aggregators and curators of content, as well as producers. The philosophy, learned from Google, seems to be that if a news site does a good enough job sending people away, they will come back for more. In distilling this new ethos, journalism professor Jeff Jarvis proposed a golden rule for linking: "Link unto others' good stuff as you would have them link unto your good stuff."

It shouldn't surprise that good, hygienic hyperlinking, like good writing, is largely about clarity, accuracy, and consistency. Readers should not have to hunt through links, confused about what they might do for them. You cannot control for every possible user experience, but you can be clear, accurate, and consistent, which will be rewarded by readers who return for more.

WWGD (What Would Google Do)?

Because, like all search engines, Google looks for key words, digital writers and editors rely on them to write headlines and subheads. As Chapter 3 emphasized, digital editors should think in terms of key words when hyperlinking, anticipating and using the vocabulary of our readers. Perhaps a useful metaphor here is rock climbing. Interactors set out to scale mountains of information. The more key words digital writers can provide—the more words that jut out even slightly from the rest—the more places the reader can grab onto, step up on, and keep moving from. These key words also provide Google's and the other search engines' algorithms with the means of finding information and ranking it in their findings. Digital writers and editors can check how popular any keyword might be, and get suggested alternatives, by using Google's AdWords Keyword Tool or paid services like WordTracker.com or Keyword Discovery.com.

Google, in particular, relies on key words, particularly in the title bar that sits on top of a browser window, in metatags in the HTML code that created the page, and also within the content itself. Check out Google's Trends (www.google.com/trends/top-charts) to see, in near-real time, what computer users nationally are searching, by category.

Types of Links

Next, a digital writer should think about what kinds of links to employ. Each type operates a little differently, but all determine where a reader goes when clicked or touched, whether to a point within the same site or page, or off to a new page or site.

Embedded links are by far the most common type of link, and they are usually placed behind a word, a selection of words, an object (image, button, icon) or a "hot area." If the word or object is clicked, the visitor will be redirected somewhere else. And though most embedded links are embedded in text with HTML, other elements can serve as embedded links, such as buttons and icons, navigation bars, and image maps.

A **hot area** typically is found in or on an image, diagram, or other graphical object in which an HTML image map has been placed. Moving the cursor over the hot area

A set of easy-to-take tests at Harvard, part of its Project Implicit, will help us do this. I'd like each of us to take at least two of these Project Implicit tests, and choose any two **other than** "Weapons" or "Presidents." Each test takes approximately five minutes.

FIGURE 4.6 An embedded link in red redirecting interactors to a bank of online tests at Harvard.edu.

activates one or more embedded links. Below, HTML code is shown that embeds individual African country links into a larger map of Eastern Africa, a graphical file named "navbar":

```
<P>
<OBJECT data = "navbar.png" type = "image/png" usemap = "#mapA">
<OBJECT data = "navbar.gif" type = "image/gif" usemap = "#mapA">
    <MAP name = "mapA">
    <P>Navigate the map:
    <A href = "sudan.html" shape = "poly" coords =
        "0,0,118,28">Sudan</a> |
    <A href = "chad.html" shape = "poly" coords =
        "118,0,184,28">Chad</A> |
    <A href = "ethiopia.html" shape = "poly" coords =
        "184,200,60">Ethiopia</A> |
    <A href = "uganda.html" shape = "poly" coords =
        "276,0,276,28,100,200,50,50,276,0">Uganda</A>
    </MAP>
</OBJECT>
```

So, moving a mouse cursor over the section of the map labeled "Sudan," which is pinpointed on the graphic using coordinates, then clicking or touching, would take a site visitor to an HTML page file named "sudan.html," a webpage with more information on or about Sudan.

Inline links, by contrast, do not send the visitor somewhere else but bring content from somewhere else to the page being viewed. There is no need, therefore, to embed the link or the content. Images and graphics are the most common inline link content. In fact, almost all images on the web appear courtesy of an inline link, which positions the photo on the page and makes it appear that the photo is a part of the page. The image file is actually located somewhere else. Images appearing in blogs frequently appear using inline links, meaning that the blogger is merely linking to a graphic elsewhere on the web with HTML that makes it appear as if it is part of the blog page being viewed.

FIGURE 4.7 This
graphic shows
two hot areas, one
for cubanxgiants.
com and one
to redirect
interactors to
WanderingRocks.
wordpress.com.

FIGURE 4.8 Anchor
links are signified
by an anchor icon:
A top-of-the-page
link to "paper
topics" sends
interactors deep
into the page to
this subsection
outlining resources
for paper topics.

Anchors are in-page or within-document navigational links, redirecting a visitor to another part of the same document or page. They are commonly used to create top-of-page navigation to sections below, often in text-intensive or lengthy webpages, in order to minimize the need to scroll.

How Bloggers Link

Research shows that bloggers use hyperlinks differently than do news websites. Mark Coddington of the University of Texas found that while news sites link much as linking has been described in this chapter, referring thematically to supplemental sources to provide context, bloggers tend to use links to make social connections. And where news sites link to traditional, objective sources, bloggers often link to each other. Blogging journalists, Coddington found, "are found to be situated between the two groups, appropriating some practices from each" (2012). These orientations frequently lead news sites to links within their own sites, reflecting the size and sophistication of their sites, and their unwillingness to cede control, while bloggers link to the outside more than four-fifths of the time.

A History of Hyperlinking

Given how central hyperlinks are in how we read text today, it might be difficult to believe that when they were first introduced popularly in 1989 they sparked controversy (as a technology, hyperlinks have been around since the 1960s). Critics in English departments throughout the country believed that hyperlinking interferes with reading comprehension and understanding. Researchers found, however, that hyperlinks do not "slow down the reading process [and] do not affect text comprehension" (De Ridder, 2002). One might argue that links can actually enhance comprehension because a quick look at the links can give the reader a general sense of what the page is about. And for many of those same English professors, hypertext is helping to put their notes and data in "experientially closer proximity" (Landow 1997). Blogging is a contemporary example of exactly what Landow describes, connecting the speaker directly in touch with his or her audience, and placing the content in proximity to its source material or related material.

Though hypertext can enable completely non-linear or multi-linear texts, which can be read or accessed through multiple pathways, digital readers still seem to prefer the traditional narrative format. While many authors have experimented with producing elaborate, narratively complex, multilayered writings in hypertext, the traditional story arc of beginning–middle–end still reigns.

Creating hyperlinks is relatively easy; maintaining them, however, is another story. Broken links are a common problem for any site with large collections of links. And broken links chip away at a publisher's credibility, a sign of age and neglect. Hyperlinks must be periodically checked to make sure they are still active. Most web authoring software does this automatically. Additionally, if the link is still active but the URL owner has changed, the original purpose for the link might be subverted.

One final consideration: rabbit holes. Once a digital reader has linked out through a rabbit hole to another site or source or world, she rarely returns—in fact, less than half of the time. Determining when, how, and to what to link, then, are important decisions. A feature story on a cancer survivor, for example, shouldn't be interrupted by hyperlinks, which no matter how judiciously handled are, in the end, interruptions. A story promoting a coming event, however, very likely—and logically—could link out to that event's homepage.

Chunking Text

Another way to facilitate surfing and scanning is to "chunk" content, or to think of content in discrete, short, paragraph-sized pieces. Few interactors will read long articles online on their computers, though tablets and e-readers have made this activity less uncomfortable; they will instead save or print long reads. So look for opportunities to break up text into discrete, digestible pieces or chunks. The fast growth of mobile media devices, with their teeny display screens, makes chunking all the more important.

When talking about text, paragraph size will vary depending upon the nature of the content. But think in terms of short paragraphs. Paragraphs of even 100 words can seem pretty long on a display screen or computer monitor. The shorter the paragraph, the less intimidating it is to readers, and a paragraph that's too long will make the text unwieldy.

Moving Through Pyramids: A Last Word

For traditional news media outlets, the inverted pyramid style imagines the pyramid's base at the top of the article holding the story's most important information. As the pyramid tapers off in size down to its point, the information is decreasingly important. For digital spaces, we might imagine moving *into* the pyramid. The pyramid's base faces the reader, meaning that all of the most important points are highlighted right there on the first view. As the reader moves deeper into the pyramid, or to borrow from Lewis Carroll, uses links to navigate through *rabbit holes*, the reader accesses related sidebar information. The reader travels forward into the pyramid, or sideways through rabbit holes. As web surfers approach the point of the pyramid, the reader isn't finished. Now facing the reader are more and more pyramids, facing them on their sides, their bases and their points. Headlines, headers, hyperlinks, layers, and chunks are ways of helping readers through these spaces, or forward through our pyramids. As digital writers and editors, then, we are architects of spaces and of navigational schemes through those spaces. It is a high calling.

CHAPTER ASSIGNMENTS

1 Find three examples online of poor headlines and provide their solutions. In other words, fix the headlines. Be sure to include the source for each bad headline, including that source's URL, where applicable. Example:

> Headline: Chubby Babies in Breast Cancer Link
>
> Problem: Awkward. Possibly offensive ("chubby"). No verb.
>
> Solution: Infant Size Linked to Cancer Risk
>
> Source: CNN.com, January 17, 2013
>
> www.cnn.com/2013/HEALTH/01/17/infant.cancer/index.html

2 Find at least one article online that you think could be improved by deploying lists. Submit the "before" version and your edited "after" version of the article, or edited part of the article.

3 Rewrite the headline for your Chapter 1 writing sample with this chapter informing your work. Write subheads and insert where appropriate. Add lists where appropriate.

4 To practice writing to specification, write three different headlines for the following story fragment. Make the first headline eight words and the second six words. For the third headline, provide both a headline and a subhead: a headline of about six words and a subhead of about eight words. Separate the head and the subhead with a colon (for example, "Dodgers edge Braves: Hudson's 3-hitter wasted as Atlanta bats remain silent").

The story fragment:

> ACWORTH, Ga.—An Acworth man turned himself in to police Sunday night after robbing a Motel Six here and later attempting to mug a second victim on North Main Street.
>
> Howard E. Smithton, 54, a resident of the Gazebo Park apartments on Old Cowan Street in Acworth, entered the Motel Six, also on Cowan, at 8:50 p.m. Sunday night and demanded money.
>
> The clerk on duty, who said he knew Smithton, withheld his name for fear of his safety. He said he refused to give Smithton any money. A struggle ensued. Smithton overpowered the clerk, forced him to open the cash register and left with an undisclosed amount of cash, according to the clerk. Smithton then attempted a second burglary approximately one hour later on the 4800 block of North Main.

Smithton demanded that the victim, 59-year-old Bob Wilson, a member of Acworth's board of aldermen, give Smithton his wallet. Wilson said he refused and began beating Smithton over the head with a walking stick, which chased Smithton away.

Smithton later turned himself in at Acworth police headquarters on Industrial Drive at approximately 10:30 p.m. He is being held on a $10,000 bond at the Acworth City Jail, according to Michael Rose, Acworth's sheriff.

The money from the Motel 6 has been returned, Rose said.

Online Resources

Jakob Nielsen, *Writing for the Web* (www.nngroup.com/topic/writing-web/)
This booklet, created primarily for commercial sites, contains some of Nielsen's instructions on maximizing readership.

***Web Style Guide*, 3rd edition (www.webstyleguide.com/)**
Companion site to *Web Style Guide: Basic Design Principles for Creating Web Sites*, by Patrick J. Lynch and Sarah Horton.

"The Usability of Open Source Software" (http://firstmonday.org/article/view/1018/939)
A peer-reviewed research paper from David M. Nichols and Michael B. Twidale that "reviews the existing evidence of the usability of open source software and discusses how the characteristics of open source development influence usability."

***The GNOME Usability Study Report* and the GNOME open source project (http://nguyendangbinh.org/Proceedings/CHI/2004/2/docs/2p1083.pdf1)**
Downloadable report includes a set of user testing studies and 32 design and development suggestions based on those studies.

Steve Krug's usability website (www.sensible.com)
Krug takes the individual user's perspective and is sensitive to small business and small publication owners.

▶ REFERENCES

Brian S. Brooks and Jack Z. Sissors, *The Art of Editing* (Boston, MA: Allyn & Bacon, 2000).

CERN, "New Results Indicate that Particle Discovered at CERN is a Higgs Boson," Press release, March 13 (2013), http://press.web.cern.ch/press-releases/2013/03/new-results-indicate-particle-discovered-cern-higgs-boson.

Mark Coddington, "Building Frames Link by Link: The Linking Practices of Blogs and News Sites," *International Journal of Communication* 6 (2012): 2007–2026.

Isabelle De Ridder, "Visible or Invisible Links: Does the Highlighting of Hyperlinks Affect Incidental Vocabulary Learning, Text Comprehension, and the Reading Process?," *Language, Learning & Technology* 6, no. 1 (January 2002): 123.

Mario Garcia, *iPad Design* (New York, NY: F+W Media, 2012).

Robert E. Garst and Theodore M. Bernstein, *Headlines and Deadlines: A Manual for Copy Editors* (New York, NY: Columbia University Press, 1982).

George P. Landow, *Hypertext 2.0* (Baltimore, MD: Johns Hopkins University Press, 1997).

Paul LaRocque, *Heads You Win!: An Easy Guide to Better Headline and Caption Writing* (Oak Park, CA: Marion Street Press, 2003).

Patrick Lynch and Sarah Horton, *Web Style Guide 2* (New Haven, CT: Yale University Press, 2001), www.webstyleguide.com.

Kendra Mayfield, "Reality Check for Web Design," *Wired*, October 2 (2002), www.wired.com/news/technology/0,1282,55190,00.html.

Rachel McAlpine, *Web Word Wizardry: A Guide to Writing for the Web and Intranet* (Berkeley, CA: Ten Speed Press, 2001).

Errol Morris, "Hear, All Ye People; Hearken, O Earth (Part One)," *The New York Times*, August 8 (2012), http://opinionator.blogs.nytimes.com/2012/08/08/hear-all-ye-people-hearken-o-earth/.

Jakob Nielsen, *Designing Web Usability* (Indianapolis, IN, New Riders, 2000).

Roger C. Parker, *Guide to Web Content and Design* (New York, NY: MIS Press, 1997).

Richard Perez-Pena, "A Venerable Magazine Energizes Its Web Site," *The New York Times*, January 21 (2008): C4.

Thomas Powell, *Web Design: The Complete Reference* (Berkeley, CA: Osborne/McGraw-Hill, 2000).

Jonathan Price and Lisa Price, *Hot Text: Web Writing that Works* (Indianapolis, IN: New Riders, 2002).

Sarah Quinn, "New Poynter Eyetrack Research Reveals How People Read News on Tablets," Poynter Institute, October 17 (2012), www.poynter.org/how-tos/newsgathering-storytelling/visual-voice/191875/new-poynter-eyetrack-research-reveals-how-people-read-news-on-tablets/.

Jeffrey Vern, *The Art and Science of Web Design* (Indianapolis, IN: New Riders, 2001).

5

Editing for Digital
Media II: Style and Voice

Less is more.
Mies van der Rohe, architect and designer

You cannot save souls in an empty church.
David Ogilvy, advertising executive

Man is the great pattern-maker and pattern perceiver. No matter how primitive his situation, no matter how tormented, he cannot live in a world of chaos.
Edmund Carpenter, media theorist

▶ **INTRODUCTION**

In this chapter we discuss style in two dimensions—writing styles (including voice and tone) and visual style. We also look at some principles of planning and mapping websites and webpages, principles that are applicable to other digital environments, as well. And we discuss usability and why even a little usability testing can be of great value.

▶ VISUAL STYLE

Interacting with a book, newspaper, or magazine, a reader can immediately discern the relationship with any one piece of information to the rest of that publication, or with the context in which that article or element appears. Reinforcing this orientation are these media's tables of contents and, often, an index at the end. In digital spaces, however, these relationships and contexts are more difficult to identify. Search engine findings, tweets, and re-tweets of shortened URLs, and Facebook posts encourage direct access to individual webpages; however, they are situated in larger website environments. Each webpage has to be able to stand alone, which places a premium on easily discerned, consistently presented navigation. Navigation isn't simply a feature of your website; it *is* your website. Visitors should always have a clear sense of where they are and exactly how where they are relates to the rest of the site.

For these reasons, writers and editors of digital content need to at least be comfortable and conversant with visual communication and visual design, which includes the structured and deliberative process of planning navigation and how an interactor will use a webpage. Content producers should be involved at all of these levels of web design and development to ensure that the hallmarks of this design include simplicity, service to message and service to audience. As minimalist artist Frank Stella famously said, "What you see is what you see." More specifically, content developers and designers should strive to:

▶ Present clear navigation aids throughout the site and on every page. Visitors should be able to easily return to the homepage from anywhere else in the site.

▶ Present a consistent navigational scheme. Each page should communicate through its navigational links how it relates to the site as a whole, and all the site's pages should do this in a uniform way.

▶ Give visitors direct access. Provide interactors with what they want in the fewest possible steps.

▶ Direct but not dictate. Make suggestions and be clear, but allow interactors to access information in the order and to the degree they wish.

▶ Keep it simple and scannable (KISS). Navigation should be simple, quickly familiar, and always logical.

The repetition and consistency advocated in this list will help to orient interactors and reassure them, however imperceptibly, by enabling them to predict the locations of information they seek. When laying out and mapping your content, when choosing and using graphics and typefaces, and when building your navigational scheme, strive for consistency. All of your webpages should look (and read) as if they came out of the same mind, because of their consistency. Using the same basic library of elements, from typeface to photography, contributes to this uniformity.

This repetition of elements produces a basic reading rhythm or pacing of information as the interactor accesses the content. At MiniUSA.com, for example, most pages render a large photo, a paragraph of text, and then it's on to the next page. This quick rhythm is deliberate, but in an overall environment that is relatively quiet and uncluttered. Repetition doesn't have to be boring, and it can give a site a consistent graphic identity that reinforces a distinct sense of "place."

As an analogy, think of your favorite print magazine and note the ways in which the selection and placement of text and images determine the rhythm or pace for the reader. The typography and text size, the use of color, how much visual and textual information is on the page—all set a mood and establish a rhythm. Readers of *Cosmopolitan*, for example, will quickly breeze through the issue, pausing for a few seconds on the larger images, but moving quickly because they are invited to read very little. *New Yorker* readers, however, will likely linger, with longer articles and features and relatively few graphics or photos. These design considerations work similarly in digital environments.

A Case Study: MiniUSA.com

The MiniUSA site (www.miniusa.com) for the Mini Cooper automobile line demonstrates many of the principles we've been discussing. (MiniUSA would not allow screen grabs to be published in any form.) Visit any one page in the site and that page's relationship to the rest of the site is readily discernible. The presentation, which details a fairly complex topic (a motor car), is easily scanned and navigated. Visual elements help to simplify navigation and index content. Perhaps the site's greatest strength is how seamlessly it reconfigures information depending on what is clicked.

Keeping the site simple is its judicious use of graphics. Those that do appear are sized and positioned for maximum impact. They direct the visitor's attention by interacting with the text and by prioritizing information. In addition, the site's use of Flash and action scripting enables navigation and content to be layered, which further facilitates navigation; car shoppers can drill down as deeply as they wish, or skip on to another section or page. The use of Flash also minimizes download times, which is a key concern whenever designers contemplate graphics.

Web designers Patrick Lynch and Sarah Horton warn against what they call "clown pants," or too much graphic embellishment and clutter. It's an exquisite metaphor. Imagine the sort of first impression you make walking into a job interview wearing clown pants, oversized red shoes, and a big red nose. You'd certainly make an impression, but probably not the right one. Similarly, websites that overuse or misuse graphics, features, and special effects can also make a bad first impression by trying too hard to stand out. The MiniUSA site is understated, from its undersized logo to minimalist reverse-out text on black backgrounds, to shaded navigational text. Horizontal rules, bullets, icons, and other visual markers have their function, but they should be used sparingly and with a clear sense of purpose. Where everything is garish, nothing in particular is emphasized. In short, *less is more*.

The Gestalt of the MiniUSA site, or effect of the whole as opposed to the simple addition of its component parts, is consistent with the product it is selling. This is significant. The sophistication, unity, and usability of the website support the overall message of the brand, which is also meant to communicate sophistication and style, consistency across its product line, and ease (and fun) of use. Thus, from the MiniUSA case study, three general principles to guide your visual style:

▶ Make content easy to find (navigation).

▶ Make it easy to read (simplicity).

▶ Make it aesthetically appealing (visual design).

Another Case Study: BBC News

Another, very different website, one devoted to news, also demonstrates these basic principles, albeit in a dissimilar way. BBC News (www.bbc.com/news/) demonstrates effective visual communication by arraying its content in layers and by developing an easily perceived, consistent scheme for its navigation. Macro-site navigation is positioned at the top, and the tabular format shows clearly where a reader is located within the site at all times; the subsection in which an article appears is highlighted to indicate exactly where in the site the interactor has landed. The site's layers are therefore easily perceived:

▶ top layer: BBC News home;

▶ second layer: sections of the site;

▶ third layer: subsections of the selected news section;

▶ fourth layer: the selected story.

More on This Story

Related Stories

Formidable power of anti-Shia militants 11 JANUARY 2013, ASIA

▶ Dozens dead in Pakistan attacks 15 JUNE 2013, ASIA

In pictures: Pakistan attacks 15 JUNE 2013, ASIA

Anger over Pakistan 'failures' 17 FEBRUARY 2013, ASIA

Pakistan country profile 05 JUNE 2013, SOUTH ASIA

From other news sites

Telegraph
Pakistan mourns dead after
weekend of bloodshed
5 hrs ago

MSN Philippines
Weeping families identify Pakistan
victims
8 hrs ago

East African Standard
Pakistani in shock after double
bomb attack
11 hrs ago

Yahoo! UK and Ireland
Sunni militants claim twin Pakistan
attacks
12 hrs ago

CBC
Pakistan bomb, gun attacks kill 22
22 hrs ago

FIGURE 5.1 BBC.co.uk's top-line navigation.

Once inside an individual page, for a specific article, the interactor can readily see related content on both the right side in an all-text sub-menu, as well as at the bottom in special sections that group related content. It is worth noting that BBC articles typically lack hyperlinks within the text; the site prefers to group linked content in these subsections or menus to its own content to the right and below, and to other news organizations at the bottom just below links to its own content. It is also worth noting that the BBC uses boldface in its first paragraph and for its headlines and subheads in order to slow its readers just enough. Virtually every story also has a video or photo element, adding another important layer of information and another way to experience the story. These elements are arrayed in clear layers, typically one on top of the text story, and one following the text story, which allows a reader to make decisions about what to read or view and in what sequence, while suggesting by its layout a 1–2–3 sequence.

In terms of layout, the BBC News is a model of simplicity. Using a main center gutter means the content will be easily viewed regardless of monitor or screen size, and it means that content will flow relatively easily into the BBC's mobile app. Too often web and graphic designers create page grids that look great on their jumbo monitors, forgetting that most users cannot display more than about half of the designers' layouts at any one time. The BBC's straight-ahead layout facilitates the kind of scrolling that mobile apps encourage while eschewing horizontal scrolling or movement, which web readers and smartphone users simply won't utilize. And though advertising does appear, the ads don't scar the page as they do on most newspaper websites. They are easily ignored,

FIGURE 5.2 Layered navigation at BBC.co.uk.

FIGURE 5.3

appearing on the page in those places that are least viewed regardless, according to Poynter Eyetrack findings.

▶ PLANNING THE PAGES

The minimalist elegance of the MiniUSA homepage and the straightforward utility of the BBC News site are not accidents; good sites and good pages are the products of planning. Site mapping is the equivalent to creating an architectural blueprint before any mortar is mixed. Even the activity of developing a site map forces the developer to think through how individual pages, sections, and elements are going to relate to each other. These decisions will go a long way in determining the navigational scheme. Manifesting these decisions visually in the form of a site map can clearly communicate these inter-relationships.

The site map in Figure 5.4 plots the pages and sections of a site, visually representing the relationships among and between pages, sections, and individual files to show what will link or connect to what.

After mapping out a site, a good next step is to begin storyboarding individual pages (see Figure 5.5). The term "storyboard" comes from a practice in filmmaking in which

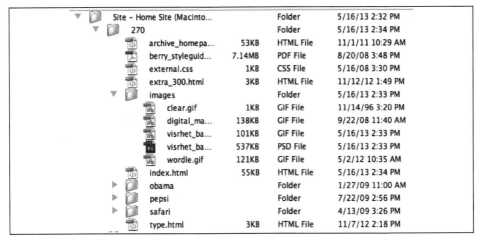

▼ 📁 Site – Home Site (Macinto...		Folder	5/16/13 2:32 PM
▼ 📁 270		Folder	5/16/13 2:34 PM
archive_homepa...	53KB	HTML File	11/1/11 10:29 AM
berry_styleguid...	7.14MB	PDF File	8/20/08 3:48 PM
external.css	1KB	CSS File	5/16/08 3:30 PM
extra_300.html	3KB	HTML File	11/12/12 1:49 PM
▼ 📁 images		Folder	5/16/13 2:33 PM
clear.gif	1KB	GIF File	11/14/96 3:20 PM
digital_ma...	138KB	GIF File	9/22/08 11:40 AM
visrhet_ba...	101KB	GIF File	5/16/13 2:33 PM
visrhet_ba...	537KB	PSD File	5/16/13 2:33 PM
wordle.gif	121KB	GIF File	5/2/12 10:35 AM
index.html	55KB	HTML File	5/16/13 2:34 PM
▶ 📁 obama		Folder	1/27/09 11:00 AM
▶ 📁 pepsi		Folder	7/22/09 2:56 PM
▶ 📁 safari		Folder	4/13/09 3:26 PM
type.html	3KB	HTML File	11/7/12 2:18 PM

FIGURE 5.4

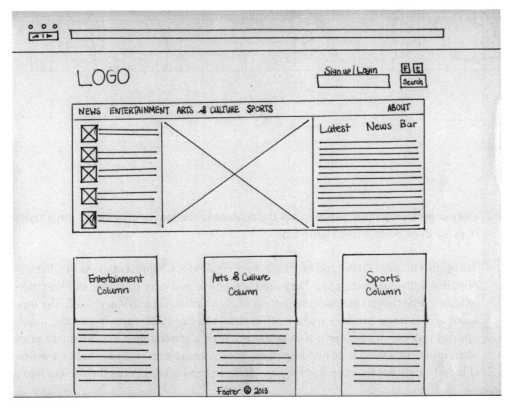

FIGURE 5.5

FIGURE 5.6

story conceivers graphically map out the content of the movie—the story—on a series of placards or posters (see Figure 5.6).

These storyboards can be, and often are, very crude visual representations of what will populate individual webpages. They are inexpensive and easy to make, and they take relatively little time to generate, so there is really no reason not to storyboard. The time spent at this stage can save quite a bit of time and headache further into the development process. Wading into web authoring with a general idea but no storyboards often results in wasted time building pages or even entire sites that later prove unworkable and/or are not scalable. Rookie page designers end up designing themselves into a corner. Storyboarding allows them to spot imbalances and to see problems and issues relating to unity before these problems are knitted into the page design.

Storyboarding places and positions design elements and content on paper, even if it is merely positioning the major pieces. To the degree possible, both the elements and the content should be described, including typeface choices, rough sizes of content elements, and—wherever possible—color. Each storyboard should lead a reader's eye through the page's content. Readers will first see only basic shapes, dominant colors, and big masses of text. They will discern the foreground first, then mid ground and background content. Only after this orientation will they see specific elements and text, deciding at that point on what to focus attention. A storyboard helps the designer see what readers will see, and in the same order. To these ends, storyboards should provide:

▶ a basic hierarchy for headlines and subheads;

▶ cues for consistency in color and typography;

▶ a logical map or path for the reader's eye.

Text should be broken up, and there should be some breathing room for the page's elements. This visual relief, or "air," is all important. Pages and sites that are too busy, cluttered, and noisy will send interactors away. Graphics, therefore, should be used only in service to the intent of the page and never to merely decorate a page.

In developing storyboards, a good rule of thumb for internal pages is for content to account for between 50 and 80 percent of a page's design space, leaving no less than 20 percent of the space for navigation. This guideline does not apply to homepages, however, where introducing the navigational scheme might require more space. To prioritize the content, Jakob Nielsen's usability studies suggest a useful method: Evaluate all of the design elements on the page by eliminating them one at a time, if only hypothetically. If the design works better or even the same without the element, leave that element out. *Less is more.*

Unfortunately, there is no way of knowing the size of the screens that interactors are using to view your pages, and no way of determining their monitors' color sophistication. For this reason, a "lowest common denominator" approach is recommended, unless you are targeting a specific group or audience about whom more is known regarding their computers or devices, browsers, and connections. Assume a low baseline and use resolution-independent pages, which allow designs to adapt to the screen size. Using percentage-based sizing in frames and tables rather than fixed, pixel-based sizes, for example, can be an effective way to accomplish a flexible design format. Of course, table cells that are not fixed are also unpredictable and therefore will rearrange or reconfigure your page designs. Good designers test and re-test their pages on a variety of machines, devices, and browsers.

After you have finished storyboarding, evaluate your plans to make sure each of the following is included on every webpage:

▶ **What:** a title, such as the text that appears on the browser's top bar and the text that appears when users add the site to their "favorites" lists. This heading should make absolutely clear what the page is about or includes.

▶ **Who:** somewhere on each page should be its author's identity and institutional affiliation.

▶ **When:** when the page was created or last revised.

▶ **Where:** clear, uniform navigation.

▶ WRITING STYLE

This chapter began with visual style because whatever is written for digital environments will live in a larger, visual context. With some parameters of that context established, it's time to turn to writing style, voice, and tone. The web puts unique burdens on the writer, in particular because the exercise of "reading" is so fundamentally different in digital spaces. Early research on web reading conducted by Jakob Nielsen indicates that web users read about 25 percent more slowly via computer screens than they do ink on paper. This means, of course, that they also read less, much less. The implication, then, is that writing for digital spaces must be concise and direct. Nielsen has recommended a word count for online writing that is about half the standard word count for a similar piece of writing developed for a print publication. Recognizing that there is little agreement on word counts among web writers and editors, the important point Nielsen makes is that we have to facilitate scanning.

If site visitors read less, if they are in a hurry, if they most often are on task, then putting the most important information up top would seem an obvious step to take. The first screen of information, or about 30 text lines on most computer monitors, should organize and telegraph what is in the rest of the space, recognizing that users do not like to scroll. Visitors will use the information presented first—for example, the headline—to help determine whether they want to read any further. For this reason, as Chapter 2 emphasized, the inverted pyramid style used by most newspapers for hard news is a useful style online, as well, one that addresses the need for writers to present the most important facts or ideas first. Surfers are often hunting, searching for information on how to lose weight, or save money, or where to find a good airfare to Las Vegas. Rarely are they aimlessly browsing in search of beautiful prose. They will choose your content because it helps them, and because that utility is immediately perceptible.

Dialing Into Your Voice

Part of your writing style for digital spaces is your voice, or the personality that is expressed in your writing. For some, this voice comes naturally. For others, it takes work. And the format or context of your writing should play a role in determining or adapting that voice. For example, one of the great promises of social media is their capacity to communicate obviously, authentically human voice. More specifically, with its 140-character limit, Twitter is ideally suited for quick rejoinders, for short, pithy commentary, and for referring people to sites and pages. Some writers have personalities for which this communication channel is a perfect fit, making the translation of this personality in the writing a relatively easy exercise. For other digital writers, the longer text-intensive format of most blogs might be a better match in terms of personality, voice, and pace.

Because social media are designed primarily to facilitate conversation, and because conversation typically requires communicating in authentically human voices, the capacity of social media to express this humanity presents big organizations with a powerful opportunity to put a human face on what otherwise can be perceived as an unthinking, unfeeling bureaucracy. Common on these social media platforms and in these digital environments are more casual or informal styles of writing, styles encouraged by the platforms themselves. It is this informality that can be a great advantage. Vanderbilt University Medical Center, for example, uses Twitter to reach out to its patients and their families. On Vandy's Twitter feed are responses from individuals within the medical center, real human beings who have been authorized to address specific problems and who have information on how to address those problems. Informal banter, a sense of humor and fun, and, most importantly, a human voice are hallmarks of the conversations taking place on the center's Twitter feed.

The decision of who to tweet on behalf of the hospital was an important one. Vanderbilt Medical Center could have appointed someone with experience with Twitter, someone who has already developed a natural voice for Twitter. Ideally, this person is authorized to tweet about more than just the brand or organization, because anyone who tweets about one and only one thing will inevitably become boring and repetitive. This official tweeter should be liberated to share his or her passions and interests, within limits, of course, and thereby integrate this personal information as he or she deems it appropriate and natural.

Implied in Vanderbilt's use of Twitter is a larger strategy of deliberate, specific communication that reaches several target audiences in ways relevant to the medium. You don't see merely re-purposed content from other channels and publications on Vandy's Twitter feed. You don't see Twitter used simply as another form of RSS or email push. This is important, because Twitter followers are tech-savvy. They will intuit when they are getting re-purposed pablum, when Twitter isn't adding any value. The goal, then, is empowering real people to say and tweet (or Facebook or blog) authentically human things in situationally appropriate ways.

Using Typeface as a Guide

How do you determine or decide your voice and, more generally, your persona? How do you do this in a larger organizational context? First, recognize that while you can be informal, casual, and therefore more human in social media environments, your writing must still be professional and consistent with the overall ethos of your organization, company, or cause. Second, let's think about voice metaphorically by looking at descriptions of various typefaces. Because typography doesn't have its own vocabulary or vernacular, typefaces are often and even typically described as if they were human, or at least had human characteristics. "Oh, that typeface is a bit frilly." Or, "this typeface looks formal, as if it were wearing a tuxedo." So choosing (or at least trying out) a voice might be as simple as choosing (or trying out) a typeface. Consistently communicating in the chosen voice is another matter, but knowing your voice's hallmarks and characteristics is an important first step. It's suggested here that determining your chosen voice's characteristics by looking through type descriptions can be a useful, time-saving exercise.

Our first case study is the Gotham typeface (see Figure 5.7) on President Barack Obama's official campaign website, which uses Gotham as its primary display typeface.

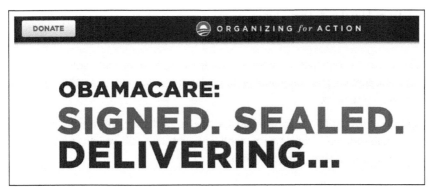

FIGURE 5.7

Here is a description of Gotham as written by its developer, the Hoefler & Frere-Jones type factory in New York (or Gotham) City (emphasis added):

> Gotham is that rarest of designs, the new typeface that somehow feels **familiar**. From the lettering that inspired it, Gotham inherited an **honest** tone that's **assertive** but **never imposing, friendly but never folksy, confident but never aloof**. The inclusion of so many original ingredients—a lowercase, italics, and a comprehensive range of weights—enhances these forms' **plainspokenness** with a **welcome sophistication**, and brings a broad range of expressive voices to the Gotham family.

These bolded words describe a voice that would likely be effective in digital spaces for many organizations, companies, or news organizations. As a set, these words hopefully describe the voice of this textbook.

For a comparison of a very different voice, here is the description of the typeface Tungsten, which also comes from Hoefler & Frere-Jones:

> Tungsten is a **compact** and **sporty** sans serif that's **disarming** instead of pushy—**not just loud, but persuasive** . . . one that employed **confidence** and **subtlety** instead of just raw testosterone . . . **more Steve McQueen than Steven Seagal** . . . **whiskey highball, not a martini** . . . a tight family of **high-impact** fonts **that doesn't sacrifice wit, versatility, or style**.

Tungsten's descriptors present a very different voice and persona, one that might best suit Twitter. It might also work in blogs, depending upon the larger communicative goals of the organization, company, or cause. Here are a few more typefaces, with their descriptions, from Hoefler & Frere-Jones, as examples of personas or voices for your writing:

▶ **Forza:** succinct geometries make for an expressive type family that's ardent, disciplined, shrewd, and commanding. In twelve styles, from the crisp Thin to the powerhouse Black.

▶ **Vitesse:** engineered for responsive handling and a sporty ride, Vitesse is a 21st-century slab serif that's agile, steady, confident, and suave. Six weights from Thin to Black, each with a matching italic.

▶ **Whitney:** signage fonts favor clarity, editorial ones demand space efficiency. Our Whitney family tackles both challenges—and now features extensions into the Greek and Cyrillic alphabets, covering more than 200 languages worldwide.

▶ **Sentinel:** for everyone who wishes Clarendons had italics, and everyone whose favorite slab serif is shy a few weights: Sentinel is a fresh take on a lovely and useful historical style, a thoughtful and complete family that's serviceable for both text and display.

FIGURE 5.8 The stylish Neutra typeface on a café in Paris.

▶ **Verlag:** from out of the six typefaces originally created for the Guggenheim Museum comes Verlag, a family of 30 sans serifs that brings a welcome eloquence to the can-do sensibility of pre-war Modernism. Three widths, each in five weights, all with matching italics.

Choosing a typeface to dial into voice is one way of determining or perhaps finding or *discovering* your voice. Another might be to develop a frequently asked questions (FAQs) page or list for your company, organization, website, or cause. To demonstrate two very different voices, take a look at some FAQ lists found on the web, one an example of a "just the facts, ma'am" approach and one from Rosie O'Donnell that expresses her own brand of saucy insouciance.

Example 1: Gmail (excerpted):

1. What makes Gmail different?

Yes, Gmail is another email service. But it's different in lots of ways, starting with a philosophy: that communications can be made simpler, more efficient, and more fun. When building Gmail, we looked at the frustrations people were having with email, and started with our product from scratch. The result is something that's faster, cleaner, and more intuitive. For example, Gmail automatically groups an email and its replies into a conversation, so you can easily follow the back and forth of an email exchange. It's just like you were chatting. And now, you can chat in Gmail too.

There are no pop-ups or banner ads in Gmail, and very little spam. With Google search, it's easier for you to find the things that matter to you. And Gmail even has some personality. But don't take our word for it, try it yourself. Think of it as a fresh start.

2. How do I sign up?

You can get a Gmail account if you're invited by someone who already has one. Or, you can sign up for an account using your mobile phone.

Example 2: Rosie O'Donnell (excerpted from www.rosie.com):

is this the frequently asked questions page?
yep

are you sure?
positive

how do you make the movies?
on a mac
use iphoto slideshow
or imovie
it's ez—u can do it 2

why can't I see the movies?
try this
Mac: www.apple.com/quicktime/download/mac.html
Windows: www.apple.com/quicktime/download/win.html

why and when are comments off?
no rhyme or reason
just my mood

why don't you use punctuation?
just lazy i guess

Your objective in developing a FAQ list is to think for your audience(s) and anticipate their questions and needs, as well as to speak to these questions in a voice appropriate both for those audiences and for your organization. In this exercise it is the process that is most important, not the product, so don't worry too much about design or layout or aesthetics. Should you adopt an authoritative, institutional voice, or a more interpersonal, informal voice? Or something altogether different?

A third mental exercise for determining voice is to essentially role-play. Let's break it down into steps. First, identify the voice you wish to communicate in a word or two—a label or category that distills its essential characteristics. Next, generate a list of the attributes of that particular voice. Finally, role-play with expressions of that particular voice by writing something in that voice. Let's take a look at a few examples of this three-step process.

Example 1: Professional Voice

Attributes:

▶ direct;

▶ strong;

▶ authoritative;

▶ fact-based;

▶ journalistic.

Role: Chief executive:

Nearly 75 percent of our employees are voluntary members of the BlueTeam, an organization that helps grow our healthcare facility and better serve our community. This section of the BlueTeam website connects members to more information about the organization's activities and with ways to immediately get involved.

Example 2: Fun and Friendly

Attributes:

▶ witty;

▶ clever;

▶ funny;

▶ quirky;

▶ attention-grabbing.

Role: Co-worker, colleague or friend:

Ice cream, flash mobs, and rock bands may not be the first things that come to mind when you think about fundraising, but they are what the BlueTeam is all about. And you've got to see it to believe it. Come out to Ridge Ferry Park this Saturday to see the BlueTeam in action, and please consider joining us in reaching out to the community. We guarantee you'll have fun, and you can keep the volunteer t-shirt as a memento of a great day spent with new friends.

Example 3: Direct

▶ simple;

▶ functional;

▶ personable;

▶ refreshing;

▶ concise;

▶ easily understandable.

Role: Coach or teacher:

> We need your help. If you'd like to be a part of something that serves our com-
> munity and raises money to provide healthcare to those who most need it, please
> contact me about joining the BlueTeam. It's a volunteer organization that's put a
> priority on making sure at-risk residents in our community get the healthcare they
> need, regardless of whether they have insurance or not. We've touched a lot of
> lives since we formed in 1983, and we'd love to have you as part of the team.
> Email me, Lisa Simpson, at lsimpson@BlueTeam.org, or call or text me at 706-369-
> 6844. I can help you get up to speed and contributing in no time.

Taking the Right Tone

Research shows that web users are turned off by "the pitch," or by language easily identified as advertising or marketing. These interactors tend to rank sites that use what could
be called "marketing-ese" as less credible than sites that do not, which implies that a
more objective tone will be more effective even when the goal is to sell, or market, or
persuade. Digital writers have to earn a reader's trust, which can be lost or blocked by
exaggerated claims, boastful language, or obvious sales pitches. Marketing slogans and
unsupported claims, particularly in content otherwise designed to be or presented as
neutral information, are perceived as tacky and unprofessional. Short sentences, active
verbs, direct statements, and inverted pyramid presentations will contribute to the
right tone.

Digital content is accessed and read globally, in all time zones. Like the caution against
marketing-ese, this global reach strongly suggests writing that is simple, straightforward, and clear and free of jargon. Another less practical option is to translate the copy
into several foreign languages. Fortunately, about 1 billion people name English as their
second, third, or fourth language, thus a good start is plain English—no confusing acronyms, colloquial expressions, culturally bound metaphors, or gobbledygook terms. No
legal-sounding verbiage, slang, or idioms. Rein in phrasal verbs, or those that consist of
two or more words, such as pick up, pick away at, let on, and go on about. And avoid
ambiguous pronouns, particularly gender-based pronouns: Not all languages handle
these in the same ways. Use short sentences and simple, common, concrete words.

▶ USABILITY

You were careful planning, mapping, and storyboarding your content. You determined your voice and tone. You were sensitive to a potentially global audience. Now, after development, you will still need to demonstrate great care by making sure everything works:

- ▶ Do the graphics appear in the right places and render in correct ways?

- ▶ Do all of the hyperlinks work?

- ▶ Are there formatting or layout issues across machines, devices, browsers, and apps?

Usability expert Steve Krug advises that even a little usability research is better than none, so asking even one other person to test your pages and read your content can generate valuable feedback to inform updates and changes.

A real-world example: When undergraduate students of a web design class at Berry College in Mount Berry, Georgia, were asked to develop a site for the local Habitat for Humanity chapter, the class first met with the chapter's executive director to discuss his goals for the organization's site. To guide that discussion, the class prepared a list of questions, a list that might help you better serve your organization, company or cause, and a list that has value in developing mobile apps, as well:

1   What do you definitely want the site (or app) to do?

2   What do you definitely want the site (or app) *not* to do?

3   When are you hoping to have a working site (or app) up and active? What deadline do you suggest?

4   Who will host the site (or maintain the app)? How will we publish the site to the web?

5   What graphics or art do you have already? What art do you want to use (logos, photos, charts)? What art do you know you do not want to use, or cannot use?

6   What content do you have or are planning to get?

7   Of these elements, what will be frequently and/or routinely updated?

8   Which parts of the site (or app) will be temporary, such as an event of the month, and what will be permanent (or at least long lived)?

9   What are your expectations for this site (or app)? What are your expectations for our involvement in developing the site (or app), both now and longer term?

10   How complex does the site (or app) need to be? What functionality do you want it to have (e.g., enabling supporters to donate online, to volunteer online, etc.)?

11   What tone, mood, or attitude should the site communicate? What tone, mood, or attitude should be avoided?

12   Do you have examples of sites (or apps) you like, sites similar in approach or philosophy to what you want?

13   What are your plans for usability testing?

14   Who is going to maintain and update the site (or app)?

The class next designed and developed a website for the Habitat chapter that is easy to navigate, one with an obvious design structure and navigational scheme. Habitat wanted site visitors to be able to "get it" without having to ask, "Where do I start?" or, "Can I click on that?" So the students eliminated or otherwise attempted to anticipate user questions. Good website usability design means that visitors will not have to ask:

▶ Where am I?

▶ Where should I begin?

▶ Where did they put _____?

▶ What's most important here?

▶ Why did they call it that?

Users glance. They scan. They click. They do not always choose the BEST path on the page to take them where they want to go. It is up to you to make the pathways to their destinations immediately clear. With these priorities in mind, the Habitat site design team's goals included:

▶ creating a clear visual hierarchy on each page;

▶ taking advantage of conventions;

▶ breaking up pages into clearly defined areas;

▶ making it obvious what is and what is not clickable on each page;

▶ minimizing noise and distractions.

In addition, the development team sought to make sure that the elements users see on the page, including search boxes, links and nav (navigation) buttons, accurately convey their importance and utility. The more important the content, the more prominently it was placed.

Krug points out that navigation is not just a feature of a website, it *is* the website. The top priority, then, is clear, predictable, uniform, ubiquitous navigation. There are two types of users: hunters and gatherers. The search-dominant hunters ask, "Where's the search box?" The information gatherers instead ask, "Where are the links?" Layout and design should help both types of users get from one place to another and orient them within at all times. They should signal what is available, and they should transparently reveal the content. Think of the kinds of maps you typically find in shopping malls or subway terminals, those that clearly show "YOU ARE HERE." Implicitly, these maps also communicate how big a place is and they situate you in relationship to everything else within that place or space.

A good model of a clear navigation scheme can be found at MLB.com, the website for Major League Baseball. Finding a box score for the latest Yankees game, for example, is intuitive and simple, and the path to do it is clearly displayed: Home >> Scores >> Yankees >> Box. The reader knows precisely where he or she is in the site in relation to the rest of the site, and is able to return to any previous part of the site with just one click.

So, at a glance, a homepage should be able to quickly and clearly:

- ▶ establish identity and mission;
- ▶ show site hierarchy;
- ▶ show where to start;
- ▶ show what's there;
- ▶ indicate shortcuts to main, most desired pages and sections;
- ▶ convey the big picture;
- ▶ avoid clutter.

Several institutions and organizations have conducted comprehensive usability studies that inform other, more local usability evaluations. The National Cancer Institute (NCI), for example, published its *Usability Guidelines*, a document describing what the institute has learned about its own usability, which is quite a bit. The NCI's site is quite sophisticated. The development phases that this site recommends are also helpful: Plan, Analyze, Develop, Test and Refine. Other topics covered in this comprehensive usability help site include:

▶ What Is Usability?

▶ Why Is It Important?

▶ How Much Does It Cost?

▶ Can Usability Be Measured?

FIGURE 5.9

The NCI offers research-based guidelines for page layout, navigation, links, text appearance, graphic design, accessibility, and search, and it provides a toolbox of templates and examples (www.usability.gov/).

CHAPTER ASSIGNMENTS

1 Choose a website you visit regularly, one where you read a lot of the content. Imagine that you have been hired as the site's new editor-in-chief. Make specific recommendations to improve the presentation of content at the site, integrating and referencing the chapter as much as possible.

▶ Is the voice effective?

▶ Is the tone appropriate?

▶ What elements or features promote use of the site?

▶ How are graphics and visuals incorporated, and do they encourage or discourage use?

▶ How do they do this?

▶ How much thought was given to navigation throughout the site?

▶ Are the elements—graphical, navigational, and metaphorical—consistently applied throughout the site?

▶ Is the tone or rhythm of the site consistent throughout?

▶ Do these dimensions match the audience(s) for the site?

Here is a categorical checklist of site dimensions to critique:

▶ navigation;

▶ page layouts (balance/contrast/unity);

▶ consistency;

▶ tone and voice;

▶ writing quality;

▶ site organization.

Length of your critique: approximately 750 words.

2 This next assignment is also presented as an exercise in this chapter. Create an interactive FAQ help page for some entity (publication, company, or organization), preferably one with which you have some connection. Your frequently asked questions section should anticipate common problems and questions that users, customers, or clients might have about that publication, organization, or company.

The primary objective in this assignment is to think for your audience(s) and anticipate their questions and needs. It is the process that is most important, not the final product. So, don't spend too much time on the design or layout or aesthetics of the list. As the chapter described, this assignment is also useful in determining or deciding the appropriate voice for the entity, or for you writing for that entity. Before working on your list, go online and read some FAQ lists for organizations similar to that for which you are writing.

Online Resources

Identifont (www.identifont.com/)
Online directory of typefaces. Can be used to select type or to identify type.

Jeff Jarvis's Buzz Machine blog, specifically his "Golden Rule of Links" (www.buzzmachine.com/2008/06/02/the-ethic-of-the-link-layer-on-news/)
Jarvis teaches journalism at The City University of New York.

Typography Deconstructed (www.typographydeconstructed.com/)
Provides an anatomy of type.

▶ REFERENCES

Carolyn Dowling, *Writing and Learning with Computers* (Camberwell, Australia: Acer Press, 1999).

Anders Fagerjord, "Rhetorical Convergence: Studying Web Media," in Gunnar Liestol, Andrew Morrison, and Terje Rasmussen (eds) *Digital Media Revisited* (Cambridge, MA: MIT Press, 2003): 293–326.

Jeff Glick, "When, How to Tell Stories with Text, Multimedia," Poynter Institute (2004), http://poynterextra.org/eyetrack2004/jeffglick.htm2.

Steve Krug, *Don't Make Me Think* (Upper Saddle River, NJ: New Riders Press, 2000).

Patrick Lynch and Sarah Horton, *Web Style Guide 2* (New Haven, CT: Yale University Press, 2001).

Rachel McAlpine, *Web Word Wizardry: A Guide to Writing for the Web and Intranet* (Berkeley, CA: Ten Speed Press, 2001).

John Morkes and Jakob Nielsen, "Concise, SCANNABLE, and Objective: How to Write for the Web" (1997), www.useit.com/papers/webwriting/writing.html.

Jakob Nielsen, *Designing Web Usability* (Indianapolis, IN: New Riders, 2000).

Jakob Nielsen, "How Users Read on the Web," www.useit.com/alertbox/9710a.html.

Anthony Tedesco, "Adapt your Writing to the Web," *The Writer* 114, no. 5 (May 2001): 16.

Nathan Wallace, "Web Writing for Many Interest Levels" (1999), www.e-gineer.com/articles/web-writing-for-many-interest-levels.html3.

6

Designing and Building Spaces and Places

Your audience gives you everything you need. They tell you. There is no director who can direct you like an audience.

Fanny Brice, entertainer

The world is full of obvious things which nobody by any chance ever observes.

Arthur Conan Doyle, *The Hound of the Baskervilles*

▶ INTRODUCTION

The best publications are those that are most relevant to the people they aim to serve. In this chapter, the focus is on audience and on learning as much as possible about the information needs, sensitivities, interests, and objectives of a desired audience. This knowledge can then be used to plan and build digital spaces and content in those spaces for our audiences. In order to guide site planning, this chapter also covers how to develop an audience-specific style guide, which will help ensure consistency and familiarity.

CHAPTER OBJECTIVES

After studying this chapter, you will be able to:

▼

plan webpages and websites;

▼

apply grid-based design principles;

▼

understand audience needs and how to satisfy them;

▼

attract interactors to a website and keep them coming back;

▼

develop and use style guides.

▶ **PRE-PLANNING**

Before we write a word of content, we need the answers to at least two fundamental questions. First, who is our audience? Who is the website, blog, Twitter feed, or Facebook group supposed to reach? Second, what is the informational purpose of the content? The more contact we have with our interactors, the better the planning will be. As intuitive as this is, most site development still occurs in a vacuum, with little or no contact with the intended audience(s). If we can involve real users in planning, development, testing, and updating, the digital publication has a better chance of succeeding.

As a starting point for the discussion, as you consider the kind of site (or digital space) you are developing or for which you are producing content, try to place that site on an information spectrum. At one end of the spectrum are information-rich sites; on the other are sites that are sensory oriented and, therefore, are relatively light on information. YouTube, for example, lives at the sensory extreme by emphasizing the visual and, with almost exclusively short videos, creating impressions and evoking emotions. Similarly, Instagram, Pinterest, and Snapchat are mostly sensory, allowing users to share or trade photos. On the other end of the spectrum, we might put corporate intranets, reference sites such as the Library of Congress, and sites by and for institutions of higher education. In the middle are those sites that provide some information but also seek to provide an experience of some kind, like most news sites. Knowing where your project fits on this spectrum can inform the kinds of content that should be developed and the ways in which that content should be presented.

On the sensory end of the spectrum, consider an interactive feature at the *Chicago Tribune*'s website that is powered by a rather simple Flash movie and that enables baseball fans to display their names on an online version of Wrigley Field's scoreboard. Before adding the feature, *Chicago Tribune* site developers knew they wanted something to provide an experience, something entertaining that could deliver near-instant gratification. The marquee-generator could be considered an amenity not unlike a ride at a carnival or a bench at a public park. Knowing the purpose and the audience—in this case, the newspaper's many Cubs fans—in turn informed the development of the feature. To drive traffic, the newspaper sent alerts about the new feature via Facebook.

On the other end of the spectrum might be a webpage designed by the Centers for Disease Control and Prevention to help parents diagnose cerebral palsy. Not surprisingly, given the subject, this page is very high on information and very low on entertainment or emotion. Appropriate, then, are a sober tone, logical organization of the information, and a clear demonstration of credibility and authority.

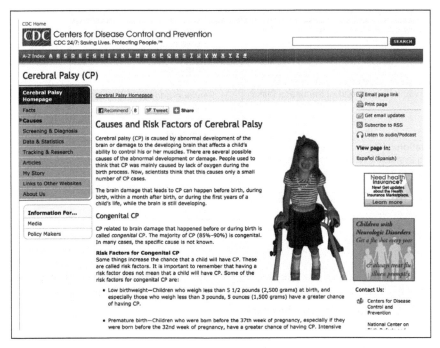

FIGURE 6.1
Source: www.cdc.gov/ncbddd/cp/causes.html.

▶ MAXIMIZING CONTENT FITNESS

Once you've determined how information-heavy your site should be and to what degree visitors are looking for a sensory experience, consider your audience in terms of the kinds of information they are looking for, or how the information you present might fit into the larger puzzle that your audience is trying to piece together over time. Quality information researchers call this "fitness." Research has shown that information quality has little to do with technology and everything to do with the fitness of the information as determined by interactors. Information science researchers Kuan-Tsae Huang, Yang W. Lee, and Richard Y. Wang found that when people visit a site, they base their judgments of the quality of information more on how well that information matches what they are seeking than how sophisticated the site is in terms of its technological bells and whistles. The research suggests four dimensions of information quality (see Figure 6.2).

The IQ dimensions identified and organized in the study provide a useful checklist for evaluating the fitness of content for the audience you are trying to serve. Are they visiting your site to buy something? If that's the case, access and security, or Accessibility IQ

INFORMATION QUALITY (IQ) CATEGORY	IQ DIMENSION
Intrinsic IQ, or information that has quality for the user in its own right	• accuracy • objectivity • believability • reputation
Contextual IQ, or information that must be considered within the context of the user's tasks	• relevancy • value-added • timeliness • completeness • amount
Representational IQ, or user issues surrounding systems that provide information such as databases	• interpretability • ease of understanding • concise representation • consistent representation
Accessibility IQ, or user issues surrounding the provision of information	• access • security

FIGURE 6.2

dimensions, will rank highly. Are they looking to you for information on cerebral palsy? Intrinsic IQ dimensions are going to rank at the top. A news site will need to score well on nearly all of the dimensions in the chart.

▶ CONTENT DEVELOPMENT

After determining the kinds of information for which your audience is looking, next think about who you hope will visit your site. Once again, it might be helpful to think in terms of categories. Occupational types, demographics, gender, culture, and age ranges are good places to start. Be as specific and as comprehensive as you can, which will help you to determine not only the substance of your content, but also the degree of detail and abstraction. Think of the webpage on cerebral palsy. With a primary audience of very concerned parents, writers for this page knew the content needed enough detail and substance to truly inform, but not so much that the information overwhelms the reader. They also knew that abstraction was not an option. Similarly, readers in professional fields, such as business, science, or technology, likely will expect a wealth of empirical data, perhaps supporting charts and graphs, as well. Consider the information challenges your audience might have. Information technology professionals, for example, get too much information; they are overwhelmed. Your challenge is to stand out and to offer expertise found nowhere else.

Does your audience need "how to" information? You'll likely develop sequential content, or demonstrations that walk a reader through a process step by step. Does your audience need to collaborate? What social networking tools and communication environments will you offer? Are they looking for pleasure or efficiency, advice or participation in something meaningful?

Where does your audience live? Are they local, national, international? Does the answer have implications for your content in terms of cultural, ethnic, or linguistic considerations? Will you need to avoid idioms and slang? Depending upon the people groups your content might reach, your color choices, too, could have important implications. Red, for instance, means entirely different things to different cultural and ethnic groups. The color red in:

▶ Thailand ranks as the most popular color;

▶ China connotes prosperity;

▶ Malaysia symbolizes valor and might;

▶ the Ivory Coast connotes mourning;

▶ many African countries connotes death;

▶ the United States grabs attention and connotes passion, blood, and life.

What kinds of sites, publications, and documents does your audience use already? Where do your readers and potential readers go to satisfy their information needs? Think of specific sites, newspapers or magazines, radio and television programming, newsletters and competitors. You can learn both what to do and what not to do from evaluating these other sources. What conventions can your designs borrow from these other types of information sources? Familiarity will make your content more appealing, and you will spend less time in design and development.

How often do you anticipate visitors coming to your site? Once, daily, weekly, monthly? The frequency will determine how often your site's content should be updated or refreshed. How will you drive traffic to the site? Is your audience already active on Facebook? Twitter? Instagram, LinkedIn or Google+? You will have to go where they are already and join their conversations to attract visitors to your content. Join the groups and platforms they already use. Read everything you can about your audience. Spend time with and among the members of your audience in social networking contexts.

Knowing your audience's technical limitations can help to determine the kind of content you develop, even the media formats you might choose. What browsers and operating systems are your visitors using? Firefox and Explorer, for example, are very different; often what works on one browser will not function properly on the other, or at least not in the same way. The PC–Mac divide, too, can cause compatibility and operability issues, as can the Android–Apple dichotomy. What is their connection speed? Broadband? What kind of broadband? Are they accessing from home or from work? What advanced browser features do they support? What kinds of plug-ins will they need to access your content? Based on your audience, do you even need a website, or does going solely with mobile make more sense?

As you consider graphical elements, think through how they might be interpreted in different parts of the world, or even in different regions of the country. What are your alternatives, either textually or visually, that might be more culturally neutral? For example, if you are writing about the political strife that has colored daily life in Northern Ireland for more than 40 years, when choosing photography you might be tempted to include a Celtic cross. It is, after all, a rather stereotypical image of Ireland. But remember: the article focuses on Northern Ireland. To about half of the residents of the country, the half that is Protestant and loyal to the British crown, a Celtic cross would very clearly communicate Catholicism, the Republic of Ireland, and Irishness.

FIGURE 6.3 A mural on the side of an apartment building in Northern Ireland, where iconography typically is freighted with political, sectarian meaning.

Others might opt to show some of the political murals found on buildings throughout Belfast and Derry, Northern Ireland. These murals are laden with political commentary and therefore can be quite provocative. Great care should be taken when choosing which murals to present and how to present and describe them.

▶ INFORMATION ARCHITECTURE

Once you know your audience and the types of information that visitors hope to find on your site or page, after you've carefully considered what this audience needs and how visitors are accustomed to getting it, the next question is how to present that information in a logical manner that makes it easy for users to find. Planning how information will be organized and how this organization will be revealed to users should be an early step in any website design. This planning and organization of information is referred to as information architecture, a process complex enough that there are entire academic departments dedicated to its study. At its most basic level, the aim of information architecture is to determine an information hierarchy for a site by grouping related information. These groupings should be presented according to some hierarchy of importance, which can then determine page layouts and site tree development. A site tree is a graphical representation of how a site's parts relate or link to one another. Once the hierarchy has been determined, map it out graphically on paper for the beginnings of a site tree (see Figure 6.4).

There are many possible models for site architecture, some linear or sequential, and some non-linear. Again, it might be helpful to think in terms of a spectrum, with a 1–2–3 sequence or linear model at one end and a highly interconnected web model at the other. Slideshows, for example, are sequential. Sites that walk users through a procedure, skill, or practice are, as well. They have a predictable structure and are, therefore, fairly simple to plan.

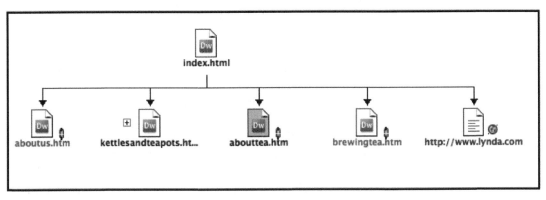

FIGURE 6.4

On the other extreme is a site like Wikipedia, which has no discrete beginning and no determinate end. Pages interconnect and cross-reference, providing a deep, rich web of information accessible in an almost infinite number of different sequences. Wikipedia is flexible and scalable, changing all the time. Wikipedia is, therefore, a very complex site, but its architecture permits and facilitates this interconnectedness and its ability to continually expand.

Some sites and many intranets combine these models. In the aggregate, most corporate intranets are webs of interconnected, hyperlinked information. But you're likely to find a section or two for training, sections that follow a sequential progression. *The New York Times* site has a clear beginning—the front page or homepage; but a reader may wish to access a wide variety of different kinds of articles in any number of sequences. The *Times* site therefore is organized into sections and areas of interest rather than by sequential order.

Basics of Page Layout

Let's shift focus from the site level to that of individual pages, or from site architecture to designing and laying out individual pages. Many of the skills and sensibilities that produce good print pages are also valuable in webpage design. These same principles can also guide, at least generally, the layout and design of mobile applications. A page's layout, whether digital or print, should create a consistent visual rhythm to pace the reader as she moves through the page. This rhythm is established in the placement and repetition of shapes, colors, typefaces, textures, and spatial relationships, as well as by the sheer number of elements. If quick and lively is the rhythm you seek, you might use lots of small, closely placed shapes. If, however, solemn and dignified is a more appropriate rhythm, you will likely use large, solitary shapes.

As a thought experiment, imagine reading through your favorite print publication: *Wired, Cosmo, Transworld Skateboarding, Southern Bride*—the choice is yours. Now reflect on what kind of rhythm that publication has. How fast or slow is the publication's pace? How is that rhythm manifested? What libraries of elements does the publication use? What kinds of layouts are common? What is consistent throughout the publication? What kind of tone does the publication establish, and how consistent is that tone throughout? How are these choices informed by knowledge of the intended audience?

The primary tool in print page design is the grid. Whatever visual rhythm you choose, it can be plotted out on a grid, which can be indispensable in planning out *all* of the space, including the white space, the margin areas, and the areas of visual rest. Text, photos, illustrations, and logos can also be placed on a grid. There are a lot of grids from which to choose (see Figure 6.5).

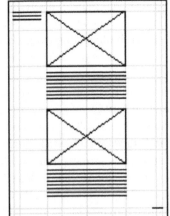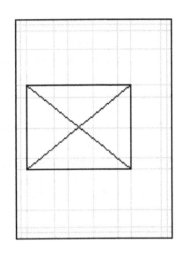

FIGURE 6.5

For a homepage, Figure 6.6 provides an example of plotting basic content layout on a grid.

FIGURE 6.6

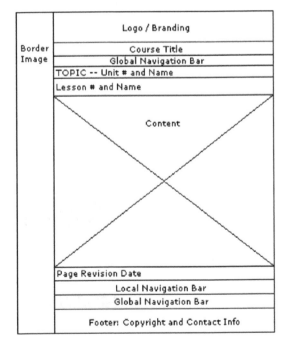

The complexity of the grid should depend upon the complexity and quantity of design elements; so, determining what you have to work with and what content elements you have is a good place to begin thinking about what kind of grid you will need. The more elements you have, the more choices you will have to make. Keep it as simple as possible.

More than ever before, the web is something we carry in our pockets and handbags. Thus, there is a fundamental shift in web design to mobile-first approaches, or designs that think first about how content will flow into smartphones. This approach calls on layouts to be modular and stackable, allowing a series of largely squares and rectangles to stack on top of one another in a smartphone scroll. In September 2013, for example, Salon.com, Slate.com, and the City of New York each unveiled site redesigns to render effectively on desktops, on iPads and tablets, and on smartphones. All three take a very modular, grid-based approach to design.

Whether designers think first about the phone or the desktop, more are taking what is called a "responsive design" approach that lays out content depending upon the device through which that content is being accessed. Responsive design relies on media queries that target specific devices and viewport sizes, and that allow a website to communicate with a user's device to determine how to accommodate a range of different devices and screen sizes.

FIGURE 6.7 A navigational section on the City of New York's new mobile-first website.

Mobile-first would mean writing CSS code first for mobile devices, then using media queries to selectively serve up additional styling as the viewport size increases. Salon, Slate, and New York City take desktop-first approaches, but their sites' CSS coding utilize media queries to accommodate other smaller screen sizes and devices. Thus, laying out these sites using grids is simpler, at least conceptually—but writing the code to translate those layouts into working sites across browsers, machines, devices, and screens? A daunting challenge.

The point here is that with an increasingly complex landscape of devices and screen sizes, web designers are having to adjust with layouts and plans that are adaptive and flexible. Fluid grids, flexible images and image sizing, and media queries are the tools being used to translate layouts into content that works on desktops, tablets, and on the go.

One of the simpler layout patterns across media and media formats is the "Z" path that guides the human eye through most text documents from the upper left to the right, then down diagonally, then again left to the big finish at right. To define a path, you need an entry point or focal point, an obvious point of entry that inspires and motivates the reader to keep moving along the path you have charted.

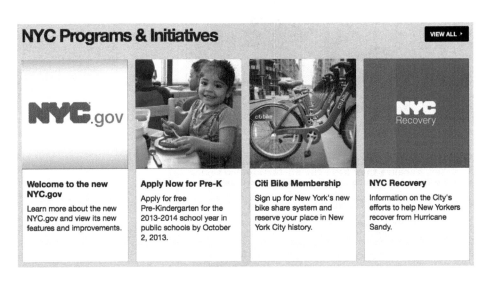

FIGURE 6.8
Additional menus at nyc.gov.

FIGURE 6.9 Smartphone-ready content at nyc.gov.

Find Local Events

SEE ALL EVENTS ▸

DATE
Select a Date

BOROUGH
Select a Borough ▾

CATEGORY
Select a Category ▾

CMJ Music Festival
OCT 15, ALL DAY EVENT

Hester Street Fair
OCT 12, 10AM TO 6PM

Archtober
OCT 7, ALL DAY EVENT

Village Halloween Parade
OCT 31, 7PM TO 11PM

FIGURE 6.10

The mockup in Figure 6.10 for an automotive ad clearly uses the Z path that Western readers' minds instinctively want to follow. We begin in the upper left, sweep right, then down diagonally following the incline of the car itself, then left to right to take in the details. This ad also uses an inverted pyramid, delivering the main message with a dominant visual and a headline first. The secondary information is at the bottom of the ad.

This ad for a ship line (see Figure 6.11) provides another example of the Z pattern to plot out content. The elements here are a company name, headline, dominant visual, body copy, and sidebar information. A three-column, four-row grid was used to map out these five elements.

With a rough map or grid of where your content is going to go on the page, next apply some basic page design aesthetics to make sure you have achieved excellence in what is called "The Big Four": **balance**, **contrast**, **unity**, and **symmetry**.

FIGURE 6.11

Balance can be briefly described as a state of equilibrium, or as the appearance of rest. A well-balanced page will typically be easy to read because all of the elements of the layout appear to be in the right place, with no particular element competing too strongly for our attention. An imbalanced layout, with visual "weight" improperly distributed, will give the reader a vague feeling of uneasiness or discomfort. For example, a top-heavy page with a "heavy" object on top of something lighter—a photo on top of a paragraph of text, for example—lacks balance and appears unpleasant to the eye of the reader. The ship ad in Figure 6.11 works because there is plenty of body copy and a heavy back-screened box to support a fairly small representation of the ship, which otherwise is a very heavy visual object. Notice how little water there is, contributing to a "lightness" in the graphic.

Generally, the "weight" of design elements, from heaviest to lightest, is as follows:

▶ photos;

▶ graphics;

▶ headlines;

▶ subheads;

▶ main body text;

▶ white space.

Contrast is the difference between or "unlikeness" of two or more things. This difference in page layouts creates variety, interest, drama, and unpredictability. Any layout needs emphasis, which will then contrast with everything else on the page. Contrast's enemies are dullness, boredom, and sameness, but this isn't to say that contrast should come at the cost of consistency and progression. Your tools in achieving contrast are color, headlines, and headline sizes, typeface and typeface sizes, photography, element placements (isolation, clusters, symmetry, asymmetry), borders and edges (even ragged ones), shapes (including unusual ones), and congruity/incongruity. An oversized graphic can provide contrast while at the same time reinforcing the text. Like-sized photos, on the other hand, can simply blend into or even become a background, like uniformed soldiers anonymously marching by on parade. Imagine an auditorium stage covered with high school or university students walking in a graduation ceremony, all in the same color robes and mortarboards, except one. He's wearing a gorilla suit and holding a giant placard. Who do you think will be noticed in this processional? It's all about contrast.

FIGURE 6.12

Zen's yin-yang symbol demonstrates classic contrast, as well as the other elements of the Big Four: balance, symmetry, and unity. With sharp contrast, the white and black are perfectly balanced, flowing in and out of one another for complete unity. In fact, unity is the semantic point of the symbol.

Unity is perhaps the easiest dimension to understand but the most difficult to achieve. The term refers to the sense that all the parts of the design and the layout belong together and work in harmony with one another. Unity requires more than balance, although balance is an important ingredient of unity. Synthesis, cohesion, and *Gestalt*, or the notion that the whole is greater than the rote or pure mathematical sum of the parts, are the hallmarks of unity. *Gestalt* is a German word that is translated as "form" or "wholeness." The term describes an early 20th-century German movement in psychology that focused on perception. In particular, these psychologists found that our perception of form depends not just upon seeing individual parts, but on the organization of the whole. We see the whole first, then we start breaking it down into parts. For example, what do you see in this next diagram?

Do the dots in Figure 6.13 suggest a square? That's *Gestalt*, because each dot is merely a single dot, but together, lined up as a unified group or battalion, they give the appearance of a square.

Symmetry is proper proportion of the parts to one another and to the whole with regard to size and form. Symmetry is an excellence of proportion, in other words, and is therefore very closely related to balance. For page design, this means practically that each page has a vertical axis that can be used to map out content either symmetrically

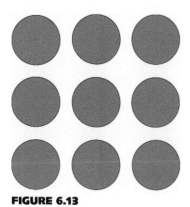

FIGURE 6.13

or asymmetrically. Symmetry is most often used for traditional presentations and asymmetry for playfulness, informality, and attitude. An exquisite ad for the Louisville Ballet, for example, depicted a ballet dancer's toe-shoe adorned foot, on pointe, on top of an egg, which was also vertically positioned. These two elements appeared with only the words, Louisville Ballet. The simple message here is perfect balance and that message depends upon perfect symmetry in the layout. Balance and symmetry make up the whole point of the ad, a point emphasized by the pointe ballet shoe that with the egg visually resembles an exclamation point. To achieve this, the designer started (and ended) with the page's vertical axis.

▶ DEVELOPING A STYLE GUIDE

For consistency and efficiency when creating, editing, and displaying content, embrace the idea of developing a publication-specific style guide, which in this context is a manual that governs how webpages and their content should be written and presented. We are not talking about writing style or tone, as we did in the previous chapter, but about style guides. The terms *style guides* and *style sheets* can also refer to the system of HTML code used by programmers to ensure that the pages they are creating are consistent in behavior and appearance. Here we are speaking of editorial style guides, not those used for programming and coding. Perhaps the best-known editorial style guide is the *Associated Press Stylebook*, which for more than 60 years has provided guidance on, among other things, spelling, capitalization, grammar and punctuation, and usage. Style guides often include special topical sections, as well, such as those in the *AP Stylebook* on business, social media, sports, punctuation, and Internet-related terms.

Here's how a style guide can help. Let's say you are working on an article that refers to the popular Bebo social media platform. Should the company or site name be presented as "bebo," as it appears on the site itself, or as the more conventional "Bebo," or perhaps "Bebo. com"? Is the term "email," no hyphen, or "e-mail"? Web page or webpage? Do you need to spell out Universal Resource Locator on the first reference, or is URL sufficient? A style guide entry for Bebo (and ebay and amazon.com) will settle this question once and for all.

Digital editors turn to stylebooks to answer these questions and, in aggregate, to contribute to consistency in the content. Consistency is perhaps even more problematic online, where file names, file types, computer code, and tags are so important and abundant, and where even a single capitalization mistake can shipwreck an entire webpage. Stylebooks can govern webpages, digital content, and the use of technology-based terms, both for presentation and for the coding or building of pages and sites.

Online stylebooks typically are written to complement a conventional stylebook. *Wired* magazine's stylebook, which is applied both to the monthly print magazine and the magazine's companion website, began on a single sheet of paper. Copy editors simply documented style questions as they cropped up, along with the answers to those questions as they were negotiated on the fly by the publishing company's editorial staff. That single page evolved into a lengthy computer file, which ultimately produced a book: *Wired Style: Principles of English Usage in the Digital Age.*

Like all style guides, the one in use at *Wired* continues to evolve. The staff wrestles with terms and words, and when a new term, buzzword, or acronym emerges, the publication's editors debate its style and proper usage. Somehow out of all the email messages and debates, agreement emerges on usage and proper *Wired* style. As examples, here are two terms and their style explained from *Wired*'s usage book:

FDDI
Pronounced "fiddy" and standing in for "fiber distributed data interface," this fiberbased network architecture offers a faster and more dependable alternative to Ethernet or Token Ring. (It transmits at 100 Mbits per second over LANs and MANs.) Of course, with gigabit Ethernet on the horizon, the future of FDDI looks bleak.

file name
Two words, like "screen name" and "domain name." In the early DOS days, computers wouldn't allow spaces in names and forced users to make file names one word. But "file name" was never closed up—in DOS or in English.

Embedded in any style guide are assumptions about the readers, assumptions that may include age or perhaps generation, interests, technological proficiency, and expertise in the area(s) addressed by the content. Once again, primacy is placed on knowing our audiences. To illustrate this point about assumptions, here are a few examples of how a style guide might handle style and usage questions common to webpages, and how the entries assume a level of sophistication concerning multimedia:

> When presenting file names, use only lowercase letters. Examples:
>
> florence.wmv
>
> asparagus_recipe.doc
>
> siena.jpg
>
> verona.pptx
>
> On first reference, put technical terms in italics:
> "Viewing this movie requires a *Flash plug-in*."
>
> Except when beginning a sentence, follow proprietary company name conventions. Examples:
>
> amazon
>
> bebo
>
> ebay
>
> General Motors
>
> When presenting URLs, use only lowercase letters: http://cubanxgiants.com.

For a comparison, here are a few entries from the *Associated Press Stylebook*, all from the "A" section at the front of the volume. These entries make far fewer assumptions about the guide's readers:

> ▶ **academic degrees**—Put an apostrophe in bachelor's degree and master's degree. This is to show possession. The degree belongs to the bachelor or master (that's you). Even when shortened to bachelor's and master's (no "degree" afterward), you keep the apostrophe.
> ▶ **addresses**—Abbreviate the words street, avenue and boulevard (think S–A–B), but only if they appear after a numbered address. Also abbreviate compass directions, but only if they appear with a numbered address. So, you'd write 50 S. Court St.,

but if you leave off the house number, you'd write South Court Street. Got it? Never abbreviate drive, highway, place, or any of the other words that might follow an actual street name such as Court, Union, Ventura, Lombard, Pennsylvania or whatever. Let's use this system for Utah addresses: 1160 E. 100 South St.

Is style a big deal? Consider this usage example taken from *Eats, Shoots & Leaves*, a one-time bestseller in the UK on the subject of punctuation. The example hopefully underlines how important every jot and tittle, every comma and colon can potentially be:

"A woman, without her man, is nothing."

"A woman: without her, man is nothing."

The only difference in the two, besides their entire meaning, is one colon and one comma.

As with most things, keep your style guide as simple as possible, allowing it to evolve and grow over time. Including examples can help to provide general parameters, as well, though no style guide is all inclusive or complete; all are works in progress. The *AP Stylebook* is updated with a new print edition annually, and it is updated more frequently for subscribers online.

The goals of style guides are the shared goals of good writing: clarity, concision, and consistency. In the *AP Stylebook*, for example, for the first 15 years of the Internet, the term "Web site" was two words, with an uppercase "W." In *Wired* magazine's style guide, however, the term has been "website" almost from the beginning. The Associated Press switched to "website" in 2010, and this book for the most part conforms to AP style. Whether the term is "Web site" or "website," "Bebo" or "bebo" is not all that important; what is important is that you use one and only one term or style for that term in all references. Toggling between two or more variations or versions of any term is unsettling for readers, and it suggests carelessness with language.

This consistency is needed wherever type appears, so style guides often stipulate specifications or guidelines for headlines, deckheads, subheads, and photo cutlines. These stipulations might include typeface designations, including one for headlines and another for body copy and perhaps still another for cutlines. In saving time by avoiding having to decide these in each and every instance, stylebooks and guides are an online editor's friends. They help a site and its staff achieve and maintain consistency, keep everyone on the same proverbial page, and free up time for more important tasks than deciding between Bebo and bebo. In anticipating and answering questions, stylebooks sweat the small stuff so editors can spend their time on bigger problems.

Here's the description from the Associated Press (www.apstylebook.com) of its own style book:

> The journalist's "bible," the style manual is an essential tool for all writers, editors, students and public relations specialists. It provides guidelines on spelling, capitalization, grammar, punctuation and usage, with special sections on business and sports. Included is a guide on media law, with practical guidelines on libel law, privacy, copyright and access to places of information, and a special section on Internet and computer terms, a comprehensive effort to unify spelling and usage of computer-related terms, from website and email to URLs and "cyber-" prefixes. This segment also offers Internet searching tips and cautions.

Another standard style, *The Chicago Manual of Style*, emerged more than a century ago when one proofreader began writing down on a single sheet of paper a few basic style rules. This list became a booklet, then in 1906 the first edition of *The Chicago Manual of Style* was published. The 16th edition checked in at a whopping 1,026 pages. One reason this style is so strong, besides its detailed instructions, is the manual's balance between establishing rules and allowing the author or writer or publisher flexibility. Freedom and flexibility are stated goals of the manual, at the heart of which is a "respect for the author's individuality, purpose, and style, tempered though it is with a deeply felt responsibility to prune from work whatever stylistic infelicities, inconsistencies, and ambiguities might have gained stealthy entrance" (*The Chicago Manual of Style*, 2010, Preface, p. viii).

To speed development of a style guide, you might choose an existing one as a base or foundation, then add to that foundation over time. The traditional choices include the *Associated Press Stylebook and Briefing on Media Law*, *The Chicago Manual of Style*, and *MLA*. These guides are designed almost exclusively for print. The *AP Stylebook*, for example, does not address issues such as displaying links, writing link text, and writing page titles. *E-What: A Guide to the Quirks of New Media Style and Usage*, by EEI Press, does, to provide another contrast. This textbook relies on the *AP Stylebook* for text and Lynch and Horton's *Web Style Guide* for its visual style. Using a traditional style guide and supplementing it with other resources and personal experience can direct students in developing a customized guide that addresses both the big picture *and* the little details.

The University of North Carolina (UNC) School of Journalism and Mass Communication created an addendum to the *AP Stylebook* to govern usage specific to UNC. Here's that addendum's entry on academic degrees, an important and recurring subject for reporters and editors covering the university:

> **Academic Degrees:** In general, reserve the title Dr. for M.D.s and other medical degrees. Use Ph.D., LL.D. and other degrees to establish a person's credentials. The preferred form is to use a title or phrase. (John Bruno, assistant professor of marine ecology and conservation.) Do not precede a name with a courtesy title for an academic degree and follow it with the abbreviation for the degree. Wrong: Dr. Jane Smith, M.D. Use an apostrophe with bachelor's and master's degrees, but not in Bachelor of Science or Master of Arts. Avoid academic degree abbreviations; use the reference in a phrase (Gayle Smith, who has a doctorate in medicine). Examples of degrees awarded at North Carolina include:

- ▶ bachelor of arts (B.A.) (a bachelor's);
- ▶ bachelor of science (B.S.);
- ▶ doctor of education (Ed.D.);
- ▶ doctor of law (J.D.) (a doctorate);
- ▶ doctor of medicine (M.D.);
- ▶ doctor of pharmacy (Pharm.D.);
- ▶ doctor of philosophy (Ph.D.);
- ▶ doctor of public health (Dr. P.H.);
- ▶ master of arts (M.A.) (a master's);
- ▶ master of business administration (M.B.A.);
- ▶ master of public health (M.P.H.);
- ▶ master of science (M.S.).

The *News & Record* newspaper in Greensboro, North Carolina, has done a similar thing, augmenting the *AP Stylebook* with its own wiki-hosted stylebook at http://nrcopydesk.wikifoundry.com/. In addition to entries on Greensboro-specific topics such as O. Henry and the Atlantic Coast Conference, the copy desk wiki lists names, titles, and contact information for local government officials, and it lists alphabetically local companies and organizations, such as the Winn-Dixie grocery chain and the North Carolina Zoo. Also helpful is a listing of trademarked names, including, from the "L" section:

Liquid Plumr drain opener;

Lite light beer by Miller;

Little League baseball sports services;

Little Tikes preschool toys;

Loafer shoes;

Lotus 1–2-3 computer software;

Lucite acrylic resin, paints;

Lycra spandex fibers.

If your organization, company, or site decides to develop its own style guide, there are several sections you will want to consider, including:

- ► vocabulary;

- ► abbreviations and acronyms;

- ► italics, bolds, quotation marks, and parentheses;

- ► hyphens and dashes;

- ► punctuation;

- ► capitalization;

- ► headlines and subheads, including colors and font types and sizes;

- ► hyperlinking protocols (active, visited, etc.);

- ► ordered and unordered lists;

- ► graphic design issues;

- ► photo captions;

- ► numbers;

- ► spacing;

- ► logos, slogans, taglines.

Digital writers' style guides will vary, of course. A site with medical information, for example, is going to be very different than one providing help in real estate, and both will be different from the UNC addendum excerpted earlier. Terminology; graphics, photography, and diagrams; tables and charts; and level of formality in writing will all be very different. But front-end work developing a style guide will save a great deal of time and headache later, and for however many people you have writing, editing, and creating for that site or publication.

CHAPTER ASSIGNMENTS

1 Identify a publication, company, or organization for or about which you will create online content. This entity can be real or imagined, corporate or non-profit, local or national or international: *Outside Magazine*, *The New York Times*, *Coin Collector's Digest*, Coca-Cola, Habitat for Humanity, International Association of Business Communicators, the Miami Dolphins. The entity you choose should be a publication or organization with which you have or want to have some connection or affiliation, one are already familiar. It can be the one for which you already work or want to work in the future.

Prepare a two-page summary of the audience needs for the publication or organization for which you will be writing and editing content. Do some research. Your summary should include:

▶ **Audience profile.** Who will be reading the content?

▶ **Purpose of publication.** Is it for entertainment, for news, for something else?

▶ **Frequency of publication.** Is it a monthly magazine? A mobile site updated on the hour?

▶ **The competition.** What are the sites and publications competing for the same audience?

▶ **Style issues.** Will you maintain the current style guide of the publication or organization, or is there need for a new one?

▶ **Information challenges.** What does the audience need to know, or what information does the organization need to broadcast? Do any special obstacles stand in the way of communicating that information quickly and clearly?

▶ **Your response to the information challenges.** How will you overcome any barriers and get your content out there?

If you have access to database providers such as Hoover's, Lexis Nexis, or Bloomberg, run some searches on competitors who serve the same audiences as those you seek. Learn what you can from what these competitors have experienced and are doing.

2 Secondly, detail the online content you will create for your organization or publication. What you write and develop is up to you, so you have the flexibility to do what makes sense and to write what can best serve you where you are now—in school, on the job, or on the job hunt. Possibilities for this assignment include:

▶ a news story or series of news stories;

▶ a feature story;

▶ criticism, such as restaurant review, play or movie review, book review;

▶ an interactive press release;

▶ a how-to feature.

These are just a few of the possibilities. Keep your publication's audience first and foremost in your mind. Identify the topic or angle of your proposed piece, making sure the topic is relevant and timely. This is a story or piece you will actually write, develop, and produce. You will gather the information, do the reporting, conduct the interviews, see the play—whatever is necessary to produce the copy.

3 Third, using a grid-based layout, deconstruct a favorite website by laying out on the grid its major elements. One way to learn good design is to reverse-engineer examples of good designs. This might be why the U.S. Navy Seals destroyed a downed stealth helicopter during the assassination of Osama bin Laden in Pakistan; the Seals didn't want to give any enemies the ability to reverse-engineer the navy's stealth technology.

FIGURE 6.14 A layout grid.

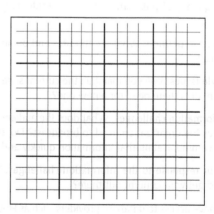

So, for this assignment, you don't have to deconstruct an entire site, just the homepage and a representative page or two from inside, including perhaps a sectional front page. This would also be a good exercise for learning how top-selling mobile apps are designed, as well. If you want to take a crack at that, run a search on "best-selling mobile apps." Apple, for example, charts them across multiple categories at www.apple.com/itunes/charts/. Choose one and reverse-engineer it.

4 Finally, develop and complete the content piece you detailed in assignments 1 and 2. Develop and present the piece for online readership by using the techniques and tools we've discussed so far. Do not merely post a large block of text or cut-and-paste from Word. This assignment asks you to apply what you have been learning. Be sure to spend plenty of time editing, including fact checking, spell checking, and editing for grammar, punctuation, and organization.

Length: About 750 words.

Online Resources

American Copy Editors Society (www.copydesk.org)
Resources at the site include reference materials, quizzes and help in discussion.

Associated Press Stylebook (www.apstylebook.com/)
Chicago Manual of Style Online (www.chicagomanualofstyle.org/home.html)

Dictonary.com—Style Guides (www.dictionary.com/Dir/Arts/Writers_Resources/Style_Guides/)
Online listing of style guides and manuals, including a handful of guides specifically for digital usage.

Guide to Grammar and Style (http://andromeda.rutgers.edu/~jlynch/writing/)
Online guide to grammar, style, and usage by Jack Lynch, associate professor of English at Rutgers University.

InfoDesign (www.informationdesign.org/)
Articles about information design.

Oxford Dictionaries (http://oxforddictionaries.com/us)
The online version is frequently updated, providing a rich source when determining style on newer terms and slang, such as "twerk" and "srsly."

The Slot: A Spot for Copy Editors (www.theslot.com)
Site of Bill Walsh, long-time copyeditor and author of several books on editing.

Society of News Design (www.snd.org)
This society is for designers in journalism, and the site offers resources selected for the group.

W3's *Style Guide for Online Hypertext* (www.w3.org/Provider/Style/)
This document was written in the early days of the web, defining such terms as "webmaster," the "www.name.com" convention, and a few basic points which are just as valid today. Readers should note that the site has not been updated to discuss recent developments in HTML, and it is out of date in many places.

▶ REFERENCES

The Chicago Manual of Style, 16th edition (Chicago, IL: University of Chicago Press, 2010).

Irene Hammerich and Claire Harrison, *Developing Online Content: The Principles of Writing and Editing for the Web* (New York, NY: John Wiley & Sons, 2002).

Susan Hilligloss and Tharon Howard, *Visual Communication: A Writer's Guide* (New York, NY: Longman, 2002).

Kuan-Tsae Huang, Yang W. Lee, and Richard Y. Wang, *Quality Information and Knowledge* (Upper Saddle River, NJ: Prentice Hall, 1999).

Steve Krug, *Don't Make Me Think: A Common Sense Approach to Web Usability* (Indianapolis, IN: Macmillan, 2000).

Patrick Lynch and Sarah Horton, *Web Style Guide 2* (New Haven, CT: Yale University Press, 2001), http://info.med.yale.edu/caim/manual/contents.html.

Roger C. Parker, *Guide to Web Content and Design* (New York, NY: MIS Press, 1997).

Thomas A. Powell, *Web Design: The Complete Reference* (New York, NY: McGraw Hill, 2000).

Lynne Truss, *Eats, Shoots & Leaves* (New York, NY: Gotham Books, 2004).

Wired Style: Principles of English Usage in the Digital Age (New York, NY: Broadway Books, 2002).

7

Writing for Blogs

It's easy to write poorly, but it's hard to write poorly every day . . . It's hard to write every day.
Rebecca Blood

Change starts at the edges.
Francis Pisani, in *Nieman Reports*

Whether explaining or complaining, joking or serious, the human voice is unmistakably genuine. It can't be faked.
Doc Searls, *The Cluetrain Manifesto*

▶ INTRODUCTION

The Supreme Court ruled in the landmark case *Branzburg v. Hayes* (1972) that the First Amendment's protections applied as much to "the lonely pamphleteer" as to the "large metropolitan publisher." Until only recently it really helped to have a printing press. With digital publishing platforms, tools, and software, however, now "the lonely pamphleteer" is anyone with a blog, Twitter feed, or even Facebook page. Digital media have profoundly reordered the media landscape, and blogs and blogging have been at the center of that reordering. By bringing the cost of publishing even to large readerships to the vanishing point,

CHAPTER OBJECTIVES

After studying this chapter, you will be able to:

▼
understand the limits and capacities of the blog format;

▼
write specifically for blogs;

▼
develop a policy for making corrections;

▼
apply a systematic understanding of ethics to blog writing and publishing;

▼
describe the role of blogging in journalism;

▼
Live blog an event.

and as part of a broader trend toward participatory "we" or "me" media, blogs and blog-gers daily influence changes in public opinion, how brands and products are perceived, and how political campaigns are won. The blogosphere is a key piece of digital real estate, and blogs offer a longer form for writing than most social media. Blogging should be thought of, therefore, in a larger digital media context, one that includes and incorpo-rates social media and social networks.

▶ BLOGS: A BRIEF HISTORY

Not a term that tumbles gracefully off the tongue, a "weblog" or "blog" is simply a website powered by software that makes it easy to publish to the web, typically posting content as entries in reverse chronological order. The most recent or newest posts, therefore, typically appear on top. Some other common attributes of blogs include archives, per-malinks (or hyperlinks to specific posts and the comments posted in response), time/ date stamps, tags (or key word identification), and blogrolls (hyperlinked lists of other blogs). Blog posts typically connect their readers with source materials mentioned or used by the writer, a cross-referencing that provides layers of information and, by both displaying and providing access to source material, serves to build credibility. When, for example, a blogger is commenting on a political speech, it is customary to link to a transcript of that speech or to an audio recording of the speech, making it transparent to the reader where fact leaves off and opinion begins.

The multiplicity of ways in which blogging can take shape makes broad categorizations difficult. Blogs range from personal digital diaries to major news sites to single-author opinion pages. The term "blog" means nothing more than the collection of the few attri-butes described above, thus it is a value-neutral medium or media format for publish-ing online. This chapter is most interested in blogs dedicated to news, information, and opinion rather than those used to relate personal events and private thoughts. But the skills and perspectives of this chapter are applicable to all blog formats.

A useful metaphor here is the ink pen. Using the pen to write a diary, the writer becomes a diarist. Using the pen to do journalism, the writer perhaps becomes a journalist. Ink pens are used for all sorts of purposes, from signing checks to journaling to drafting manuscripts for the next great novel. As a technology, there is nothing about the ink pen that makes it more or less capable of producing exquisite literature or pure drivel. A blog is no different. Thus, blogging is a lot like writing. The way the blog format is used defines blogging as practice.

The best blogs create for their readers a sort of "targeted serendipity," as pioneering blogger Rebecca Blood has called it, or a shared point of view and information and sources a reader perhaps did not even know he or she wanted to read. (Blood started her blog *Rebecca's Pocket* in 1999, when the format was just emerging, and she wrote one of the first books about blogging, *The Weblog Handbook*, in 2002.) One of the best at this is BoingBoing.net, where the top posts during late summer 2013 were a plague devastating California's black squirrels and a decision in England to put Jane Austen on the £10 note. Blogging should be seen, then, as an expression of community, allowing individuals to communicate and congregate around shared ideas and interests.

Big Blog Moments

Josh Micah Marshall's "The Talking Points Memo" blog got a great deal of attention in December 2002 for raising questions about then Senate Majority Leader Trent Lott's views on race. In doing so, TPM (www.talkingpointsmemo.com/) legitimized blogging as journalism, or at least established that blogging and the mission of journalism are not necessarily at odds or in any way mutually exclusive. Both bloggers and traditional journalists have debated ever since whether or when and under what circumstances blogging can be considered journalism.

In the wake of Lott's statement on national cable television that the United States would have been better off had Strom Thurmond been elected president in 1948—when Thurmond ran on a segregationist platform—Marshall revealed a history of what could be described as racist statements made by Lott. The Mississippi senator previously compared court rulings in 1981 upholding affirmative action programs at colleges to the dating ban between black and white students at Bob Jones University, according to TPM.

After a full weekend of silence, during which only TPM blogged on the subject, mainstream news media picked up on Marshall's analysis, piecing together Lott's record. The media coverage fueled a national debate that ultimately led to Lott's removal as majority leader, but not before the surreal occurred: Lott appearing on BET to apologize to the nation's black community. Lott's capitulation or, more accurately, Marshall's attention to an overlooked political story proved a watershed moment for blogs, which were still considered by many at the time to be a minor league publishing option.

It is important to note that politically, Marshall and his blog are on the left, and, even more importantly, that he has always been candid and transparent about this political orientation. He began publishing TPM in November 2000 during the Florida presidential election vote recount; since then TPM has been dedicated to a form of watchdog investigative journalism that is in danger of vanishing as ever-larger media companies stress entertainment and ad sales over service to the public interest. TPM quickly found a loyal audience—several loyal audiences, in fact: TPM launched its second site, TPM-Cafe.com in 2005, and TPMMuckraker.com and TPM Election Central in 2006.

Though Marshall is proud to be a blogger, he says he also believes that what he and his reporters do is journalism. TPM, after all, is credited with investigative reporting on the firing of eight U.S. attorneys, reporting for which TPM received the Polk Award for Reporting (another groundbreaking moment for blogs as a format). Importantly, TPM's coverage of the U.S. attorney scandal utilized crowd-sourcing. TPM pursued tips from readers, synthesized the work of other news outlets, provided its own original reporting, and solicited and received the help of thousands of readers in sifting through piles of documents released by the Bush administration. "There are thousands who have contributed some information over the last year," Marshall told *The New York Times*, referring to TPM's crowd-sourced U.S. attorney coverage.

In 2006, when watchdog groups that monitor federal spending wanted more information on nearly 2,000 pork barrel projects buried in a Congressional spending bill, they listed the projects on the web and asked readers to do some research. Readers did, and information began pouring in. Similarly, also in 2006, Porkbusters.org enlisted readers to find out which senator had blocked legislation that would create an online database of federal grants and contracts. Ted Stevens, R-Alaska, and Robert Byrd, D-West Virginia, were uncovered as the obstructionists in a matter of days. The wisdom of the crowds was leveraged to shine more light into the dark places of government, and blogs have made it easier to publish the results.

Memogate

The political right has been busy, as well. It was self-avowed conservative bloggers in 2004 who first called into question the authenticity of four documents presented by Dan Rather of CBS News on the TV news magazine show *60 Minutes*, supposedly from President Bush's commanding officer in the Texas National Guard. The documents described efforts to get preferential treatment for the (then) future president. Bloggers pointed out that given the equipment on which the memos were composed, they couldn't possibly have been written in the early 1970s, as was being alleged by CBS News.

Just hours after *60 Minutes* aired an Atlanta man with the username "Buckhead" posted a comment on Free Republic (www.freerepublic.com), observing that the CBS memos, which had been posted online, had been typed in a proportionally spaced font that was unlikely to be found on or from a 1972-era typewriter. A blog called "Power Line" (www.powerlineblog.com) reprinted Buckhead's speculations, along with comments from readers who claimed knowledge of IBM typewriters, fonts, and superscripting. A reader who had been a navy clerk/typist and another who had been an air force personnel manager weighed in on military typewriters, paper sizes, and procedures. Power Line's initial post quickly listed 605 trackbacks, meaning that 605 other online sites linked to the blog's analysis. Again, crowd-sourcing generated smarter coverage than any one reporter likely could have produced.

Meanwhile, CBS News and Dan Rather stuck to their story. Rather stated on air:

> ▶ The story is true. The story is true. I appreciate the sources who took risks to authenticate our story. So, one, there is no internal investigation. Two, somebody may be shell-shocked, but it is not I, and it is not anybody at CBS News. Now, you can tell who is shell-shocked by the ferocity of the people who are spreading these rumors. (September 10, 2004).

The story was not true as reported, and CBS News ultimately admitted this, making the episode an important point on the timeline of blogs. For one, the episode pitted traditional or mainstream news media against new media, specifically bloggers, and it was bloggers who won the day. A few days after *60 Minutes* made its claims, a former CBS executive vice president, Jonathan Klein, sneered at CBS's critics who claimed the old memos had to be modern forgeries written on a computer: "You couldn't have a starker contrast between the multiple layers of check and balances (of professional journalists) and a guy sitting in his living room in his pajamas writing," Klein told Fox News on September 10, 2004.

Bloggers had become reporters of a kind. Thousands of blogs picked up the story. Type designers, computer workers, and former military clerks joined the debate. Mainstream news media other than CBS News joined in, as well. Professional journalists interviewed document experts, who raised the same questions as the bloggers. Then CBS's own experts revealed that they had never bothered to authenticate the memos. As the *San Francisco Chronicle* noted, many mainstream journalists were reading the blogs to track the discussion and find sources. "The Internet has empowered ordinary citizens to become fact checkers and analysts. People with a wide range of experiences can collaborate online, sharing knowledge, sources and ideas, and challenging each other's facts," wrote the *Chronicle*'s Joanne Jacobs.

Doing Journalism

The case studies mentioned above highlight how blogs can be used to do journalism, or to fulfill the mission of journalism, which is to give an electorate the information it needs to govern itself. First, note that the bloggers mentioned above do not use their blogs to merely dump onto the web what has already appeared in print, as most news media organizations did with their first blogs. An early exception was a blog launched by the *Seattle Post-Intelligencer* in 2003 and written by technology reporter Todd Bishop.

Bishop's blog quickly became a daily extension of an important Seattle beat—covering the software giant Microsoft, which is based in the Seattle area. The newspaper's print edition and traditional website remained the places or spaces to break news, but Bishop said the blog gave him space to follow up on print stories with information that perhaps did not require a full story. His blog also became a place to give readers valuable context for the print stories, expanding and extending coverage for those who wanted to read (much) more about Microsoft. (Bishop left the paper in 2008.) "After writing a story about liability for software flaws," for example, Bishop said, "I posted an entry that gave readers access to a lot of the material that helped me understand the issue and put the story together."

Bishop's blog posts also helped him to collect sources for future stories, identifying people whom, he says, he would not have found without the blog. One reader emailed him in response to a post about Microsoft's software patching strategy, a reader who turned out to be the person responsible for patching his own company's PCs. The next time Bishop covered the issue in print, he contacted his new source for comment.

A journalist's blog can also be a useful repository for information that has been edited or cut out of a story to fit the available space in the newspaper or on the broadcast, such as an observation, anecdote, or extended quoted material. Long, unexpurgated interview notes shouldn't be simply dumped online, obviously, but addenda and sources such as interview notes or excerpts can extend the coverage. *The Daily Show*, for example, routinely posts full interviews with prominent guests after editing down those interviews for the show's 30-minute TV format.

Because blogs typically favor writing in a conversational voice, they leverage digital's unique capacity for interpersonal communication, or communication very different and much more personal than any mass media can deliver. Delivered via the web, however, the potential reach of this otherwise interpersonal communication is global and immediate, matching the capacity of traditional mass media. The more informal, personal nature of most blog writing is due to the fact that most blogs are by a single author. This places priority on voice.

A journalist's blog can be used to aid reporting by soliciting information. If a reporter cannot make it to a public meeting or event, a post (and/or a tweet or Facebook post) can notify your readership community of that event and let them know why you think it might matter. Perhaps someone in your readership can attend the meeting, ask questions, and even provide some reporting on what happened. Asking readers to post their reactions to the event or meeting gives readers ownership of the coverage and can strengthen the bonds of the community. Of course, the obligation to check facts remains for the journalist, even when—especially when—presenting news gathered by interactors.

A journalist's blog can also be used to pose questions to a readership. Open questions that identify concerns about a particular issue or event can build community and inform reporting over the long term. Using a blog in this manner can also help the journalist to gauge the readers' interest in certain issues and to determine which stories to continue reporting on, resisting the daily print impulse to write and publish a story and then move on without following up.

Community building is an essential element of successful blogging. Blogging journalists should be actively thinking of ways to engage readers, to begin and continue conversations, and to create and sustain loyal audiences. One of the most powerful ways to build community is to foster communication and interaction between readers themselves. Some of the best conversations can be started with very brief blog entries that ask for input and reactions. Of course, starting the conversation is half the battle: a good blogger will also continue to facilitate the conversation by getting involved, steering the line of inquiry, responding to posts and participating.

▶ HOW TO BLOG

Whether they are used for journalism or not, there are at least three hallmarks of most good blogs. First, they are updated frequently, perhaps very frequently, depending upon the audience and the nature of the subject. A fast-moving story might lend itself to several updates per day, as information streams in, perhaps amplifying or building on tweeted updates. Regardless of the topic, the blog should be frequently, regularly updated, which is, after all, the reason blogging software was developed—to make it easy to publish.

Second, most blogging software automatically puts the most recent post at the top, or in reverse chronological order, so readers do not have to scroll or hunt for the latest information. The medium (or media format) is, in other words, built for breaking news. Good blogs are timely.

Lastly, good blogs tag posts, or identify them with key words that can be used to find related posts and that search engines use to catalog the blogosphere. A post on the next World Cup in soccer, for example, might be tagged with the key words "World Cup," "soccer," "futbol," and "FIFA." For similar reasons, the post's headline should spur interest and invite reaction.

As they have been discussed so far in this book, the principles of good writing for digital spaces all apply when writing for blogs. Layering content, making it scan-able, breaking information up into easily read chunks, and linking to relevant material elsewhere on the web are the very things for which blogs were designed. If you are thinking about presenting something in long form, consider summarizing it on the blog instead, then linking to the longer piece in .pdf or .doc form for those readers who wish to read on. This promotes both scanning and provides layers for drill-down. A few ideas or examples of list-worthy information:

▶ components of a bill or law;

▶ requirements for submitting or applying for something;

FIGURE 7.1 The author's blog, at WanderingRocks. wordpress.com.

▶ aspects of a candidate's background;

▶ details of a legal decision;

▶ supplies needed for a project;

▶ ingredients for a recipe;

▶ product features;

▶ subsections of a long or multi-page article;

▶ directions on how to create or complete something.

Wordpress or Blogger.com?

The two most popularly used blog formats, Wordpress and Blogger.com, offer slightly different blends of strengths and weaknesses. Google-owned Blogger.com's chief benefits are that it is free, almost fully automated, and simple to use. The learning curve for Blogger is short and shallow; users can be fully up and blogging in minutes. Wordpress also offers a free version that is easy to use, but Wordpress's strength is a pay version that is a self-hosted blog format robust enough to become a content management system, an e-commerce website, or a fairly sophisticated website. However, Wordpress's free version is more than most bloggers need, offering 3 gigabytes of space, full automation but with the ability to tweak the HTML code running behind, and access from mobile apps on virtually all smartphone brands.

FIGURE 7.2
Blogger.com's interface for generating a post.

A Blogger.com account, not surprisingly, is integrated with other Google products, including YouTube, Gmail, and Google+. This integration is either a positive or a negative, depending upon a user's pre-existing relationship with Google and its many services. But Google has been intentional in favoring its own services and offering much less flexibility with non-Google products.

Wordpress, on the other hand, is superior when it comes to social media integration. Automatic post-and-share features include connecting to Facebook, Twitter, LinkedIn, and Tumblr. Wordpress bloggers can also facilitate sharing via StumbleUpon, Pinterest, and Reddit by adding buttons to their Wordpress blog posts and pages.

In short, either blog software is easy to use and can accommodate nearly all a blogger's needs. Both have been stable, with no major changes in user interface over the years, and both allow for a high degree of customization. And both allow bloggers to integrate photos and video.

Ten Steps to Better Blogging

You know the hallmarks of a good blog, and you can appreciate how blogs can be a powerful tool in the quiver of journalists and people who do journalism. Building on

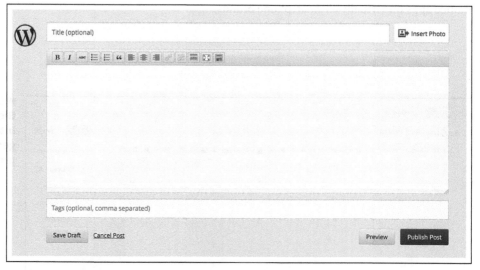

FIGURE 7.3 Wordpress interface for generating a post.

that foundation, here are ten practical steps or, more accurately, good habits that will produce a better blog:

1 **Write every day.** In arguing for frequent, regular blogging, Rebecca Blood wrote, "it's easy to write poorly, but it's hard to write poorly every day. . . . It's hard to write every day." Write frequently and regularly and your writing will surely grow stronger with the practice.

2 **Schedule your blogging time.** Like establishing any new habit, blogging requires planning and commitment, so determine when in the day or night you can consistently blog, then to stick to that time. Some will prefer to write early in the morning, coffee in hand, with energy reservoirs at their maximum. Others prefer the reflection of late evenings, after the day's events have played out.

3 **Be authentic.** A jazz music deejay in Greensboro, North Carolina, in the 1990s, daily signed off his broadcasts with the call to, "Be yourself so you won't be by yourself." The best blogs have an authentically human voice that is distinctive, even idiosyncratic. Don't worry about pleasing everyone from the start. Instead, write for an audience of one—yourself. This will help you to cultivate the authenticity, transparency, and voice you need. The networked and Google-searched web will connect your area of interest or expertise with readers who share a similar point of view and/or interest, as will your activities on Twitter, Facebook, and other referral systems. Sites like Google, Storify, Technorati, Digg, Reddit, Del.icio.us, Stumbleupon, and Slashdot will pick up on what you are posting and make your writing known to larger and wider audiences.

4 **Carve out a niche.** The best bloggers focus on specific interests—the narrower the topic, the better. This leverages their own expertise and experience in the area. Larry Lessig, for example, is a Stanford law professor specializing in intellectual property law. His widely read blog, at www.lessig.org/blog, focuses on intellectual property law, the First Amendment, and the open source movement, though he comments on other subjects such as pop music and technology. Readers can count on his blog to keep up with the major news and events in intellectual property law as they relate to digital media and digital content.

5 **Be curious and take lots of notes.** Not every thought is blog worthy, so keep a notebook or temporary file of your musings, thoughts, ideas, links, and articles of interest—anything that might inform your blogging. When you keep your daily appointment to write, you can relax knowing you have a file or folder of goodies to get you going rather than having to stare at an empty template postbox and write from scratch a pithy or provocative post. This is a really useful tip for writing in general, and many if not most good writers practice this (just look for their Moleskine journals tucked inside a pocket or backpack).

6   **Engage.** When you get comments, tweets, and Facebook "likes," respond to them. Encourage them. Affirm your readers and continue the conversations your posts have begun. This is about community-building, which was discussed in the previous section. Participate on other people's blogs, include their blogs on your blogroll, and link to other posts when appropriate. Share their content. The blogosphere operates on the principle of reciprocity, so make sure you are creating plenty of social capital by being interested and engaged with the ideas of others in your blog circle or community. If you are not prepared to engage at this level, there really is no point to starting up a blog.

7   **Learn the software.** You don't have to become an expert coder, but you can devote an "upgrade day" every few weeks or so to learn more about the software you're using to power your blog. Experiment with its newer features and play with the settings. Learn more about what your blog can do. You could also use this planned time to tag or retag posts to better organize your content and to make it easier to find specific posts. This is a good time to check for broken links, as well.

8   **Promote yourself.** Don't be shy. Market your blog. Tweet out. Integrate it into your Facebook activity. Register your blog with Technorati, which indexes and provides blog search. Register with the major search engines. Set up RSS and email feeds of your site to have your content delivered to anyone who wants to subscribe. Google Analytics is a free tool any blogger can use to see how people are finding you and what terms they used to locate your blog, which can inform how you tag content and the kinds of headlines you write.

9   **Break up the text.** This is a theme of this textbook. Though your writing may be Pulitzer worthy, your readers will still need some visual relief. Follow the basic graphic design and layout principles covered in previous chapters, and use boldface, lists, photos, graphics, cartoons, breakout diagrams, and illustrations to elaborate your post and break up what otherwise might be an overwhelming storm of words.

10   **Be ethical.** Think through and hold to a code of ethics. An old adage advises that the best time to plan what you would do with a lot of money is when you don't have any money, because when you are flush with cash, your values will likely change based on your appetites. Similarly, planning ahead for ethical challenges by adopting a code of ethics will allow you to have a set of carefully deliberated priorities, goals, and values to turn to in times of crisis, when decisions about content need to be made quickly and resolutely.

▶ BLOGGING ETHICS

The tenth and last habit or step is one that is often overlooked, and critics of bloggers have often pointed to the fact that bloggers do not share a set or code of professional, standardized ethics. Lawyers who violate their profession's code of ethics can be disbarred. Physicians also can be prohibited from practicing medicine for serious ethical breaches. But journalists? Writers? Bloggers? Shame is really the only punishment. (Of course, much-publicized breaches, such as Jayson Blair's plagiarism and fabrication of stories at *The New York Times* during 2002 to 2003, can lead to so much public pressure that the writer either resigns or is forced out, but these instances are rare.) So subscribing to any code of ethics is voluntary. To maintain or preserve a writer's freedom of expression, it would have to be. Most print journalists follow the Society of Professional Journalists' (SPJ's) Code of Ethics, a list of standards that translates well to the blogosphere. In fact, some bloggers have developed standards based on the SPJ code, which is excerpted here:

> The SPJ code calls journalists to:
>
> ▶ Seek Truth and Report It
>   Journalists should be honest, fair and courageous in gathering, reporting and interpreting information.
>
> ▶ Minimize Harm
>   Ethical journalists treat sources, subjects and colleagues as human beings deserving of respect.
>
> ▶ Act Independently
>   Journalists should be free of obligation to any interest other than the public's right to know.
>
> ▶ Be Accountable
>   Journalists are accountable to their readers, listeners, viewers and each other.
>   —Society of Professional Journalists' Code of Ethics
>   (www.spj.org/ethicscode.asp)

Rebecca Blood codified her relatively short list of good blogger behavior in her book *The Weblog Handbook* (2002, pp114–120), this way:

> 1 Publish as fact only that which you believe to be true. If a statement is merely speculation, it should be so stated.
>
> 2 If material exists online, link to it when you reference it. Readers can judge for themselves and a founding principle of blogging is exercising freedom of expression and the marketplace of ideas. Online readers "deserve, as much as possible, access to all of the facts," Blood writes.

3   Publicly correct any misinformation. Typically entries are not rewritten or corrected, but later entries should correct inaccurate information in those earlier posts. Inaccurate and erroneous information on other blogs should also be corrected in the spirit of the greater blogging community's responsibility to one another and to its readers.

4   Write each entry as if it could not be changed; add to, but do not rewrite or delete, any entry. "Post deliberately," Blood advises.

5   Disclose any conflict of interest.

6   Note questionable or unbiased sources.

So you see, Blood's list and the Society of Professional Journalists' Code of Ethics share some significant characteristics. Both Blood's and the SPJ's code espouse:

▶   publishing the truth;

▶   supporting arguments with credible sources;

▶   being accountable;

▶   spending time writing as though changes could not be made;

▶   disclosing conflicts of interests, articulated by the SPJ as acting independently.

Blogger Martin Kuhn devised a widely distributed code of ethics for bloggers that is general enough to encompass most forms of blogging. His code includes imperatives to:

1   Promote interactivity:
    ▶   Post to your blog on a regular basis.
    ▶   Visit and post on other blogs.
    ▶   Respect blog etiquette.
    ▶   Attempt to be entertaining, interesting, and/or relevant.

2   Promote free expression:
    ▶   Do not restrict access to your blog by specific individuals or groups.
    ▶   Do not self-censor by removing posts or comments once they are published.
    ▶   Allow and encourage comments on your blog.

3   Strive for factual truth:

  ▶   Never intentionally deceive others.

  ▶   Be accountable for what you post.

4   Be as transparent as possible:

  ▶   Reveal your identity as much as possible (name, photo, background informa-
      tion, etc.).

  ▶   Reveal your personal affiliations and conflicts of interest.

  ▶   Cite and link to all sources referenced in each post.

5   Promote the human element in blogging:

  ▶   Minimize harm to others when posting information.

  ▶   Promote community by linking to other blogs and keeping a blogroll.

  ▶   Build relationships by responding to emails and comments regularly.

Jimmy Wales, founder of Wikipedia, and *Web 2.0*'s Tim O'Reilly began soliciting recommendations for blog behavior in 2007, refining the list over time and hoping to come
up with a code that balanced free expression, allowing even "mean-spirited comments"
with the widely shared belief that some objectionable expression should be censored,
deleted, or otherwise removed. "One of the mistakes a lot of people make [is] believing
that uncensored speech is the most free when in fact, managed civil dialogue is actually
the freer speech," O'Reilly wrote in 2007.

The code that Wales, O'Reilly, and their contributors came up with, which can be
accessed at http://blogging.wikia.com/wiki/Blogger's_Code_of_Conduct, states that
bloggers should:

1   Take responsibility for our own words.

2   Write nothing we wouldn't say in person.

3   Connect privately first.

4   Take action against attacks.

5   Not allow anonymous comments *or* pseudonymous comments.

6   Ignore the trolls (or those wishing harm).

7   Encourage enforcement of terms of service.

8 Keep our sources private.

9 Demonstrate discretion when deleting comments.

10 Do no harm.

Each of these codes has great value, and it isn't terribly important which one holds sway in any particular organization. The more important thing is that the organization has one. In fact, a code can be read as distilling an organization's values as much as prescribing good behavior.

What To Do About Corrections

One of the recurring ethical concerns for bloggers over the years has been how to handle corrections of mistakes. The ease of publishing and the absence of editors in the blogosphere have combined to yield a high rate of error relative to that for print media. The imperative for print journalism has been to write, edit, vet, and then publish. In the blogosphere, the paradigm is turned on its head: Publish, then let readers do the vetting. But print journalists typically don't have the option to make a correction directly in the article they've published, instead relying on corrections written by editors that are published in subsequent issues of the newspaper or magazine, often in a small "Corrections" box toward the front of the publication. There is no way to ensure that readers of the first erroneous article will see or read the correction.

In digital spaces, however, a writer has the option of making a correction or change directly to a story he or she has posted, with or without noting the fact that a change has been made. The option to effectively "erase" mistakes has caused concern for blog writers and their readers. Changing or correcting the record without alerting readers to what has been changed threatens a writer's credibility by undermining the very transparency the media format is so good at facilitating and that contributes to credibility. How corrections or changes should be handled, therefore, is an important question. As the Wales–O'Reilly collaboration underlines, in the blogosphere it is considered bad form to delete anything, including and especially reader comments, but particularly when it is done without notice or explanation.

Clearly, when published statements or posted comments are libelous or illegally invade a person's privacy, they should be taken down. If something has to be corrected, however, a blogger has several options. He or she could:

▶ Include a note at the bottom of the original post with the new information.

▶ Include the new information in the post while striking through the old or incorrect information (and displaying the strikethrough). This isn't an aesthetically pleasant option, but it does demonstrate maximum transparency.

▶ Write a new post with the updated or corrected information, a post that links to and refers to the original post.

▶ Delete the problematic post and replace it with the updated, corrected information, with or without notice that a replacement has been made.

When deliberating over these options, remember that interactors have repeatedly demonstrated that they will reward transparency, even a willingness to be transparent. Digital writers who are forthcoming, candid, and open earn their readers' trust as interactors place more trust in those whom they perceive as having nothing to hide. Relative to other online writers and content producers, bloggers very conspicuously took the lead in capitalizing on transparency by disclosing their personal politics and biases, regularly providing links to original source material to allow readers to judge the material for themselves, engaging in public conversations with readers that invite critique, and admitting and correcting errors quickly when they made them. It is these demonstrations of transparency that build and maintain credibility online.

So, after something has been posted, editing should be limited to fixing typos, smoothing out grammar, and modifying unfortunate word choices, but no more. The most conservative or safe way to edit, and a method that bloggers typically use if they find an actual inaccuracy or fact error, is to leave the incorrect text, cross it out, and add the new corrected version. If the correction is more substantial, a line or two explaining what the changes are and why they were made is typical, perhaps with a label of "Updated" or "Correction" above the explanatory note.

For a different point of view, Robert Stacy McCain, a career journalist and a late convert to blogging, quotes an old adage of English teachers: "Writing is re-writing." He wrote in 2010 questioning "the blogger concept that the first draft—the version of the post as it existed when you initially hit the 'publish' button—must be preserved inviolate." He publishes, then corrects typos. He corrects a more substantial error when learning of it from readers, but seldom acknowledges the error, the correction, or the reader who alerted him to the error, because to do so would "detract from the reading experience." He writes that his object is "to present the clearest expression of my thoughts to the reader, not document the writing process. Not only is the latter messy and potentially confusing, almost nobody will care about it."

McCain's position is not typical in the blogosphere, and it is not the recommendation here. Transparency is a peek behind the veil to see the writing (and reporting and editing) process, to acknowledge errors and how they were handled, and to credit those who help produce a fuller, more accurate account, all of which marks the blogosphere as a place different than mainstream media and that point to a very different paradigm for credibility of information in digital spaces.

A Word About Bias

Admittedly, it is one thing for an individual blogger writing for him or herself to offer complete disclosure of his or her associations and views, and to be completely transparent about affiliations, biases, and even agenda, and a very different thing for journalists working within traditional news organizations who are asked or who volunteer to blog for or as part of that news organization. The company might tell the journalist he or she has near or complete freedom and autonomy in writing the blog, but the reality might turn out to be tragically different, with institutional limits on expression corresponding roughly with the company's own editorial positions or biases or with the biases of his or her superior.

Religious or political views, sexual preferences, and even dietary practices could potentially be used against a person in a news media setting. And influence can be more subtle, too, of course, with bloggers receiving an implicit message that they should embrace or gravitate toward one set of views when talking with one executive, but a very different set of views when talking with another. For these reasons among many others, many reporters rightfully believe that they should not reveal everything, including, for example, how or for whom they vote.

A mini-case study: An editor in the Washington bureau of a major newspaper chain donated money to a political campaign in a way that could be (and was) traced. Bloggers scoured the databases of campaign contributions and cross-referenced the results with lists of media employees. The result was outing the editor. (Journalists are typically asked to be objective; donations to a particular candidate or campaign undermine this objectivity, or at least the perception of it.) The editor kept her job, but she could no longer donate to campaigns, at least not in traceable or visible ways. Transparency, in other words, was not high on this media company's list of values.

Another mini-case study: A newspaper editor responded to a top executive's request for ideas on how to make the company better by suggesting the company review its less than ideal website search utility. The result? The editor was reprimanded for "criticizing" the newspaper online and warned to "be careful" about what he posts (the "conversation" occurred via a website open to the public). The implicit message: Don't be honest. Don't be transparent. It might cost you your job.

Thus, an organization's commitment to transparency has to be genuine, and that commitment likely will be a greater commitment to truth and to an authentic diversity of ideas. It is consistent with journalism's mission, which is to inform a self-governing public and to facilitate that public's participation in civic life.

▶ LIVE BLOGGING

The simplicity and low or even no cost of blogging, and the spread of wireless Internet connectivity have made live blogging a popular genre or category of blogging and an important addition to reportage of crises and events. Live blogging is simply blogging in real time, while a news event is taking place. As a form, live blogging provides a visceral account of the event, usually from the point of view of the individual blogger. As such, live blog accounts typically include the personal opinions and observations of the blogger, making these accounts highly idiosyncratic, personal, and qualified.

Given these qualities, it makes the most sense to live blog where no video of the event will be made available. Because it is "live," there is typically a higher tolerance for error; live bloggers are trading accuracy for timeliness. Live blogging is an important, relatively new weapon in the reporter's digital arsenal. After all, journalism has been called the first draft of history, so a good journalistic live blog can serve as the first draft of journalism.

One of the first high-profile examples of live blogging was by the *Virginian-Pilot* newspaper in its coverage of the Lee Malvo–John Allen Muhammad sniper trials in Virginia during October 2003, one year after the series of killings the year before. The newspaper's Kerry Sipe live blogged from the media room in the Virginia Beach municipal center, tracking everything from jury instructions and testimony to his impressions of Muhammad's mood. Connected to the courtroom through closed-circuit video and to the rest of the world through a wireless Internet connection, he published posts on the *Virginian-Pilot*'s website. Sipe's minute-by-minute updates gave readers the closest thing they had to real-time news because the trial's judge barred video coverage of the proceedings. At the time of the trials, Sipe was the *Virginian-Pilot*'s online news coordinator and one of only a relatively small number of writers using blogs to report the news. Along with Sipe's unfiltered copy came an unfiltered experience, one that left the burden of assessing the news to readers. These readers rose to the challenge, passing along corrections to the record and forming something of a community around Sipe's accounts. It is also important to note that Sipe's blog was just one part of the *Virginian-Pilot*'s trial coverage, and not even that coverage's centerpiece. Other *Virginian-Pilot* writers covered the story in more traditional ways. Thus, blogs have not replaced other forms of journalism, but have added a new, unique layer of coverage.

Most news organizations rely on blogs, and many have added live blogging to their breadth of coverage. The Associated Press and CNN launched their first blogs for the Democratic National Convention in July 2004, and *The New York Times* very prominently launched a live blog for the presidential primary season in 2008.

Time To Live Blog

Once you have decided that a live blog is the way to go and have committed to doing it well (because there are few things worse than a live blog badly done), here's how.

First, live blogging requires preparation. Find out whether you will have Internet or mobile access at the event, which often means getting in touch with the venue. If they do, will you have to pay? If mobile is all you will have, you might need to verify signal strength and reliability. In short, find out what options you will have for connectivity.

Depending upon what you find out about how to connect, you can then decide from what machine or device to write and post—a laptop, netbook, tablet, or mobile phone. Factoring into this decision is whether you plan to include other media in your posts, such as photography and/or video. For photo-heavy live blogs, a smartphone might be the best option. For largely textual accounts, a laptop and its full-size keyboard is likely the best choice. Of course, a laptop presumes a seat and a surface, like a table or desk, while a smartphone or tablet does not. (A note from experience: Make sure you take a charger and/or a backup battery for whatever device or machine you will be using.)

When determining where to publish, you might default to an existing blog, or you might set up a new blog or blog feed for the event. Free blogging services like Blogger.com, Tumblr.com, and CoverItLive.com are options. Tumblr works particularly well with smartphones, while Posterous.com can be done via email. Both Tumblr and Posterous have apps for both the iPhone and Android, as well. One of the leaders, even pioneers, of the blogging movement, Meg Hourihan, co-founded Pyra Labs to develop a blogging software now known as Blogger.com, which Google acquired along with the rest of Pyra in May 2003. Blogger.com's software is one of a number that automate the blog publishing process and, therefore, eliminate the need for users to write any code or install any sort of server-side software or scripting. Once launched, Blogger.com's blogs use templates and a Word-like toolbar to make writing and submitting posts a simple exercise.

That anyone with a Google username and password can begin writing and publishing to the world from his or her own URL in a matter of minutes at no cost is momentous, on a scale similar to Gutenberg's liberating of knowledge with moveable type. While website publishing has long been available to anyone willing to learn HTML coding or WYSIWYG design, the advent of blogging software gave tens of millions of individuals a simpler way to maintain webpages. Other popular blogging software tools include TypePad, LiveJournal, WordPress, and MovableType. Some, like Blogger, are remotely hosted, while others, such as MovableType, are installed on the user's own computer.

Proper preparation can take a lot of the stress out of what can be a very stressful experience, because there are so many demands on your attention. Once you are on site, plugged in, powered on, and connected to the Internet one way or another, you are ready to blog. In your first post, you will want to set up the rest of the account. Where are you? Why? What exactly are you covering? What aren't you covering, and why? Why is this event important, and what do you hope to accomplish or convey in your live blog? What does the venue or room or site look like? Who else is in attendance? Place the event into a broader context.

In short, you want to take your readers there. To do this, you want to leverage the live blog's capacity for immediacy and vicariousness, and you will want to provide in your account detail, texture, and reflection. Give readers a sense of what happened and what you thought about what happened. This is visceral, immediate, onsite reporting from a particular point of view—your point of view. So you can and even should use first-person voice. Hyperlink where appropriate. Include a photo where you think suitable, especially in the scene-setting stage.

Here are more tips for reducing the stress and getting the most out of your live blog experience:

▶ Relax. Key in your notes as unfinished sentence fragments, then go back when you have time and flesh out the narrative.

▶ Provide a transcript if you are covering a speech or panel discussion, if possible. Though tedious for most, for a few who could not attend, this transcript will be a valued resource.

▶ Write a short blurb about a part of the event you couldn't get to and link to someone who did, someone who provided a report or transcript.

▶ Post a retrospective or more comprehensive commentary piece once the event is over. Put the event, or your take on the event, into context.

▶ Know that the biggest challenge is paying attention to the event while writing at the same time. You can take advantage of this challenge by allowing the activity to focus your writing and your attention, placing you in the middle of the stream of events washing over you. What you live blog today can become the basis for a more analytical piece tomorrow.

▶ Know up front that you will probably annoy or distract someone near you. Clacking away on a keyboard really can be obnoxious. Planning where you sit can help, as can congregating with other bloggers and keyboard clackers. You should also turn your phone to "vibrate" and avoid flash photography.

BOX 7.1   *Liveblog*

The following are excerpts from a live blog account of a Republican Party rally in northwest Georgia. The blogger, John Druckenmiller, does what a good live blogger should:

• He introduces readers to the event and what is about to take place. He brings readers in with description, and he introduces the participants.

• Druckenmiller then provides a near real-time account of what takes place, with plenty of rich detail and some of his own reactions throughout.

• He sticks with it to the end, then provides closure with a wrap-up post.

The live blog's posts are presented in reverse chronological order, which is typical:

Senate candidates make their pitches at packed GOP rally

Posted on August 17, 2013 by hometownheadlines •

Hometown Headlines *spent midday Saturday at the Floyd County GOP's annual rally at the Tillman Hangar. Our speaker-by-speaker coverage is below. We're about to add a photo gallery from the event. Please check back by 3 p.m.*

1:22 p.m. Speeches end. Time for the straw poll results. Gingrey wins the poll by 34.4% followed by Handel at 26.7, Broun at 18.3, Kingston at 13.7, Perdue at 5.3, Grayson at 1.5 and no votes for Yu.

1:16 p.m. Eugene Yu: Vote for Yu—for you. That's what Yu says his pitch is. Says do you want a senator who's one of 100 or one of a kind. Says he's one of a kind. Says he might look and talk a little different but "I am proud to be an American . . . I will deliver your voice in Washington." Says the American dream is slipping away; he wants to save it for his children and grandchildren. Says once elected, leaders forget what got them to Washington and what reasons. Talks about the balanced budget and whips out his wallet as an example. Says common sense will solve budget woes.

1:07: Paul Broun. Very rousing speech including a call to "close down the EPA." Talks about making any legislation pass his four-way test: it is fair, is it constitutional and can we afford it among the key points.

. . .

12:57 p.m. Phil Gingrey. Thanks those who have supported him here. Says he will serve the state with the same heart and intensity as he did with the old 11th Congressional District (and current one). "We don't need a senator who is sort of conservative . . . we need someone who will stand on Georgia values." Says Gingrey: "The Constitution doesn't adjust to the times, the times need to adjust to the Constitution." Key issues: Jobs, jobs and jobs. The debt. And Obamacare. Calls Obamacare the "worst piece of legislation ever enacted" by Congress. Adds Gingrey: "We Republicans are not working to shut down the government . . . that ball is in their court (Democrats/ administration).

12:53 p.m. David Perdue next. Says we watched the Soviet Union collapse and wonders if we'll watch the United States crumble as well. Cites $17 trillion in national debt. Says federal debt is a huge threat to our national security. Says there is a critical need to fix tax code and healthcare. "We have an opportunity to dig out of this mess."

12:50 p.m. Karen Handel talks about her success in local and state offices (including secretary of state). Wants a meaningful plan to fix government, to "get moving on the Fair Tax now." Wants Obama on defunding Obamacare. Says the state needs fresh leadership to make needed changes. "I will not resign myself to an America of mediocrity."

. . .

12:38 p.m. Wait. David Pennington goes first as gubernatorial candidate. No straw poll on governor's race today. He chides Deal—not by name—for not being here (hence, no poll). Talks about Dalton's ranking as a fast-growing community in terms of city incomes. Preaches limited government on the state level, citing how it has worked in his city. (Applause from the Tea Party's Mike Morton.) Pennington says the state has great resources. "If we put those type assets with true limited government principles," the state's economy will take off, he says. Gets a warm response and a few stood as well.

12:35 p.m. Finally, the Senate candidates.

Now hearing from others involved in the party representing different groups. Nice touch but this crowd is anxious to hear the Senate candidates and perhaps David Pennington, who's challenging Deal in the GOP primary.

. . .

11:37 a.m. First speaker is U.S. Rep. Tom Graves. The District 14 congressman comes in low-key dress, oxford shirt and blue jeans. He jumps into Obamacare and how it is being delayed by the administration. "It's too dangerous for American people. . . . It's time to defund Obamacare." Graves talks about "29ers," those working less than 30 hours a week to avoid rolling into Obamacare worker mandates. He askes the crowd, "Are you ready to stop the train wreck?" Rousing support from this partisan crowd.

11:34 a.m. Floyd County GOP Chair Layla Shipman greets the crowd following the presentation of the colors by the Boy Scouts. She introduces local elected officials.

. . .

11:23 a.m. Some of the side conversations are on the "general purpose" SPLOST issue to be on the Nov. 5 ballot. If we were taking bets right now, you'd have more in the "won't pass" category. The main issue: The Tennis Center. And those are comments from more moderate Republicans, not the Tea Party members. Big miss not having some of pro-SPLOST push here today.

11:15 a.m. Lots of networking but no candidates at the mic yet. But the candidates are working the crowd, including Senate hopeful Karen Handel.

11:01 a.m. The candidates and officeholders make the rounds. Insurance Commissioner Ralph Hudges is here as is U.S. Rep. Tom Graves. Also on site: County Commission Chairman Irwin Bagwell and Commissioner Rhonda Wallace. Tax Commissioner Kevin Payne. State Rep. Christian Coomer. Lots of side issues on display including a big turnout by Fair Tax supporters.

10:54 a.m. Earl Tillman is greeting guests as they arrive at this hangar for the rally. Lots of campaign paraphernalia, from signs to paddles. It looks like primary season. The barbecue from Duffy's is drawing the biggest crowd so far.

THE ORIGINAL REPORT TODAY: And we're off. On a mid-morning that feels more like the final month of the campaign rather than 10 months out, **Floyd County Republicans** are welcoming the most impressive list of political hopefuls the state has seen this year.

Among those likely facing Democrat **Michelle Nunn** in the November 2014 general election are: **Paul Broun, Phil Gingrey, Derrick Grayson, Karen Handel, Jack Kingston, David Perdue and Eugene Yu**. All flooded the still-forming GOP primary ballot after U.S. Sen. **Saxby Chambliss** surprised most by declining to seek a third term.

Also attending are gubernatorial hopeful **David Pennington**, Dalton's mayor and the perceived Tea Party favorite, as well as Kingston resident **Dr. John Barge**, currently Georgia's school superintendent and rising political rival of **Gov. Nathan Deal**. Barge had yet to formaly enter the race; expect an announcement soon. Citing scheduling conflicts, Deal did not attend today's rally but did send a campaign team. Also not attending: Lt. Gov. **Casey Cagle.**

The undercard, if you will, includes just about every other statewide official up for a new term next year as well as local and regional Republican officeholders—and perhaps some potential 2014 rivals.

This is the ninth year the Floyd County GOP has staged the summertime rally at Earl Tillman's hangar at Richard B. Russell Airport/Towers Field. It has grown from around 200 guests to perhaps nearly 300 today. The event, from 11 a.m. until 1 p.m., is free but guests had the option of paying $10 for a barbecue plate ($25 maximum per family). Duffy's Deli catered the event.

Reprinted with permission

▶ THE BLOGGER VERSUS JOURNALIST DEBATE

Is anyone with a blog a journalist? Is anyone with a camera a photographer? What happens to journalism when every reader can also be a writer, editor, and producer? These are but some of the questions long debated in both the blogosphere and in journalism, and still no clear consensus has emerged. The blogger–journalist dichotomy is a false one. Many journalists blog; many bloggers do journalism. Key distinctions, then, include the methods or processes employed and the purpose or goal of the content.

Where an information-gathering process includes what Kovach and Rosentiel, in *The Elements of Journalism*, call "the discipline of verification," and where the purpose is service to the public interest, then blogging could be said to be journalism. Where one or both of these is absent, the blogger would be hard pressed to claim to be doing real journalism. Original reporting that has been corroborated, fact-checked, and verified, reporting that seeks to inform a self-governing electorate, whether on a blog or any-where else, must be called journalism.

Most blogs have a different mandate than does journalism, however. Most blogs are dedicated to some form of commentary or opinion. To the extent that a blog lacks original reporting, it should not be considered as doing the primary enterprise of jour-nalism. For most bloggers, a high value is placed on the act of expression, on providing in the aggregate a diversity of voices. Also important in the blogosphere are writing or publishing with speed, offering transparency of sourcing and of the opinions that influenced the writing, and decentralizing information and knowledge. For journalism, by contrast, great value is placed on providing a filter for information, editing the con-tent, fact-checking, ensuring accuracy and fairness, setting the agenda, and centralizing news dissemination. In some cases, then, the value sets of the blogosphere and of jour-nalism are in tension if not utter conflict. The vetting and editing process typically used in print, for example, comes at the expense of speed and of single-voice authenticity, hallmarks of the best of the blogosphere. Blogging's priority usually is to publish, then to begin filtering; journalism's priority is to filter, then after and only after to publish. Blogging, then, can be seen as a thoroughly postmodern form of expression and pur-suit, and postmodernism rejects objectivity as a goal or ideal. This rejection pits many bloggers against the guild of journalism, which still strives for objectivity, at least in its methods if not in its products.

The filtering and editing in journalism is possible because of daily printing cycles and large editorial and production staff. With large, capital-intensive printing presses and a prohibitively expensive distribution system, newspapers, in fact, require substantial staff. Organized hierarchically, the staff funnel the information out from a center. With the imperative to publish, then to filter, bloggers are as concerned with *unmaking* and testing public opinion as forming it. The ethos for news and information blogs, then, is based more on values such as immediacy, transparency, interconnectivity, and proxim-ity to the events. As a heterarchy, diverse bloggers post, cross-link, blogroll, and track back to interact in a network pulling ideas and knowledge from the edges.

An incident from the 2008 presidential primary might illustrate some of the tensions between the imperatives of most bloggers as contrasted with the mission of the profes-sional guild of journalism. A supporter of Barack Obama attending one of his rallies in California, a rally not open to the public or to the media, found herself witness to what she immediately recognized as newsworthy commentary from the candidate. Obama referred to Pennsylvania's small-town voters as "bitter," as clinging to guns and religion, and as having antipathy to people "who aren't like them." The blogger deliberated for four days whether or not to publish what she had heard.

Declaring herself to be a "citizen journalist," 61-year-old Mayhill Fowler determined to publish the news, which she did on OffTheBus.net, a cooperative news blog launched by Arianna Huffington of *The Huffington Post*, one of the web's most popular blog-format sites, and Jay Rosen, a journalism professor at New York University. Fowler's decision underlines how digital communication has changed campaign coverage in unpredictable ways. But it should not surprise. The democratization of publishing inevitably alters our political process. Obama perhaps did not think his remarks would reach beyond the ballroom; he did not know he was being blogged.

Fowler's claims to journalism notwithstanding, does her campaign rally post represent journalism? As an eyewitness account of remarks at a campaign event that most would agree was important to the race for the party nomination, Fowler's post must be considered an act of journalism. Does this make Fowler a journalist? As an avowed contributor to Obama's campaign (and Hillary Clinton's and even Republican Fred Thompson's, as well), Fowler's standing at the rally presents some real problems were she to claim to be a journalist. Most journalists would never make public their political cleavages, nor would they attend as a supporter a political event that had been closed to the media. Fowler's four-day delay before publishing points to these problems or conflicts. A journalist would not have to weigh the pros and cons of publishing news in the public's interest, at least not in the circumstances the California fundraiser presented.

Objectivity as a Process Goal (Not a Product Goal)

Few journalists or journalism professors today cling to the belief that pure objectivity is possible, at least as an attribute of journalism's products—the news. Striving for as objective a news-gathering process as possible, however, still is widely regarded as noble and good. Contributing to candidates clearly threatens and even mocks that objective process. The fact that Mayhill Fowler was criticized both by media and by her fellow Obama supporters points to this inherent conflict, bringing to life the biblical paradox of trying to serve two masters and, as a result, loving one and hating the other. As Rosen commented on the episode, "journalists, the pro kind, aren't allowed to be loyalists. But loyalists . . . may find that loyalty to what really happened trumps all. And that's when they start to commit journalism." This doesn't, however, make loyalists journalists.

According to Friend and Singer (2007, pxvi), a journalist in American society is someone "whose primary purpose is to provide the information the citizens of a democracy need to be free and self-governing; someone who acts in accordance with a firm commitment to balance, fairness, restraint, and service; someone whom members of the public can trust to help them make sense of the world and to make sound decisions about the things that matter." Journalists, including digital journalists, perform this *sense-making* role. David Simon, a former reporter and a producer of HBO's hugely successful *The Wire*, asked in the *Washington Post*: "In any format, through any medium—isn't an understanding of the events of the day still a salable commodity?" He wondered if the Internet is so profound a change in the delivery model that "high-end news," or journalism that really matters, will become increasingly scarce, rare, exotic. Jeff Bezos, founder of Amazon.com and buyer of *The Washington Post*, wondered essentially the same thing on an interview on NBC's *The Today Show* in September 2013. "I think printed newspapers on actual paper may be a luxury item," Bezos said. "It's sort of like, you know, people still have horses, but it's not their primary way of commuting to the office."

An operative term in this definition is "trust." To instill trust, traditional journalists agree to a code of ethics, however tacitly, typically one similar or identical to the Society for Professional Journalists' Code of Ethics discussed earlier. As Friend and Singer write, "a code of ethics does not create ethical behavior." Such a code can provide a compass, or a map of orienting philosophy to govern or guide behavior. Where these codes of ethics have failed to prevent lapses in journalism, bloggers have brought checks and balances of their own, serving as a sort of watchdog of the watchdogs, or a "Fifth Estate" to journalism's "Fourth Estate." Bloggers routinely criticize journalism and mainstream news media for what they see as sloppy, erroneous, and incomplete coverage and reporting. Journalism, therefore, provides these blogs with most of the fodder for the blogs' posts. The vast majority of blog content is derivative, or dependent upon journalism's original reporting. One study showed that less than 5 percent of blog content is the result of doing the legwork of journalism—original reporting, the heavy lifting required of the discipline of verification.

Bloggers instead react, commenting on issues, events, and people in coverage, and providing context and elaboration. These distinctions are not to belittle blogging; on the contrary, blogging has assumed important roles in building a vibrant, well-informed democracy. The distinctions are made to help us understand how the information landscape is changing, and how interdependent are the digital media and traditional mass media ecosystems.

Why Traditional Media Embrace Blogging

Besides the reasons already mentioned for blogging, news organizations look to blogs to accomplish other goals more difficult in print media, including:

- ▶ Connecting with audiences and, therefore, building trust. News organizations like MSNBC, the *Dallas Morning News*, *Seattle Post-Intelligencer*, *Houston Chronicle* and others use blogging as one of many channels through which to flow editorial content. Blogs help to make these organizations more accessible, answerable, and transparent.

- ▶ Building community. With blogs, readers can become active partners rather than passive consumers. Blogs can give readers a stake in the process and its product, increasing loyalty and understanding along the way.

- ▶ Providing context, additional coverage, and interaction that do not make it into the print publication or onto the broadcast. Blogs make room for content that does not neatly fit into traditional media.

- ▶ Following up on ideas and opinions that emerge first in the blogosphere. Blogs are a way of tapping into a vast, networked media ecosystem.

- ▶ Giving reporters and writers, who by nature love to write and to express themselves, another avenue for that expression.

- ▶ Selling (more) advertising.

The popularity of blogging globally is emblematic of broader trends toward participatory, grassroots media and personal publishing. Not surprisingly, journalists see opportunities in blogging for a type of commentary, immediacy, and intimacy impossible with or through other forms.

▶ CORPORATE BLOGGING

The cover story for *BusinessWeek* magazine on May 2, 2005, read: "Blogs will change your business." Blogs, indeed, have changed business, and now many years after that article, corporate America's embrace of them continues. Blogs offer businesses the opportunity to build informal, lasting relationships with customers. As a digital media academic told *The New York Times*, "There's a conversation going on out there about every company and every brand, and talking with people engenders better relationships." A quick search in

November 2012 on the blog search engine Technorati for mentions of "Ikea," for example, turned up nearly a half million blogs, and that was in a single day of blog publishing.

Bloggers can generate buzz. For small businesses, blogs can be particularly powerful in shining a spotlight on a product or aspect of the business that deserves attention. As a side benefit, the corporate blog creates additional inbound and outbound hyperlinks that in their aggregate also serve to raise a company's search profile with the big search engines. Of course, it helps if you have something to say. This is the hard part. Anyone can start up a blog technically, but few can write well enough, with enough substance, to make it a worthwhile read over a sustained period of time.

As an unfiltered, conversational, personal, transparent, and interactive media format, blogs are powerful tools in establishing a dialogue with customers and clients. Blogs are humanizing, which remedies one of the chief problems of businesses, bureaucracies, and organizations in projecting any sort of relatable face. Good corporate blogs create a dialogue by providing writing that is candid, simple, concise, and often amusing. Successful corporate blogs do not try to sell anything, at least not overtly, and they don't preach or teach. They speak plainly and transparently.

CHAPTER ASSIGNMENTS

1 Live blog an event, a trip, a conference, or a meeting. Take your readers there. Use several brief posts to give your readers an account of that event. Hyperlink where appropriate. There is no minimum or maximum for the number of posts. Follow the guidelines detailed in this chapter.

2 Find a handful of blogs on a subject of your choosing. Read them over some extended period of time to get a sense of how each of the bloggers "covers" or writes about the subject you chose. To find the blogs, you could use Google's blog search (www.google.com/blogsearch); Alltop, a blog directory (alltop.com); or Technorati (http://technorati.com/), a blog search and ranking site. Write up a review of 750 words or so describing the strengths and weaknesses of the four or five blogs you chose. Be sure to discuss:

▶ voice and writing style;

▶ transparency and disclosure;

▶ linking;

▶ usefulness;

▶ social media integration.

3 Think about your career aspirations, your research interests (senior project, papers for your classes), and your political/religious/philosophical inclinations and interests:

(a) Search for news/commentary blogs (not social, personal journal blogs) that line up with one or more of your interests or pursuits.

(b) Identify three blogs you might actually read on a regular basis. This assumes a few things: quality and style of writing, currency, presentation, point of view, just to name a few.

(c) Prepare a tip sheet for the rest of the class that will look something like this (one entry per blog, three blogs/entries for the assignment):

Blog name or title: TalkingPointsMemo

URL: www.talkingpointsmemo.com

Author: Josh Micah Marshall

Brief description:

Left-leaning political commentary with an impressive record for accuracy and for beating the media elites on breaking stories. Widely read and commented on, this blog is among the very best nationally at what it does, which is why it was among the first blogs to sell advertising and make a nice little career out of blogging for its author.

Why I like this blog (include why you chose it, what about the blog matches up with your own interests or pursuits)**:**

I like to follow politics, and I like the behind-the-scenes. I distrust the elite media's handling of the major political parties, so I look for alternate sources of coverage. The Daily Show is fun, and it actually does a good job providing insights into the faults and flaws of the powerbrokers, but it's purely for fun. Josh Micah Marshall consistently puts meat on bones served up by The Daily Show. As a fellow blogger writes of Marshall's posts, this blog does "exactly what on-line web journalism is meant to do: Challenge the other guy to go one better. Keeping the competition honest" (www.chrisnolan.com/archives/000605.html).

(d) Make sure your submission is typed up and printed out.

(e) To find the blogs, you could use Google's blog search (www.google.com/blog-search); Alltop, a blog directory (http://alltop.com); or Technorati (http://technorati.com/), a blog search and ranking site.

Online Resources

Blog Communities, Software, and Platforms

▶ Blogger: www.blogger.com/.

▶ Ikonboard: www.ikonboard.com.

▶ Movable Type: www.movabletype.org/.

▶ Tumblr: www.tumblr.com.

▶ WordPress: www.wordpress.org.

A Few Good Blogs

The Committee to Protect Journalists (www.cpj.org/)
Defending journalists worldwide.

Cyberjournalist.net (http://news.cyberjournalist.net/)
Digital journalism blog by Jonathan Dube.

Dooce.com
A personal blog written by Salt Lake City resident and "Mommy" blogger Heather Armstrong.

Manhattan Nest (http://manhattan-nest.com)
A blog started in 2010 by Daniel Kantor, an interior decorator and writer in New York who writes about "do it yourself" thrifting and home decorating.

The Pioneer Woman (http://thepioneerwoman.com/)
In the author's own description, she is "a desperate housewife. I live in the country. I channel Lucille Ball, Vivien Leigh, and Ethel Merman. Welcome to my frontier!"

Poynter Institute's Mediawire (www.poynter.org/category/latest-news/mediawire/)
Group-authored blog focusing on media industry news.

Romenesko (http://jimromenesko.com/)
Journalism insider blog by Jim Romenesko.

Scobleizer (http://scobleizer.com)
Technology-focused blog by Robert Scoble.

The Shifted Librarian (www.theshiftedlibrarian.com)
Librarian and information science blog by Jenny Levine.

Stupid Cancer (stupidcancer.org/blog)
A blog written by and for cancer survivors and cancer patients.

Talking Points Memo (www.talkingpointsmemo.com)
News and political commentary.

The Monday Morning Quarterback (TMQ) (http://search.espn.go.com/gregg-easterbrook/)
Gregg Easterbrook's colorful sports blog at ESPN.com.

The Volokh Conspiracy (http://volokh.com/)
Law blog by Eric Volokh.

▶ REFERENCES

Paul Bausch, Matthew Haughey, and Meg Hourihan, *We Blog: Publishing Online with Weblogs* (Canoga Park, CA: Hungry Minds, 2002).

Rebecca Blood, "Weblogs: A History and Perspective" (www.rebeccablood.net/essays/weblog_history.html).

Rebecca Blood, *The Weblog Handbook* (Cambridge, MA: Perseus Publishing, 2002).

Branzburgv.Hayes(1972),www.law.cornell.edu/supct/html/historics/USSC_CR_0408_0665_ZS.html.

John Cassidy, "The Online Life: Me Media, How Hanging Out on the Internet Became Big Business," *New Yorker* (May 2006).

Trevor Cook, "The Death of Quality Journalism," *Unleashed*, March 12 (2008), www.abc.net.au/unleashed/stories/s2186777.htm.

Daniel W. Drezner and Henry Farrell, "Web of Influence," *Foreign Policy*, (November/December 2004), www.foreignpolicy.com/story/cms.php?story_id=2707&page=0.

Cecilia Friend and Jane B. Singer, *Online Journalism Ethics: Traditions and Transitions* (Armonk, NY: M. E. Sharpe, 2007).

Joanne Jacobs, "The Way It Is Today Isn't How It Was: If the Facts Aren't Right Bloggers Are All Over It," *San Francisco Chronicle*, September 26 (2004) (URL no longer available).

Bill Kovach and Tom Rosenstiel, *The Elements of Journalism: What Newspeople Should Know and the Public Should Expect* (New York, NY: Three Rivers Press, 2007).

Staci Kramer, "Journos and Bloggers: Can Both Survive?" *Online Journalism Review,* November 12 (2004) (URL no longer available).

Nicholas Lemann, "Amateur Hour, Journalism without Journalists," *New Yorker* (August 2006).

Robert Stacy McCain, "Blogging is Re-blogging," *The Other McCain* (blog), February 11 (2010), http://theothermccain.com/2010/02/11/blogging-is-re-blogging/.

Chuck Salter, "Hyperlocal Hero," *Fast Company,* November (2006), www.fastcompany.com/magazine/110/open_hyper-local-hero.html.

Cass R. Sunstein, "Fragmentation and Cybercascades," in Erik P. Bucy (ed) *Living in the Information Age* (Belmont, CA: Wadsworth Publishing, 2005): 244–254.

The Today Show, NBC-TV, September 25 (2013), www.today.com/video/today/53101083.

Jessica Wapner, "Blogging—It's Good for You: The Therapeutic Value of Blogging Becomes a Focus of Study, *Scientific American,* May (2008), www.sciam.com/article.cfm?id=the-healthy-type.

PART THREE
Contexts

8

Journalism for a Digital Age

In any format, through any medium—isn't an understanding of the events of the day still a salable commodity?
David Simon, writer and executive producer of HBO television series *The Wire*

The revolution will not be televised. The revolution will be live.
Gil Scott-Heron, songwriter

In times of profound change, the learners inherit the earth, while the learned find themselves beautifully equipped to deal with a world that no longer exists.
Eric Hoffer

▶ INTRODUCTION

Newspaper presses and the massive rolls of newsprint that feed them are fast becoming as quaint as steam engines and whale oil. In his monologue at the National Press Club dinner in 2013, Conan O'Brien quipped, "A lot of people say no one's reading newspapers anymore. I say that's ridiculous. Just ask my blacksmith." In *The Beautiful Cigar Girl*, author Daniel Stashower delivers a non-fictional account of a murder in New York City in 1841 popularized a few years later by Edgar Allan Poe. The murder of a beautiful cigar girl gave the city's penny presses a carnival of twists and turns, suspects, clues, and police mistakes. James Gordon Bennett, editor of the *New York Herald* and a man called the father of the penny press, claimed his newspaper would "outstrip everything in the conception of man. . . . What is to prevent a daily newspaper from being made the greatest organ of social life? Books have had their day. The theaters have had their day. The temple of religion has had its day. A newspaper can be made to take the lead of all of these in the great movement of human thought." This chapter explores the implications for journalism of the revolutionary changes the digital age has wrought.

▶ SAVING THE WHALE

Because of tremendous challenges in terms of the changing habits of interactors and the punishing instability of business models, traditional news media must evolve. Those that are surviving the shifts see themselves less as newspapers and TV stations and more as information providers and community builders and facilitators. As organizations adapt to a fast-changing media ecosystem, they suggest a metaphor. The newspaper industry is in some ways like a giant whale threatened with extinction. This whale historically has supported an entire ecosystem of plankton, smaller fish, and barnacles that depend upon the beast for sustenance. Now the ecosystem is changing, and the great whale has to evolve, change, adapt. Whales don't do this very easily, willingly or quickly, yet an entire Fourth Estate ecosystem depends upon this evolution's success. What should the whale become next? What new appearance should it take? The stakes for democracy are high. MSNBC TV personality Rachel Maddow said in an August 2013 airing of her self-named show, "You need to pay and subscribe to your local newspaper. Whatever it is, your local paper needs you. It needs to exist. It needs to have enough reporters on staff, to have enough subscriber income to pay for local reporters and to pay for editors so you can actually get coverage of what goes on at these usually pretty boring meetings in your county and in your town, because sometimes they're really important."

That the whale is dying is little disputed. Newspaper readership, circulation, and market penetration numbers have been in steep decline since the 1960s; market penetration peaked in the 1920s. The 2008 economic bubble burst was a watershed year, with McClatchy Newspapers, once the nation's most consistently profitable newspaper company, shedding 1,400 jobs throughout the country. And that was just one in a string of such announcements. In the same month, the Tribune Co., owners of nine newspapers including the *Los Angeles Times*, the *Chicago Tribune* and the *Minneapolis Star-Tribune*, announced it would cut 500 newspaper pages across its holdings in response to falling advertising revenues. In 2013, Amazon.com founder Jeff Bezos paid US$250 million for the *Washington Post*, a newspaper once worth several billion. Just prior to that, Boston Red Sox co-owner John Henry acquired the *Boston Globe* for just $70 million; *The New York Times* acquired the *Globe* for $1.1 billion in 1993. And in 2011, *Newsweek* magazine was sold for $1 (plus about $40 million in pension obligations).

With the widespread availability of free information online, news media companies face unprecedented competition at the same time that their revenue streams are being threatened and diluted by dwindling readership. This diminishing is due to both competition and the aging of what could be the last generation of newspaper readers. A boom in interest in and use of social media coincided with the 2008 collapse and with some of the economic pressures on the newspaper industry. This further upheaved the industry, which responded by closing publications, reducing circulation, and, of course, laying thousands off.

The decline in newspaper readership is part of a general shift away from push media (newspapers and broadcast television sending the news out) to pull media (aggregators and filters such as Pulse, digg.com, and Twitter that allow interactors to pull in what they want). According to a study from the Shorenstein Center on the Press, Politics and Public Policy: "Our evidence suggests that the Internet is redistributing the news audience in a way that is pressuring some traditional news organizations. . . . Product substitution through the Web is particularly threatening to the print media, whose initial advantage as a 'first mover' has disappeared." Interestingly, the study also found that while traffic to many of the national "brand name" newspapers is growing, the same is not true for the sites of local newspapers.

Part of the problem for traditional print newspapers transitioning to digital publishing models is perhaps related to self-perception. What business are newspapers in, exactly? The newspaper business? Or, considering how dependent they are on their delivery trucks, the transportation business? In 1960, Theodore Levitt analyzed the railroads' then current economic problems in a *Harvard Business Review* article entitled "Marketing Myopia." Levitt wrote that the railroads thought of themselves as being in the railroad business rather than the transportation business. The railroads thought they had a monopoly but failed to see new competing forms of transportation collectively eating away at their core business, just as newspaper companies have seen in suffering a death of a thousand cuts.

Similarly, newspapers have faced new competition on every front. Websites such as Craigslist and Monster.com have devoured newspaper revenue from classified advertising. Google News, My Yahoo!, and a host of other sites and portals have largely commoditized news. Thousands of sites specializing in business news and numbers, sports, weather, and entertainment diminish the need for a printed newspaper each morning, making a product printed overnight seem even quaint.

Journalism professor and author Phil Meyer explained in his book *The Vanishing Newspaper* that newspaper publishers have essentially four choices for survival:

1 Think of another use for their product. Baking soda manufacturers, for example, faced extinction by marketing their product as an air or refrigerator freshener. Their product's main purpose—cleaning teeth—was usurped by toothpaste.

2 Write and edit for those who are still buying and reading the printed product: the elderly. (This obviously is not a good long-term strategy. The newspaper industry is not replacing its older readers with younger ones.) Jim Roberts, digital editor at *The New York Times*, told the blog Portfolio.com in May 2008 that the newspaper "is not going to be obsolete in print for a long time. So whatever it takes to keep breathing life into it, we're going to do. We are blessed, in a sense, because in Manhattan there are people who will not give up their papers. It's like the Charlton Heston quote— 'We'll have to pry it from their cold, dead fingers.'

3 Enter the substitute (or encroaching) industry, which for newspapers is online news and digital information.

4 Or, as many corporate media companies are doing, harvest the business for whatever can be salvaged before the enterprise goes under. Raise prices. Reduce quality by laying off editorial staff. Reduce circulation and frequency of publication. Take the money and run.

Evidence of the popularity of the fourth option are the 2,400 jobs lost by the newspaper industry through the first six months of 2008 and ranking in 2012 by LinkedIn of the industry as the one that had shrunk the most during 2007 to 2011. LinkedIn and the Council of Economic Advisors crunched data from LinkedIn's nearly 150 million members, finding that newspapers were "the fastest-shrinking U.S. industry." There was some good news: Online publishing ranked among the fastest-growing for that same period. Since mid-2008, *Newsweek* sold for US$1 and subsequently shut down its print version, and *The Atlantic* magazine was acquired only to use the name and website as a platform for conferences. The whale is dying, begging the question of whether it can evolve fast enough to survive. The stakes are incredibly high. As Tom Rosenstiel and Bill Kovach argued in their book *The Elements of Journalism* (2007), journalism serves democracy, citizenship, and community by providing citizens with the information they need to be free and self-governing. The future for most newspapers in the United States is not good, and this is a national tragedy. But where a newspaper still is essential to its readers, it still is essential to advertisers.

▶ UNDERSTANDING "WE" MEDIA

Newspapers are learning that the Internet age is a participatory, social age. This means new and evolving roles for news organizations. One of the larger changes for traditional news media organizations is that readers are no longer merely passive receivers; they are actively involved in shaping the news agenda and in sharing and commenting on the news. New York University journalism professor Jay Rosen has famously referred to this new readership as "The People Formerly Known as the Audience," or the "writer–readers." So-called "we" media, or media in which interactors are participants and contributors, have reshaped the journalistic landscape. The ease and low cost of digital publishing and the very human impulse to network socially explain why Google acquired Blogger.com more than a decade ago, in 2003, then subsequently the video-sharing site YouTube in 2006. This impulse explains the rise of Facebook, Instagram, Snapchat, and Twitter. (Of course, not all social networking bets pay off. In 2005 Rupert Murdoch's News Corp. acquired social network Myspace for US$580 million, only to sell it in 2011 for $35 million.) What began as an internet-worked computer system for national defense, the Internet has become a thoroughly social phenomenon.

Natural disasters such as Hurricane Katrina in Louisiana and Mississippi in 2005, the Myanmar uprising in 2007, and a catastrophic earthquake in southwest China in 2008 spawned several citizen journalism initiatives that showed how socially networked the news can be in a digital age. In the aftermath of Katrina, CNN.com launched iReport, which solicits and publishes on the news website's homepage photos and video captured by ordinary people. The *New Orleans Times-Picayune*, which had to go completely digital during and after the storm, also very aggressively sought contributions, reports, video, and photography from Louisiana residents, contributions that helped the newspaper (and website) to win a Pulitzer prize for its hurricane coverage. People throughout the globe relied on participatory (or citizen) journalism to follow China's earthquake and rescue efforts in May 2008, disaster "coverage" that included widespread use of Twitter to produce a steady stream of on-the-ground reporting from the affected areas. Text messages, instant messages, microblogs, and blogs provided a visceral source of firsthand accounts of the disaster in what was a remarkable development for a country known for its censorship of media and of news reporting.

More recently, in April 2013, the Boston Marathon bombings revealed the best and worst of a news age in which anyone can contribute. Journalists turned to Twitter, of course; in fact, many *Boston Globe* staffers were runners in the marathon. Some immediately began to live tweet from the scene of the two bombings, live Twitter feeds that the *Globe* integrated into its live blog of coverage of the event and its aftermath. The *Globe* monitored its reporters' Twitter feeds using TweetDeck.

But bystanders and commentators tweeted freely, as well, adding to what was already a volatile blend of corroborated fact, hunches and intuitions, hearsay, and what turned out to be a great deal of misinformation. The *Globe* monitored readers' tweets, verifying and republishing many of them. This makes two important points. First, social media have become an integral and integrated source and channel of and for the news. Second, professional journalistic organizations are needed to sift, filter, verify, and organize the news—in short, to make sense of it all. Among the results was a huge rise in Twitter followers of the *Globe's* Twitter feed and blog.

The Boston police and other law enforcement also turned to Twitter, which served both to get the official word on the ongoing investigation out, as well as to solicit information, especially during the critical manhunt phase of the investigation.

Journalist Seth Mnookin, who also teaches at Massachusetts Institute of Technology (MIT) in Cambridge, MA, wrote about his experience with Twitter during the Boston events for Harvard's *Nieman Reports*. In his account he describes first turning to Twitter for logistics. He saw a student journalist on the scene and used Twitter to connect with the student and a photographer also there. They arranged a face-to-face meeting.

FIGURE 8.1 The second of what became a steady stream of tweets from the Boston Globe.

FIGURE 8.2

Mnookin used a police scanner app on his iPhone to keep track of police activities, and he tweeted through the night. Mnookin's colleague, Hong Qu, used Keepr, a social media monitoring software Qu developed, to capture Mnookin's tweets and to pull in the 100 most recent tweets from Twitter's API (application programming interface). Qu used Keepr to identify reliable sources who appeared to be tweeting from the scene based on four indicators of credibility: disclosure of location, multiple source verification (the tweets cited information from primary as well as other sources), original pictures or video, and accuracy over time.

Mnookin and Qu practiced a then new form of networked journalism that combined the speed and immediacy of social media with journalism's discipline of verification. Qu described Mnookin's tweets as a sort of "rolling, live-streamed press conference in which he answered followers' questions, corrected misinformation spreading via social media, and distributed important public safety updates from the police." Mnookin also leveraged the wisdom of the crowds by asking for help with his reporting.

Rather than write notes in a notebook, Mnookin turned to Twitter for note-taking, with an added benefit of having all of those notes time- and date-stamped. And as Mnookin describes it, "I knew my notes were going to be public. I spent more time thinking about whether something was important or informative or whether I was simply writing things down because I was nervous or had nothing else to do." He tweeted 483 times between April 15 and 19, and 169 times on April 18, the evening the manhunt ended.

It's also important to point out that Mnookin's reach via Twitter grew exponentially, but principally because traditional news media organizations made note of and reported what he was doing, or re-tweeted his coverage. Mnookin's number of follow-ers went from around 8,000 to 45,000 in only a few days thanks to reports in *The New York Times* and ABC News, to name a few. These news organizations serve as invalu-able filters and curators—arbiters in an otherwise free-wheeling ecosystem of news and hearsay.

Meanwhile on Reddit, the event "coverage" demonstrated how terribly wrong visceral, immediate, crowd-sourced news can become, most notoriously by mistakenly identi-fying a missing Brown University student as a suspect in the bombings. The Reddit-supplied misinformation was re-tweeted by several news organizations, including CNN and the Associated Press. Professional journalists must therefore share the blame. This same sort of amplification occurred when a student news organization wrongly tweeted that former Penn State football coach Joe Paterno had died, a tweet then re-reported by, among others, CBS News and *The Huffington Post*. As Mnookin and Qu point out, this new, higher level of uncertainty and even error is not going away, an inevitable cost of these new methods of covering, gathering, and disseminating breaking news. "Social media is not going away," they wrote. "Even though the business models of the main-stream news industry are experiencing creative destruction, demand for good storytell-ing from trustworthy news sources isn't going away either."

The use of Twitter in Boston also shows perhaps that the tendency to pit social media against traditional journalism is now obviously wrong-headed. The interplay possible between and among them can produce better news coverage. A more recent example is *The New York Times*'s integration of highly "tweetable" phrases and sentences in its mul-timedia story on the experience of auditioning for a cast member role on NBC's long-running *Saturday Night Live*. Written by Dave Itzkoff, the oral history highlighted sentences that could be clicked in order to automatically tweet them. Called "a one-off experiment" by the *Times*, the Twitter-integrated feature doesn't obligate readers to tweet what is highlighted, but tweeting a pre-designated link sent Twitter followers receiving the re-tweet to that exact point on the *Times*'s webpage. The *Times*'s editors choosing what to link for re-tweeting said they looked for "standalone anecdotes that SNL nerds like me would gravitate to and want to share around," Itzkoff said, as well as individual quotes that would fit the 140-character format. The SNL piece was selected for the experiment because its structure lends itself to dropping into the story at any point and moving from that point up or down.

Is the *Times*'s or *Globe*'s approach to social media integration *the* way to maximize the best of legacy news media and digital social media? This sort of question misses the larger point. They are good ways. There likely is no best way, and certainly not for long.

The ways people make, break, and share the news will continue to change. One online writing student likened the new role for traditional news media as overseers of a power grid: "I see news gathering becoming less centralized, as in so many facets of our society. Electric utilities now talk about a 'distributed' generation, which means solar modules on individual rooftops, all feeding the grid. The gazillion bloggers already out there and the growing use of personal electronics that turn everybody into a reporter, which we witnessed again in (terrorist attacks on hotels in) Mumbai (in November 2008), shows a parallel trend in journalism."

The student's power grid analogy recognizes that technology has enabled anyone to commit random acts of journalism. But filters are still needed. Someone will have to organize and oversee the grid. Professionals likely will continue to serve as this journalistic grid's curators and caretakers, providing a conduit through which news flows from a universe of sources and that makes some sense of it all. And hopefully interactors will continue to demand good prose, thorough reporting, and vetting that only trained and experienced writers and editors provide.

▶ WHAT JOURNALISTS DO

Regardless of what the future will mean for journalism and, by extension, democracy, the need for what journalists do will not go away. In some ways, this need will only become more acute, because journalists gather and share information, applying a discipline of verification in order to maximize truth, minimize harm, and to provide a fair and comprehensive account. By this definition, a great number of people who would not necessarily self-identify as journalists are, in fact, doing journalism. The key differentiator isn't what a person is doing, but how and why. How a person goes about gathering and sharing information, and why someone writes and publishes remain key distinctions—in any media, in all media—just as they have always been for older, traditional media.

Professional journalists are called upon to act independently, according to the Society for Professional Journalists' Code of Ethics, and to be accountable for what they write and publish. They are supposed to provide readers with the information needed to be free and self-governing. People have always craved news. As Rosenstiel and Kovach (2007) wrote, people "need to know what's going on over the next hill, to be aware of events beyond their direct experience. Knowledge of the unknown gives them security; it allows them to plan and negotiate their lives. Exchanging this information becomes the basis for creating community."

But today's journalists are being asked to be jacks of many trades rather than masters of any one. Mnookin responded to news of the tragedy by using his smartphone to tweet, to follow law enforcement's activities, to crowd-source his journalism, to geomap where he was and where the news was taking him, and to coordinate with other journalists how to cover the large and fluid story. He later wrote that he regretted not taking more photos or video, options also possible with even a smartphone. Digital journalists, then, are almost invariably more than simply writers or photographers or graphic designers. They are increasingly tech-savvy content producers familiar with dizzying assortments of software, apps, and tools. They are being asked to learn HTML, RSS, XML, FTP, Flash, video editing software, photo editing software, global positioning system (GPS)-enabled apps, social media, and a grab bag of software tools and computer languages and protocols. As Eric Hoffer wrote, "In a time of drastic change it is the learners who inherit the future."

Despite this diversification of skills necessary for digital publishing, however, the basic skills that have characterized the guild of journalism remain valuable and important. The inverted pyramid style of presenting information, for example, a style that has so dominated newspapering and that is partially credited with producing objectivity as a goal or news value, remains useful in ordering information for digital presentation.

▶ STORY STRUCTURES

The inverted pyramid orders information from most important to least, making stories easier to produce, easier to edit or cut to fit or fill a space, and it emphasizes the "who, what, when, where" fact-based approach to presenting information. As such, the inverted pyramid often is appropriate for digital spaces, as well, where information should be structured to facilitate scanning or drilling down. Historically, the inverted pyramid also accommodated wire service feeds, which came into the newsroom much as blog posts and tweets are published today, in reverse chronological order. The style has been common because it also helps to satisfy the print requirement that stories jump or continue from one page to another. Of course, with reader attention spans becoming ever shorter, providing the key information immediately, up top, will be rewarded with attention, eyeballs, likes, and shares.

The inverted pyramid also facilitates frequent updating because the top of an article can be replaced, pushing older information deeper into the article. Readers can get what they want and bail out, or keep drilling and reading deeper into the coverage. At many news organizations, due to staffing problems or simply a lack of motivation, too often

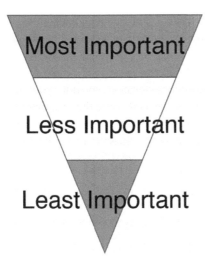

FIGURE 8.3

articles are not treated as specifically online content, or content that should change and develop over time, but, rather, merely as print poured into a new container. Articles are dumped onto the website and ignored until the next day's dump.

Other common story structures in print and online are chronological, narrative, and thematic:

▶ **Chronological stories** are perhaps the easiest to write because they follow a timeline. This structure makes sense when the story being told takes place over time, though often the climax or point of the story is presented first. Live blogging and live tweeting use this structure, one that is ideal for continuing or breaking stories.

▶ **Narratives**, by contrast, set the scene, then draw readers into that scene. Narratives follow a story arc that unifies a discrete beginning, middle, and end in a way that inverted pyramid stories do not. Narratives rely on vivid description and detail common to the novelistic style. These characteristics make the narrative style problematic online unless sparingly, opportunistically and expertly employed.

▶ **The thematic approach** organizes a complex story by theme or topic, dividing up the story into discrete pieces. For example, in a preview story leading up to the National Football League's Super Bowl, the thematic approach might first compare the two football teams' offenses, then the defenses, then the kicking games, and so on. This sort of chunking makes the thematic approach a useful one online.

When faced with a writing assignment or project, consider your answers to a few questions, questions that could be applied to a lot more than reporting and writing:

1   Why am I doing this? (A lot of writing doesn't need to be done.)

2   What will wild success look like?

3   How will I pull this off? What are specific steps I can take?

4   When will I complete these steps? What should this project's timeline look like?

5   Where will this get me (or the organization or publication) when I am finished?

Also helpful are some "commandments"—really, suggestions—for reporting and writing, suggestions that will help almost any writer with almost any writing project:

▶   The first commandment of reporting: Get out of your chair. Go get the information.

▶   The first commandment of writing: Sit your butt in the chair. Sit there daily. Write!

▶   Second: Thou shalt not be obscure.

▶   Third: Thou shalt show and not tell.

▶   Fourth: Challenge every adverb.

▶   Fifth: Challenge every adjective.

▶   Sixth: Challenge your first paragraph (delete it and read your piece again; do you need it?).

▶   Seventh: Challenge your last paragraph (delete it and read your piece again; do you need it?).

▶   Eighth: Challenge every line you love. Take out anything that is purely for effect, all that is clever, all interior decoration and ornamentation. You are an architect of meaning, not a decorator.

▶   Ninth: Challenge every exclamation point.

▶ Tenth: Challenge every use of the verb "to be."

▶ Eleventh: Circle each and every verb. Now decide, are they the right ones?

▶ Twelfth: Be alert for your pet words.

▶ Thirteenth: Read your draft aloud.

▶ Fourteenth: Proof and proof again (grammar, punctuation, spelling, consistency and clarity, economy, architecture).

▶ Fifteenth: Proof for precision (It's not a tree, it's a Liberty elm. Give things the dignity of their names.)

▶ Sixteenth: Writing is never finished, it is abandoned. Or, put another way, when is the writing assignment finished? When it's due.

Thinking About Reporting

While it's possible to overwrite—even easy to do—it is quite difficult to over-report. If you have limited time, you should spend most of it reporting. There is no substitute to boots on the ground, asking questions, doing lots of interviews, checking the databases, using the Freedom of Information Act to get information, even just hanging out and shooting the bull. In fact, with some sources, take some time *not* to ask questions. A cops-and-courts reporter in Anniston, Alabama, talked of taking cigars to the cigar-smoking local sheriff and doughnuts to the county courthouse, with no agenda in mind. When news did hit, that time spent building relationships, learning the names of sources' children, and just relating as human beings paid off with privileged access to information.

The two best questions a reporter can ask of any source are:

▶ How do you know that? Show me some evidence. If a source says, for example, that a new government program is "effective," ask for evidence of that effectiveness. How does the person in fact know that the program is effective? What demonstrable proof can be offered? Seek verification and corroboration. What does "effective" even mean in this context? Effective compared to what? As judged by whom?

▶ What do you mean? Have a source clarify if there is anything confusing about what was said. If you, the reporter, do not understand what is being said or shared, the reader has no chance. For example, if a source says sales are up

15 percent, find out what exactly that means. Up 15 percent over what or when? Up 15 percent for the year? For the week? Compared to the same period a year ago? Compared to last week? Sales are up, but are profits? How much did it cost to get that 15 percent increase?

Reporters and editors should seek to make:

▶ the familiar unfamiliar;

▶ the unfamiliar familiar;

▶ the complex somehow understandable; and

▶ the mundane, like city budgets and environmental impact studies, somehow interesting and worthwhile.

How do you report a story that one side says is a non-story and the other says is one of the biggest in a decade? Talk to as many people as you can and report what you find. Ask along the way, of everyone, "How do you know that?" Reporting is a wonderful passport to go into the world, around the world, meet people you otherwise would never meet, and learn things you otherwise would never get to know. It can be tremendously satisfying work.

As journalists, it is important to ask, "What do we stand for? No matter the technology, the fads of the day, the pressures from ownership or administration, what are and will remain our core values?" In other words, it is of great benefit to define craft excellence. How will you know tomorrow that what you've done today was a job well done?

Obviously, this is not a comprehensive guide to journalism and to reporting and writing for journalistic contexts. But it is a start. To broaden the scope, consider the roles of journalism's writers and editors. Much has not changed for a digital age.

Researcher and Guide

The sheer amount of information available today is a double-edged sword. Wonderful in theory, all proximous via digital media, and much of it free or low cost, the abundance of information is also a curse. Most people need help. Digital journalists can help by sorting, filtering, curating, and referring. Journalism students should be introduced to research and organization techniques, how to use a feed reader, how to stay on top of a specific trend via email alerts, Twitter, and search feeds, as well as how to develop source relationships via social media in much the same way as Mnookin did in Cambridge and Boston.

Traffic Generator and Entrepreneur

Digital writers and editors are learning that it helps to think about the bottom line, even though such thoughts are heretical for older generations of journalists. Good content attracts readers, and it is the reader who creates the page views, shares, and likes. This attention attracts advertisers, who generate the revenue. And it's this revenue that provides writers and editors with a paycheck. As generators of the content that nourishes the rest of the food chain, perhaps the discussion is more about roles than it is about making money.

Community and Social Media Manager

Community and social media management aren't always messy, but they are no place for wimps. This third core digital skill, which is largely absent from journalism pedagogy at the university level, has to do with how to lead and moderate and participate in communities and conversations in intentional ways. A successful forum, blog, Twitter feed, or Facebook group relies upon a robust community. However, these communities do not magically or easily form. They require an enormous amount of time, effort, authentic (as opposed to faux or automated) participation, and leadership. If you are lucky enough to develop a community, the work only gets harder maintaining and growing it. A moderator or social media manager is equal parts discussion leader, party host, and diplomat.

What does any of this have to do with journalism? In digital spaces and places, writers and editors are expected to interact. Audience interaction can yield better stories and more interesting content, but it also opens the door to arguments, mindless debates and comments so inane, so egregious, that you might want to pull the plug on the whole enterprise, as many have done. (When *Popular Science* shut off its comments sections, the site's editors explained the decision by saying that "Comments can be bad for science.") Moderators and social media managers have to swallow that first impulse, step back and remind themselves of the benefits. They need to see opportunity amidst the arguments and the story ideas amidst the flame wars. They need to lead the discussion and prod it when it falters. These community-moderating skills can only be developed through experience, and that experience should begin as early as possible.

Collaborator

Because news is turning into more of a collaboration and much more of an interactive process, the reader has more of a say in determining or at least selecting the big issues of the day. Such a collaborative, distributive ecosystem is inherently more democratic, but that does not necessarily make the more open system better for democracy or for a democratic form of government. With less powerful watchdogs, with poorer watchdogs less able to fund the expensive enterprise of investigative journalism, government is increasingly able to creep yet more into the shadows, offering but one example of the new dangers implicit in a more commercial, more recreational, more visual news media ecosystem.

Social Capital

Clearly, this changing ecosystem is enabling and rewarding participation. Through the creation and exchange of social capital via social networking and crowd-sourced journalism, blogs and other digital forms of personal publishing are encouraging and rewarding participation. (Briefly, **social capital** is the value created in and through social networks as people seek to achieve mutual goals, and it is a theory about the reciprocal relationships we create in social networks.) These venues are collectively showing that the ethos of this new ecosystem is one based on values such as inclusiveness and community, participation and deliberation, sharing and reciprocating, and free and unfiltered expression. Because it is communal and not hierarchical, this ecosystem is pitted in philosophical and strategic opposition to many traditional news media, which historically have had control.

This collaboration in some ways has been forced on traditional news media. The people formerly known as the audience use their own blogs, websites, and Twitter feeds to "correct" the record, add to coverage, deconstruct articles and coverage about them, and expose what they believe are biases. As Rosen (2006) noted, citizen journalism has moved the interview to the midpoint between source and media. "You produce things from it, and we do, too," he said. No longer are sources merely sources, as the multiplicity of professional athletes and celebrities tweeting directly to fans and publics demonstrates. "It has forced greater transparency on the part of mainstream media in how they do what they do," Rosen has written.

To illustrate this new element of the news media landscape, and to pinpoint a shift on the historical timeline, consider the ABC News *Nightline* package that aired during summer 2005 on the Discovery Institute, a conservative organization that advocates a theory of the world's origins as a product of intelligent design. The next day, in response to the coverage, which focused on the marketing of intelligent design, the institute published the entire transcript of the hour-long interview, only excerpts of which had appeared on *Nightline*. ABC News subsequently posted the entire transcript, as well, but as a reaction to Discover Institute's posting.

The institute did not accuse ABC News of error. It asked readers to examine the transcript and the program's questions, believing that they revealed a "predictable tone" of skepticism and critique. "Here's your chance to go behind the scenes with the gatekeepers of national media to see how they screen out viewpoints and information that don't fit their stereotypes," wrote an institute spokesman on the site. This transparency, forced by the source or subject of the story, asked viewers to decide for themselves, though with a strong suggestion that ABC News was, in fact, biased.

Similarly, in May 2008, the White House of George W. Bush balked at how NBC News edited an interview with the president, demanding that the network broadcast Bush's answers to some of the questions "in full." White House counsel Ed Gillespie called NBC's editing "deceitful . . . misleading and irresponsible," according to the *Wall Street Journal*. In what has become routine practice for news media, the full interview was posted after the television broadcast, but before Gillespie's criticisms, which elicited this response from NBC News's president, Steve Capus: "Editing is a part of journalism. We take the collective body of information surrounding a story, distill it and produce a report. We strive in all cases to be fair and accurate. In some instances, where appropriate, we offer interviews in their entirety—in live broadcasts, or posted on our website."

The increasingly networked, conversation-based media ecosystem is proving resistant to editing and institutional filtering, seeing in that process an incompleteness and bias. News media have responded by providing the raw materials for their reporting on their websites, a practice modeled first by bloggers. Craig Crawford, a columnist for *Congressional Quarterly*, told *The New York Times*, "We've pretended to be priests turning water into wine, like it's a secret process. Those days are gone."

▶ CROWD-SOURCED ("CITIZEN") JOURNALISM

One trend fueled by and contributing to the larger movement toward conversation and a sharing culture has been crowd-sourcing the news. In London in 2005, the Underground and bus bombings served as powerful catalysts for what has since become known as the "citizen journalism movement," if we can call it a movement.[1] For hours after the explosions, photos taken by passengers using their mobile phones were the only pictures the world could get of the scenes inside the subway system. The first-hand accounts by passengers, and the prominent placement of the video, audio, and photography from passengers on the world's news sites, boosted the profile of participatory journalism certainly in the United States and in Europe, but elsewhere in the world, as well.

During the same year as both the London bombings and Hurricane Katrina, riots on the outskirts of Paris boosted blog-driven journalism. With reporters struggling to find a way to tell the story of Paris's immigrant-crowded industrial suburbs, a Swiss magazine sent a squad of bloggers to one of these suburbs, Bondy. Working in shifts, the reporter-bloggers reported, wrote, and posted photography from a local soccer club. The Swiss blog team stayed months, long after the riots calmed down and the network news cameras moved out. For magazine writers used to writing, revising, polishing, and writing some more, the new format gave them the chance to provide a visceral, albeit tentative narrative of life in the suburb during the chaotic fight for control with French police. The writers also engaged readers in live discussion online, and they used reader feedback and readers' posts to the blogs to inform and shape their writing and coverage.

The shootings at Virginia Tech in April 2007, too, showed the power of crowd-sourcing, albeit in an unlikely place for original reporting. Wikipedia's entry on the shootings was immediate, and the entry grew exponentially in the days and weeks following the horrific shootings in May. In this event, crowd-sourced, distributed, networked journalism had another defining event, and the Wikipedia entry reflected it, with more than 2,100 contributors to the post as of late May and 119 footnotes. As an artifact of journalism, the online encyclopedia entry succeeds in providing a useful account of what happened at the university and how people were reacting to those events, and in the days just after the shooting, modeled for the world how crowd-sourced reporting and editing can produce increasingly smart journalism. The more people contributed, the smarter the entry got, generating yet better contributions and links from those who followed. The entry became its own filter, or in some ways its own editor, as contributors self-screened and added yet more nuance, layers of information, and perspectives on the events and on coverage of the events.

To call the entry its own filter is not to discount, however, the heroic efforts of the many editors who rode herd on the information as it flowed in, editing for content, tone, and taste. It is a bit like taking a standard newsroom model and expanding it out until the reporters number in the thousands and the editors in the hundreds, all disparately located, all working on no deadline, on all deadlines, on one story—much like a utility grid.

More recently, in 2012 and 2013, the Twitter, Facebook, and blog accounts coming out of Yemen, Egypt, Libya, Tunisia, Bahrain, Morocco, and Syria filled a gap left by the banning, ejections, and silencing of foreign media and the state takeovers of domestic media. Whether these socially mediated accounts helped or hurt the revolutionary ambitions of their authors and followers has since been hotly debated; but it is clear that these "citizen" journalists, or regular people committing acts of journalism in times of crisis and tumult, brought information to the rest of the world that otherwise was not available.

An ongoing question for journalists is whether participatory journalism is part of the problem of the decline of traditional news media or part of the solution. As with most binaries, this one likely is false; it is probably a great deal of both. User-generated content raises questions of libel liability, quality standards, and accuracy and fairness, among others. But pro-am marriages of professional journalists and regular people armed with smartphones and laptops can produce involvement and participation that get more people interested in the news. "The more that citizens participate in the news, the more deeply engaged they tend to become in the democratic process," wrote communication researchers Cecilia Friend and Jane Singer.

Partnering With the Crowds

Traditional news media are still figuring out how to leverage participatory journalism without diluting their standards. How to encourage and facilitate this human impulse to share news and information but still protect the professional news brand is one of the industry's great riddles. How to pay for it is another. But there are several emergent models of participatory journalism.

CNN's approach with iReport (http://ireport.cnn.com/) has been to completely segregate user-generated content into a separate site with little to tether it to the CNN newsroom or brand. The separation is clearly meant to assure site visitors that there is no "pollution" of CNN content, while still allowing a range and depth of participatory or distributed journalism and collective intelligence. A disclaimer on the separate site states: "The views and content on this site are solely those of the iReport.com contributors. CNN makes no guarantees about the content or the coverage on iReport.com!" Note the exclamation point.

CNN is attempting to build an "iReport community" around populist notions of news and how to gather and present it. In this crowd-sourced model, CNN offers to air "the most compelling, important, and urgent ones" on the network, tempting contributors with publicity rather than money.

A second model is being tried by a number of sites throughout the United States, including the New West Network (www.newwest.net/) based in Montana. New West collects contributions from its "citizens" in several cities and towns in eight states. Launched in 2005, New West states that its mission is to "serve the Rockies with innovative, participatory journalism and to promote conversation that helps us understand and make the most of the dramatic changes sweeping our region." The site publishes between 10 and 15 new stories a day, in addition to photography, video, commentary, and "conversation," or feedback via a number of reader forums.

Anyone is free to share his or her thoughts on any New West story via a "comment" button at the bottom of every story. Readers can also register with New West to be able to contribute ideas and opinions through its "Unfiltered" section. Guest columns are also solicited, as is freelance reporting. With a large and growing reader base, the site has a healthy revenue stream in display advertising, which also appears in a print periodical published by New West.

A third, nonprofit model is represented by *The Texas Tribune*, an online news organization based in Austin, Texas, that describes itself as "a nonpartisan, nonprofit media organization that promotes civic engagement and discourse on public policy, politics, government, and other matters of statewide concern." The site (texastribune.org) is funded by venture capital, grants, and by about 3,000 donors. With approximately 20 reporters and a budget of about US$1.6 million, the site is relatively small, but it has packed a powerful punch in holding government and officials accountable. Typical of the site's coverage is a 2013 series of articles on the conflicts of interest of elected Texas state officials, articles based on a large database of information that the site created to produce the coverage. Reporters there have won Murrow, Webby, and Society of Professional Journalists awards.

The Texas Tribune was built on the bootstrapping model. For example, reporters write up their stories, then email the rest of the newsroom with a request for help in editing their articles. Reporter Julián Aguilar covers immigration, Kate Galbraith covers energy and environmental issues, and Ryan Murphy covers the massive amounts of data that Texas's government generates. Murphy created a database to map out oil and gas wastewater disposal wells and Texas cities running out of water, for example. It's also worth noting that the digital news organization seeks to encourage civic engagement by hosting events, including panels and debates—no surprise—but also parties, quiz bowls, and sports events.

The Power of Crowd-Sourcing

Sites and apps such as Pulse, Feedburner, digg, Reddit, and Delicious give readers the ability to shape a very different news agenda than that of professional news editors. Traditional agenda-setting theory holds that news media can't tell us what to think, but they can influence what we think about. News media traditionally have set the agenda for what could be regarded as a national conversation, and agenda-setting theory holds that this conversation has room for about three major issues or trending topics. When a new issue emerges—say, immigration—another moves off the agenda to make room. In contrast, these smartphone apps and websites allow readers to participate in the shaping of this news agenda, even to redefine "news" in combination with professional news editors. Research has consistently shown that readers have very different definitions and priorities than does the guild of journalism.

A report from the Project for Excellence in Journalism compared the news agenda for one week as determined by mainstream news media with that found on a host of user-news sites for the same period. While the mainstream press focused on conflicts around the world and the debate on immigration, three leading user-news sites—Reddit, digg, and Delicious—were more focused on stories like the release of Apple's new version of the iPhone and that Nintendo had surpassed Sony in net worth. Many of the stories that users selected did not appear anywhere among the top stories in the mainstream media coverage studied. In addition, the sources that user-news sites draw on are strikingly different from those of the mainstream media. Seven in ten stories on the user sites come either from blogs or websites such as YouTube and WebMD that do not focus mostly on traditional news.

Hyperlocal News

Many of the same fundamentals that drive social networking have also fueled great interest in hyperlocal news. A buzz word of 2008 to 2010, hyperlocal is still quite popular, but the term is much less frequently used. A very local, community-by-community approach to news is still an important trend in journalism throughout the United States, even after some fairly high-profile fiscal disasters, such as AOL's Patch. Community news is not new, of course. News 400 years ago was shared primarily in coffeehouses and public houses, and much of it was very, very local. But using online to reach and tailor news for even individual neighborhoods is relatively new, with many of these efforts taking place in densely populated areas such as New York City's boroughs and neighborhoods, downtown San Francisco and downtown Chicago, and in small communities not served (or not served well) by a local newspaper or TV station. Global positioning satellite technology, mobile phones, and other client-specific, geocoding or locating technologies have helped to make hyperlocal news approaches feasible, and users' comfort level with being geomapped have helped to lower barriers that once included privacy concerns and fears of Big Brother-type surveillance.

Independent hyperlocal news sites like WestportNow.com in Connecticut, iBrattle-boro.com in Vermont and VillageSoup.com in Maine are thriving, according to the *American Journalism Review*, at least in terms of reader interest. As a business model, however, delivering hyperlocal news remains difficult, or financially marginal. In Rome, Georgia, the hyperlocal HometownHeadlines.com does quite well, at least in terms of attracting traffic and in providing news and "nearly news" that the local print newspaper misses for various reasons. HometownHeadlines delivers news people want, such as when and where Publix grocers is coming to town, when a cell of storms and high winds is headed Rome's way, blanket coverage of the local minor league baseball team, and the latest scuttlebutt regarding real estate development in town. In short, the site, which has a staff of two, covers its community at a granular level.

The Chitown Daily News (www.chitowndailynews.org/), founded in March 2007 with a Knight Foundation Challenge grant, uses a network of 40 or so citizen journalists throughout Chicago and software that helps to identify where this network lives and the subjects and topics its members like to cover. When a building collapsed in Wicker Park, the *Daily News* had a citizen journalist there in minutes. To accomplish hyperlocal, the site aims to put at least one citizen journalist in all of the city's nearly 80 neighborhoods, recruiting and training each one. To find these volunteers, the site has reached out using Craigslist, Facebook, and by communicating with Chicago bloggers.

The *Las Vegas Sun* (www.lasvegassun.com/) provided a clinic in January 2008 on how to do hyperlocal journalism. A fire at the Monte Carlo hotel and casino gave the newspaper and website a chance to show off its new site design and hyperlocal approach. The paper responded with, among other steps, a live blog updated by several members of the newsroom staff, an overview of the hotel's history, and a flurry of videos on the fire, all while the hotel was still burning. The site also accommodated user-contributed coverage, such as photos via Flickr and videos via YouTube. The story was very local, so the paper made it the top priority. Adequate resources were deployed, coverage was continuously updated, readers were included in the coverage, and the digital was leveraged for multimedia—in particular, for video. In short, the paper kept drilling down, as if for oil.

A pioneering father of the hyperlocal approach online is Rob Curley, who helped WashingtonPost.com to build a mesh of microsites, beginning with LoudounExtra.com in July 2007, in order to cover the *Post*'s markets one by one by one. Curley also developed video-centric hyperlocal models at the *Lawrence Journal-World* (www2.ljworld.com/), including its KUSports.com site dedicated to University of Kansas sports, and at the *Naples News* (www.naplesnews.com/studio55/) in Florida. Curley left the *Post* in May 2008 for the *Las Vegas Sun*, taking his hyperlocal Internet development team with him, and has since joined the *Orange County* (California) *Register*.

Publishers are learning that they must tailor increasingly specialized content for self-defining audiences, which could be termed narrowcasting (as opposed to broadcasting). And, yet, advertising effectiveness—and, therefore, revenues—typically depends on reach. Thus, some blend of niche content and that for mass audiences is required for sustainability.

Expression in Digital Spaces: Public or Private?

One of the more vexing problems for hyperlocal news sites, and with them sports sites, online discussion boards, and many blogs, is the erosion of civility and vitriolic, often profane discourse occurring in digital spaces. As a Chattanooga, Tennessee newspaper editor put it, newspapers online are attempting to balance free speech with the "poisonous" reality of "cruel, rage-filled, racist" comments "brimming with words you wouldn't want your mother to hear you utter." His newspaper, the *Chattanooga Times-Free Press*, explained changes to its online comments policy that included turning off comments on "fact-based articles, features or business stories, and accounts of sporting events." In another example of this devil's bargain, the *Salt Lake Tribune* decided to allow readers to individually turn off comments in response to what the newspaper's publisher called "vile, crude, insensitive, and vicious postings." The newspaper's decision came after "a thorough review of online comments" and a months-long investigation by a team of its editorial staff. In late 2010, National Public Radio announced that due to wild growth in the number of its reader posts online, NPR would outsource comment moderator duties for NPR.org. NPR cited the overwhelming number of posts: "350,000 people registered to participate in the community, with as many as 3,000 comments posted on any given day." Other news organizations are simply disallowing anonymity at all, utilizing sophisticated moderation systems, requiring real names, and in some cases even collecting credit card information for verification, as *The Huffington Post* has done.

Thus, a challenge at both theoretical and practical levels presented by much expression online is that it can be seen as having the qualities of both mass (or public) communication and interpersonal (or private) communication. Much of online expression, particularly communication in and through online social media, can be described as being fleeting or evanescent, as if it were spoken in conversation, a description that fits much of what takes place in digitally delivered social networks. In practice, much of online expression does the work of interpersonal communication, and it has been extensively studied just this way by several disciplines. The medium (or media) through which it is expressed, however, is (or are) global and immediate, creating a near permanent record of that otherwise ephemeral communication.

To make concrete the difficulties in distinguishing between public and private expression, it might be helpful to think about the kinds of expression that appear in online chat forums, online discussion boards, email, and online gaming environments. Each of these can be regarded—and have been treated across disciplines of academic study—as interpersonal communication contexts. Yet, all of them utilize or otherwise depend upon the Internet's web, which is treated by most disciplines as a mass medium or collection of mass media technologies, albeit a more interactive set of media than any previous mass medium. This hybrid nature presents problems for the law, to point to just one area. Historically, audiences for mass media have been regularly exposed to anonymous communication, for example. In more interpersonal contexts, anonymity has been far less common.

It is in some ways artificial to separate public from private, mass from interpersonal. And this blended nature of online discourse has removed to some extent the evaluation of what is newsworthy from traditional media gatekeepers and given these determinations to the lone blogger, poster, emailer, and Facebook user. The social and even civic benefits of this are unprecedented, but so are the questions these distribution methods raise.

There is perhaps no better example of the implications of essentially private communication distributed via a global publishing medium than the 2004 case study involving Jessica Cutler, a 24-year-old Senate staff assistant in Washington, DC, who blogged about her sex life pseudonymously as "The Washingtonienne." (The blog is no longer active, but archived copies are available at Wonkette, http://wonkette.com/4162/the-lost-washingtonienne-wonkette-exclusive-etc-etc.) Cutler said she created her blog to keep a few of her friends up to date on her adventures in DC, but she failed to erect a password-protected firewall because she said she thought "it would be too much trouble" for her friends. Cutler was engaging essentially in gossip meant for only a few friends, but her salacious accounts were published on a medium with global reach. Once published, Cutler's blog posts, which included detailed accounts of her sexual encounters, including those with co-workers and at least one married man, were available online to anyone in the world with an Internet connection, and they immediately were archived in multiple locations and, therefore, became searchable and quasi-permanent.

After several posts describing "nasty sex" with a co-worker named Robert, a sex partner whom she said had "a nice ass" and was "into spanking," Cutler's blog was picked up by Wonkette, one of the more highly trafficked blogs at the time. The Washingtonienne blog subsequently went viral; coverage by several major newspapers and cable TV news networks contributed to Cutler's newly found fame (and infamy). Cutler didn't seem to mind, but Robert, not surprisingly, did; he filed a lawsuit against Cutler in May 2005 for invasion of privacy for public revelation of private facts.

▶ MODERATING COMMUNITY FORUMS

Given the risks and the seemingly irresistible drift toward banality in online discussion, one of the nagging questions facing newspaper sites that offer discussion and other forms of online community is how to invite and enable the very highest levels of participation, but at the same time limit the pollution, personal attacks, and unhelpful comment. How can moderators enforce "civility," in other words, while keeping discussants on topic *and* somehow avoiding censorship in keeping things civil? As a rule, the easier it is to participate, the more monitoring that will be required. Topix.com, for example, allows anyone to post without registering. The result, not surprisingly, is a relatively high number of posts that include objectionable content.

In addition to prominently publishing and enforcing use policies and inviting users to help police the rhetoric, there are several things community moderators can do to build the community and counter attempts to undermine it. These steps include:

▶ Welcoming new users and helping to orient them.

▶ Enabling user profiles so that people can be identified and get to know one another.

▶ Being transparent. When a moderator edits or removes something, all users should be notified.

▶ Stepping in when there is trouble. Being scared to stop a thread out of fear of being called a "censor" will likely hurt more than it helps. Online spats and inappropriate threads can quickly escalate. If a moderator sees trouble brewing, he or she should warn the users and closely monitor the thread.

▶ Doing more. Moderators should not simply moderate. If community members know the moderator only as an editor or censor, they will naturally become antagonistic.

▶ Participating in discussions simply to interact with users. Moderators should always identify themselves, of course; but by participating, moderators demonstrate that they are not there to simply be the "bad guy." Similarly, moderators can highlight, reinforce, and reward the desired kind and level of participation. Celebrate good contributions.

▶ Including email address and phone number, Twitter, and Facebook information with all communications to invite and encourage feedback and to communicate accessibility.

▶ Demonstrating a thick skin. People will criticize, complain, and provoke. If the moderator is a good sport, the attitude can prevent ill will and running feuds. People can be emotional when posting online. Humor can often diffuse the situation.

▶ Anticipating problems. Realize that some topics will routinely generate hostility—topics such as sports, social issues, and politics. Actively patrolling these threads or discussion areas can help moderators to quickly respond to objectionable content.

A Case Study: The Boston Marathon Bombings and Reddit

The false identification by a Reddit user of Sunil Tripathi, a 22-year-old Brown University student, as a suspect in the Boston Marathon bombings in April 2013 and the subsequent treatment of that ID by mainstream media illustrate in stark terms how messy the media ecosystem has become. The interaction among and intermingling between mainstream or traditional news media and individuals participating with social media on their own has blurred and perhaps erased once-important distinctions between verified fact and (tweeted and re-tweeted) rumor, and between published reporting and simple speculation.

Tripathi disappeared on March 16, 2013. Because Tripathi's photo was juxtaposed with video surveillance images of what turned out later to be Dzhokhar Tsarnaev, the man eventually apprehended in connection with the bombings, Tripathi became, as far as the public was concerned, a suspect, as well. Tripathi's false identification effectively ended his family's ability to enlist the public's help in searching for him, and it led to angry phone calls, death threats, and hateful posts to a Facebook page his parents set up to facilitate the search. A Twitter user who tweeted using the handle @ghughesca reported that he had heard on a police scanner that Tripathi had been identified as "Suspect 2." Without confirming this with Boston Police, the tweet was reported by Kevin Galliford, a journalist with a TV station in Hartford, Connecticut. Galliford's report was then re-tweeted more than 1,000 times in a matter of minutes, according to *The New York Times*. Next it was BuzzFeed's turn, which sent out the false scanner information along with the confirmation, "Wow Reddit was right about the missing Brown student."

Reddit's role in this new media ecosystem is unprecedented, especially in terms of reach. For some, it is a "haven from the propaganda of the mainstream media . . . the world's most important vehicle for democratized, crowd-sourced journalism," according to the *Times*. For others, it's a messy, busy mix of rumor, chatter, and trivia. (Among its most popular categories are those for videogaming, computer programming and, of course, pornography.) Its bare-bones homepage is determined or configured by "upvotes," or popularity of content as determined by its users, which as of late 2013 numbered nearly 100 million unique users. An upvote generates "karma," which is a salute to the Slashdot online community, and karma pushes content on toward the homepage. Downvotes do the opposite. Together, these votes organize and prioritize the thousands of posts going up in Reddit's more than 5,000 categories, called subReddits. The homepage is, of course, the Holy Grail, representing perhaps hundreds of thousands of page views and the kind of attention news media, advertisers, marketers, and individual "Redditors" covet. According to one online traffic tracker, Alexa, in mid-2013, Reddit generated more traffic than either *The New York Times* or Fox News, though primarily among users 25 years old and younger.

Reddit sort of burst on the national digital media scene in summer 2012 with the Aurora, Colorado, movie theater shooting after a showing of *The Dark Knight*. Threads on Reddit opened up for breaking news about the shooting, most of it coming from individuals. One "Redditor" shot in the theater posted a photo of himself from the emergency room. Some of what got posted proved accurate, including its timeline of events; much of it turned out to be unsubstantiated rumor.

On April 23, police pulled out of the Providence River what turned out to be Tripathi's body. His family's search, which had been circumvented by accusations that Tripathi and his family were Muslim terrorists, could finally end. (They are neither Muslim nor radicals of any kind.) Some journalists apologized to the family, while others claimed that they were merely passing along information they were receiving without making any sort of truth claim. For its part, Reddit, which saw record-breaking hits, page views, and users, declared itself "content-agnostic," unwilling to intervene except in the most unusual of circumstances.

This amalgamation of public and private expression creates, as the Tripathi case study dramatically, even tragically, shows, a sort of fractal in the national conversation, a sort of hyperbolic geometric folding in on itself, to borrow a description from rubber-sheet geometry. (A fractal is a geometric object between dimensions. A Menger sponge, for example, is a cube-shaped geometric that is more than two dimensions but not quite three, with an infinite surface area but no volume.) Fueling this is the fact that people now (as they always have) form attitudes toward the issues important to them in largely private or interpersonal conversation, even gossip. And Reddit, Facebook, and Twitter thrive on and are conspicuously built to generate conversation.

What journalistic organizations must not relinquish is their duty to make sense of it all. From WikiLeaks to Anonymous and now Reddit, vast amounts of raw data are pouring into the national conversation all the time. It's the responsibility of news media to make sense of it all by applying the discipline of verification and, therefore, to be careful before passing along mere rumor under its brand and with affiliation in the same way it publishes verified facts. Not everything tweeted or posted on Reddit is worth passing along, obviously. Conversely, there is a screaming need for sense-makers to resist the tyranny of the urgent and the false god of "being first" in order to instead be responsible. As put by Jay Caspian Kang writing in *The New York Times* about Tripathi, from whom much of the Reddit–Tripathi account here comes: "If enough people with trusted media affiliations touch a bit of information on Twitter, it starts to resemble fact." Reddit isn't the problem, in other words. Reddit just amplifies the real problem, which has more to do with carelessness and insensitivity in reporting, and what is an obsession with being fast and even first.

There was some good news out of Boston. Freelance journalist Marcus DiPaola, who was among those in Watertown, Cambridge, and Boston reporting on the investigation, decided to post on Reddit a set of journalistic guidelines for journalists using Reddit. His post became the most "upvoted" comment in the Boston bombings thread.

How to Verify Social Media Content

In 2010, CNN's Middle Eastern affairs editor, Octavia Nasr, lost her job after tweeting about a Palestinian leader's death, calling the deceased "one of Hezbollah's giants

I respect a lot." Any opinion on the Middle East published via the web to a global audience runs the risk of becoming controversial, especially if the person expressing that opinion is counted on for unbiased coverage of the Middle East. Had Nasr worked for the BBC, her tweet might have been stopped before it went out. According to the BBC's social media guidelines, the network declares that "The golden rule for our core news, programme or genre activity is that whatsoever is published—on Twitter, Facebook or anywhere else—MUST HAVE A SECOND PAIR OF EYES PRIOR TO PUBLICATION" (emphasis in the original).

In September 2013, Kansas University put journalism professor David Guth on administrative leave because of Guth's tweet in the aftermath of the shooting deaths of 13 in Washington, DC's Navy Yard, a tweet that said, "The blood is on the hands of the #NRA [National Rifle Association]. Next time, let it be YOUR sons and daughters. Shame on you. May God damn you." Every writer needs an editor; every tweeter might need one, too.

Editors are also needed to verify tweets and, more generally, information being relayed via social media. So many people are generating so much content that news organizations can find themselves overwhelmed, especially during breaking news events. For its part, BBC News created what it calls the UGC (user-generated content) Hub in order to curate and verify social media content. Steps the Hub's editors take to verify video include, according to its website:

▶ referencing locations against maps and existing images from, in particular, geo-located ones;

▶ working with colleagues to ascertain that accents and language are correct for the location;

▶ searching for the original source of the upload/sequences as an indicator of date;

▶ examining weather reports and shadows to confirm that the conditions shown fit with the claimed date and time;

▶ maintaining lists of previously verified material to act as reference for colleagues covering the stories;

▶ checking weaponry, vehicles, and license plates against those known for the given country.

The screaming need for verification has provided companies like BreakingNews.com and Storyful.com a business opportunity. Calling itself the first news agency of the social media age, Storyful.com helps news organizations and digital publishers "discover, verify and distribute" material moving across social media platforms. Clients include ABC News, CBS News, Reuters, *The New York Times*, and *The Wall Street Journal*. According to its founder, Mark Little, the company blends technology with human judgment, because "algorithms, apps and search tools help make data useful but they can't replace the value judgments at the core of journalism."

As an example of the kind of verification BreakingNews.com and Storyful.com do, consider a video shared virally during the Arab Spring of 2013, footage showing a battle between riot police and protesters on the Qasr al Nile Bridge in Cairo. Storyful.com's curators discovered the video on Facebook, then contacted its creator to confirm his identity. Google Earth was used to check the location of the bridge and of the video shooter's vantage point. Using Flickr and Panaramio, Storyful.com compared the video with other user-generated content shot at ground level. Having confirmed the video's authenticity, permission was obtained to upload the video to YouTube and pass it on to news organizations.

According to Little, the company has some basic steps for verification, including:

▶ reviewing the uploader's history and location to see whether he/she has shared useful and credible content in the past, or if he/she is a "scraper," passing other people's content off as their own;

▶ using Google Street View, maps, and satellite imagery to help verify locations;

▶ consulting other news sources to confirm that events in a video happened as they are described;

▶ examining key features such as weather and background landscape to see if they match known facts on the ground;

▶ translating every word for additional context;

▶ monitoring social media traffic to see who is sharing the video and what questions are being asked about it;

▶ developing and maintaining relationships with people within the community around the story.

It should be fairly apparent that most of these steps work for verifying textual information, as well. It should also be noted how necessary collaboration and cooperation are for doing substantive verification. Mark Little describes the process of verification as putting a puzzle together. Most of the pieces can be found in the social media conversations that emerge out of big, breaking news events. By using several tools and checking in with as many people as possible, the pieces come together to give an increasingly clear indication of how likely it is that a source or artifact is the genuine article. Listening is important, but Little's team engages directly, openly, and honestly with the most authentic voices it can find, judging the credibility of a source "by their behavior and status within the community."

Where does Storyful.com look? Twitter and Facebook are fairly obvious platforms. The company also monitors YouTube, SoundCloud, Hootsuite and Audioboo. To track trends on Twitter, the team uses Tweetdeck and Trendsmap.com. To verify URLs and to check ownership of websites and online companies, Whois (http://whois.domaintools.com/) is a valuable and easy-to-use tool. Whois can tell you who registered a web address and what physical address that person or company has. TinEye (www.tineye.com/) can be used to perform reverse image searches to identify different versions of an image that may exist. Google Images also offers a version of this. To check the weather in any specific location, among other fact checks, try the WolframAlpha "computational knowledge" search engine, www.wolframalpha.com. A query for the weather on January 11, 1965 found that the high in Nice, France, reached 59 degrees that day, with a relative humidity of 74 percent.

But Little stresses that "there is no secret sauce," that verification is a painstaking process involving real people. The telephone and Skype are two of the more valuable weapons in the Storyful.com arsenal, tools that would have prevented the errors made in coverage of the Boston Marathon bombings and the Navy Yard shooting in Washington, DC. Errors in the coverage of both centered on law enforcement sources, like scanners and police reports. Misinformation flows among law enforcement sources, particularly in the beginning stages of an investigation, and a lot of that misinformation airs over scanners. These mistakes then get amplified by social media, where user-generated content often gets distributed with little or no verification.

BreakingNews.com has learned that early, anonymously sourced reports carry a higher risk of being wrong, and that news organizations tend to gravitate toward the same anonymous sources in the first few hours after a story breaks. So the company takes its time and exercises caution. When a detail carries a higher risk of doing damage if it's wrong, the Breaking News team moves even more cautiously to separate fact from fiction. "In the end, our audacious goal is to get it right at the speed of light," co-founder and general manager Cory Bergman wrote. "For now, we're content on waiting a beat when accuracy matters most."

▶ THE FUTURE (AND NOW) OF JOURNALISM

No one can give definitive answers on what the future of journalism will bring, but it is possible to learn from trends already identifiable. Journalism in the future likely will be, for better *and* for worse:

▶ delivered via devices that are mobile, portable, geomapped and always on;

▶ socially networked and, therefore, contextualized, shared, and commented upon immediately;

▶ rich in media, particularly the visual;

▶ transparent and, therefore, increasingly accountable (they are "fact-checking your ass," as one prominent blogger put it);

▶ hyperlinked, cross-linked, and meshed (for "funsies," take a look at this prediction, now eerily accurate, from 2007; just substitute Amazon.com for Google and *The Washington Post* for *The New York Times*—EPIC's Google Grid video at http://idorosen.com/mirrors/robinsloan.com/epic/);

▶ only one part of a much greater media environment or landscape, and decreasingly a destination location—a proliferation of distribution channels guarantees this;

▶ participative and collaborative (the producer–consumer, sender–receiver dichotomies are gone);

▶ open ended, in process and always in play, rather than being about finding or producing or reporting the "minted" truth;

▶ datamapped, customized, and, again, highly contextualized and atomized;

▶ a profession in which reputation, independence, integrity, and trust will still matter, and they will matter a lot;

▶ a business sector where breaking news is merely a commodity, and one that will reward perspective, analysis, sense-making, and meaning, as well as new, more interpersonal elements such as community and collaboration;

▶ de-massified, or unbundled, with single pieces of content moving to and among people rather than a broadcaster or publisher sending out a package of information, like a newspaper or TV newscast;

▶ a conversation rather than a lecture, or more like improv, with audience participation.

BOX 8.1   *Sources to Help Journalists Transition to the Digital Age*

▶ Code with me, @codewithme, two-day workshops in major U.S. cities that promise to "help journalists overcome their fear of code."

▶ Lynda.com, www.lynda.com, for website coding tutorials.

▶ Mozilla Thimble, thimble.webmaker.org, a static text editor that allows users to publish finished webpages from the site. (JSFiddle and CodePen are similar resources.) Mozilla offers several "Webmaker" tools, including a timeline-based video editing software called Popcorn Maker.

▶ Treehouse, www.TeamTreehouse.com, for help with most major programming languages, with Android and iOS development, and for project-based tutorials.

▶ Codecademy, www.codecademy.com, for an interactive method of learning to program.

▶ ENDNOTE

1 The term "citizen journalism" is problematic. Most U.S. journalists are also U.S. citizens; many "citizen journalists" are not. "Doing" journalism does not necessarily make someone a journalist any more than writing a letter or postcard makes someone a writer. Both terms, then, are imprecise. Participatory journalism or crowd-sourced journalism are more accurate terms in their reluctance to label individuals while still describing the activity.

CHAPTER ASSIGNMENT

1 Develop the online content you outlined and prepared for in Chapter 6. For this news story or press release or feature, you should report, source, write, edit, and post it online, then share it with whatever social media you are familiar. This article must have or rely upon at least three *human* sources, people you ideally spoke with face-to-face or, as a fallback, on the telephone. But know that this is a bare bones **minimum**. The more reporting you do, the better the story will be. Seek timeliness; ask yourself why the story needs to be done NOW. The story should also demonstrate impact or consequence.

Do not procrastinate. Do not wait to begin identifying sources, generating sequences of questions to ask those sources and, most importantly, to begin attempting to contact those sources. Procrastination results in sloppy, harried work, and with scarce time you risk being unable to contact sources. Build in time for callbacks, for failure to reach people. Sources are best reached early in the morning and just after 5 p.m., or after most people are gone and the phones are relatively quiet. (Yes, I wrote "phones." Do not use email for your interviews, but only to arrange interviews and for follow-up questions and fact-checking.)

Think about the journalism you've read. Have you ever seen a note like this? "This journalism is not as good as it could have been because I couldn't reach some important sources. They were out of town. I just missed them. They were really busy. Sorry." No, you haven't. So get after it, and develop contingency plans.

Beware of conflicts of interest, making sure to avoid using friends, family members, and business associates as sources. Avoid stories that could materially affect those companies and entities with which you are affiliated. This is not a public relations or marketing exercise; this is journalism.

Post with the story the questions you asked your sources, a list of the facts you checked and verified, and a list of the sources you attempted to contact (not merely those you were able to include in your story). Also identify your intended audience(s).

As you are completing this assignment, think about what might be added to your main story for publication online, including multimedia and interactive features. Because online you would have all the space you would need, consider the range of added features that could be developed, including fact boxes, an FAQ list, a video extra, interview notes and transcripts, maps, charts, a glossary, a slideshow, animated graphic, a poll, related stories and opinion, and perhaps an area where readers could contribute reactions, story ideas, photos, and comments. No need to do any of these things, but consider what might make a strong story package online.

Look also for publication opportunities. For non-journalists, if you need guidance getting started, Poynter offers a good source through its "NewsU." Look for Hot Courses on its left panel (www.newsu.org).

The five basic journalism questions:

1   WHO is involved in what you're covering?
2   WHAT are they doing—and accomplishing?
3   WHERE are they doing it?
4   WHY are they doing it in the first place?
5   HOW do they make it happen?

You can also consult Appendix A to this book: "The Core Values of Digital Journalism."

Online Resources

Best Practices for Newspaper Journalists (www.freedomforum.org/publications/diversity/bestpractices/bestpractices.pdf)
Written by Bob Haiman and published by the Freedom Forum, this pdf download was developed to help journalists achieve fairness in their reporting.

Poynter Guide to Accuracy (www.poynter.org/content/content_view.asp?id= 36518)
A collection of articles by Poynter writers to help journalists in the area of accuracy, including help in fact-checking, grammar, and punctuation, and quotations and attribution.

Principles of Citizen Journalism (www.kcnn.org/principles/)
Published by the Knight Citizen News Network, this guide provides the basic principles and covers the fundamental values of good journalism.

▶ REFERENCES

Andy Carvin, *Getting a Little Help with NPR Comments*, National Public Radio, October 12 (2010), www.npr.org/blogs/inside/2010/10/12/130513924/getting-a-little-help-with-npr-comments.

Chattanooga Times-Free Press, "Our Online Comments Policy Is Changing," *Chattanooga Times-Free Press*, January 1 (2012): A1.

Chris Anderson, *The Long Tail* (New York, NY: Hyperion Books, 2006).

Cory Bergman, "Factoring Risk and Uncertainty into Real-Time Coverage," BreakingNews.com, September 20 (2013), http://blog.breakingnews.com/#about.

Hal Berghel, "E-mail—The Good, the Bad, and the Ugly," *Communications of the ACM* 40, no. 4 (April 1997): 11–16.

Mark Briggs, *Journalism 2.0* (Austin, TX: Knight Center, 2007).

Edward B. Burger and Michael Starbird, *The Heart of Mathematics: An Invitation to Effective Thinking* (Hoboken, NJ: John Wiley & Sons, 2010), 360, 472–473.

Brian Carroll, "Culture Clash: Journalism and the Communal Ethos of the Blogosphere," *Into the Blogosphere: Rhetoric, Community, and Culture of Weblogs* (Summer 2004), www.intotheblogosphere.org1.

Tim Fitzpatrick, "Tighter Monitoring for Online Comments, or No Comments If You Want," *The Salt Lake City Tribune*, October 31 (2011), www.sltrib.com/sltrib/news/52806057–78/comments-tribune-commenting-com.html.csp.

Cecilia Friend and Jane B. Singer, *Online Journalism Ethics* (Boston, MA: M. E. Sharpe, 2006).

Celia Friend, Don Challenger, and Katherine C. McAdams, *Contemporary Editing*, 2nd edition (New York, NY: McGraw Hill, 2005).

Jolene Galegher, Lee Sproull, and Sara Kiesler, "Legitimacy, Authority, and Community in Electronic Support Groups," *Written Communication* 15, no. 4 (October 1998): 493.

Lauren Gelman, "Privacy, Free Speech, and 'Blurry-edged Social Networks," *Boston College Law Review* 50, no. 1315 (2009): 5.

Lee Gomes, "Why We're Powerless to Resist Grazing on Endless Web Data," *The Wall Street Journal*, March 12 (2008): B1.

Rich Gordon, Beth Lawton, and Sally Clarke, *The Online Community Cookbook* (Arlington, VA: Newspaper Association of America, 2008).

Frederick Hertz , "Don't Let Your Case Get Lost in an E-mail: Be Careful What You Say in an E-mail, Because You Never Know for Sure How Far the Forwarding Process Might Take It," *New Jersey Law Journal*, September 2 (2002): 30.

John B. Horrigan, "Seeding the Cloud: What Mobile Access Means for Usage Patterns and Online Content," Pew Internet and American Life Project (March 2008).

David Itzkoff, "The God of 'SNL' Will See You Now," *The New York Times*, August 22 (2013), www.nytimes.com/2013/08/25/arts/television/the-god-of-snl-will-see-you-now.html.

Joan Shorenstein Center on the Press, Politics and Public Policy, "Creative Destruction: An Exploratory Look at News on the Internet," Joan Shorenstein Center (August 2007).

Journalism.org, "The Latest News Headlines—Your Vote Counts," Journalism.org, September 12 (2007), http://journalism.org/node/7493.

Jay Caspian Kang, "Should Reddit Be Blamed for the Spreading of Smear," *The New York Times*, July 25 (2013), www.nytimes.com/2013/07/28/magazine/should-reddit-be-blamed-for-the-spreading-of-a-smear.html.

Suzanne LaBarre, "Why We Are Shutting Off Our Comments," *Popular Science*, September 24 (2013), www.popsci.com/science/article/2013–09/why-were-shutting-our-comments.

Charlene Li, *Social Technographics: Mapping Participation in Activities Forms the Foundation of a Social Strategy* (Cambridge, MA: Forrester Research, 2007).

Mark Little, "The Human Algorithm," Storyful.com, May 20 (2011), http://blog.storyful.com/2011/05/20/the-human-algorithm-2/#.UjxIJyR4NMo2.

Rachel McAthy, "How To Verify Content from Social Media," Journalism.co.uk, April 3 (2012), www.journalism.co.uk/news-features/how-to-verify-content-from-social-media/s5/a548645/.

Philip Meyer, *The Vanishing Newspaper: Saving Journalism in the Information Age*, 2nd edition (Columbia, MO: University of Missouri Press, 2009)

Seth Mnookin and Hong Qu, "Organize the Noise: Tweeting Live from the Boston Manhunt," *Neiman Reports* (Spring 2013), www.nieman.harvard.edu/reports/article/102885/Organize-the-Noise-Tweeting-Live-from-the-Boston-Manhunt.aspx.

Merrill Morris and Christine Ogan, "The Internet as Mass Medium," *Journal of Communication* 46, no. 1 (1996): 39–50.

Alex Murray, "BBC Processes for Verifying Social Media Content," BBC, May 18 (2011), www.bbc. co.uk/blogs/blogcollegeofjournalism/posts/bbcsms_bbc_procedures_for_veri.

Jenny Preece, *Online Communities: Designing Usability, Supporting Sociability* (New York, NY: John Wiley & Sons, 2000).

Simon Rogers, "The Boston Bombing: How journalists Used Twitter to Tell the Story," Twitter blog, July 10 (2013), https://blog.twitter.com/2013/the-boston-bombing-how-journalists-used-twitter-to-tell-the-story.

Jay Rosen, "The People Formerly Known as the Audience," PressThink.org, June 27 (2006), http://journalism.nyu.edu/pubzone/weblogs/pressthink/2006/06/27/ppl_frmr.html.

Tom Rosenstiel and Bill Kovach, *The Elements of Journalism* (New York, NY: Three Rivers Press, 2007).

Craig Silverman, "8 Must-Reads Detail How To Verify Information in Real-Time, from Social Media," Poynter Institute, April 27 (2012), www.poynter.org/latest-news/regret-the-error/171713/8-must-reads-that-detail-how-to-verify-content-from-twitter-other-social-media/.

Daniel Solove, *The Future of Reputation: Gossip, Rumor, and Privacy on the Internet* (New Haven, CT: Yale University Press, 2007).

Andrew Ross Sorkin, "Billionaires' Latest Trophies Are Newspapers," *The New York Times*, August 6 (2013): B1.

Daniel Stashower, *The Beautiful Cigar Girl: Mary Rogers, Edgar Allan Poe, and the Invention of Murder* (New York, NY: Berkley Trade, 2007).

Carl Straumshelm, "Who Gets It First: Twitter or the Editors?" *American Journalism Review*, February/March (2012), www.ajr.org/Article.asp?id=5271.

A. G. Sulzberger, "In Small Towns, Gossip Moves to the Web, and Turns Vicious," *The New York Times*, September 20 (2011): A1.

April Witt, "Blog Interrupted," *Washington Post Magazine*, August 15 (2004): W12.

Wonkette, "Washingtonienne Speaks!! Wonkette Exclusive! Must Credit Wonkette!! The Washingtonienne Interview!!" *Wonkette*, May 21 (2004), www.wonkette.com/politics/media/washingtonienne-speaks-wonkette-exclusive-must-credit-wonkette-the-washingtonienne-interview-9693.php, accessed November 11, 2010.

Julia T. Wood, *Interpersonal Communication: Everyday Encounters* (Stamford, CT: Cengage Learning, 2010).

Christopher Zara, "Gannett Layoffs Loom at Local Newspapers across the Country; USA Today Parent Mum On Number," August 2 (2013), www.ibtimes.com/gannett-layoffs-loom-local-newspapers-across-country-usa-today-parent-mum-number-1370079.

9

Developing a Strategy for Social Media

Internet schminternet. Revolutions happen when they happen. Whatever means are lying around will get used.
Jay Rosen, New York University journalism professor

User experience is everything. It always has been, but it's still undervalued and under-invested in.
Evan Williams, Twitter co-founder

A squirrel dying in front of your house may be more relevant to your interests right now than people dying in Africa.
Mark Zuckerberg, Facebook founder

▶ INTRODUCTION

Since the *Writing for Digital Media* textbook was written in 2008 and early 2009, so much has changed. The iPad rolled out during the book's final proofs, to name just one of the many changes since the first edition. Much of this change has been in the area of social media, about which we have a great deal of data, but not much help thinking about strategy. How do digital writers strategically think about and deploy social media in service to a message and in service to audience(s)? Answering

---

CHAPTER OBJECTIVES

After studying this chapter, you will be able to:

▼

understand how and why social media have empowered individuals;

▼

consider ethical approaches to social media use and policies for social media use;

▼

appreciate the limits and capacities of various social media models or platforms;

▼

appreciate the legal risks and considerations when using social media;

▼

use Facebook and Twitter to accomplish strategic communication objectives.

this question is the purpose of this chapter, as is exploring the ethics of social media use and how social media have changed journalistic norms and methods.

▶ THE LECTURE BECOMES A CONVERSATION

In social media, what formerly was discrete has become fluid, raising interesting questions about labor routines and job duties. Journalists, for example, are accustomed to thinking in terms of articles (or stories) as discrete products. Historically, they have also viewed "work" and "play" as distinct and separate activities, or spheres of activity. Digital has changed all of this. From the discrete article we have moved to a process of knowledge construction, one that could be metaphorically understood as more of a conversation and less of a lecture. So what is meant by "deadline" and "article" is changing as reporters are asked to stay current on Facebook, Twitter, the newspaper's online discussion board, and a raft of other socially networked platforms and channels. The "deadline" as a synchronous chronological fact has become lost in a process that is resisting routinization.

On the other side, social media spaces are growing into virtual newsrooms of sorts, or at least spaces that have, or include, news feeds and conversations about the news, newsrooms in which the primary news gatherers and sharers work for free. These interactors expend a lot of effort to inform others in their community, but they do so in exchange for social capital. In other words, what the reporter traditionally has understood as "work" has become in socially mediated spaces something that interactors regard as something other than work. Civic duty, hobby, leisure activity, perhaps volunteerism, but not work.

So the division is between those who have privileged access to events and participants in order to report on and communicate them, on the one hand, and, on the other, the majority of audience members who do not directly participate in events, who have no expert knowledge about them, and who have no privileged right of access to information is blurring or breaking down.

Also breaking down is the notion of "news" as a discrete, finished product. For journalists, the article or story historically was meant to run in a specific place for a fixed time. The story had to be current, and it had to appear in designated spaces branded by the news organization and typically bylined to indicate authorship and accountability. For journalists rooted in an analog past, digital spaces are mostly about distributing the content and transacting with interactors who are supposed to find the content, ideally by coming to the news organization's website. This general set of expectations determines how editors consider their work, including when to post new content, where to post that content, and even how to post the content.

For interactors, however, the news is more of a flow and therefore less discrete. That flow should find them. This news should be accurate, transparent, and immediate, and it should, above all, be relevant—relevant to them where they are at that moment. This news should be something interactors can and want to share, and it should be presented in ways that facilitate drilling down, digging deeper, and getting more. It's a different definition of news, therefore. Interactors see news "products" as connecting people and communities, and as something that can be customized and shared. It matters less who wrote or published it than it does how "shareable" it is.

▶ SOCIAL MEDIA ETHICS

With these changes in how even news is conceptualized, fundamental questions are being raised about journalism and its relationship to the news. What is and is not content, for example? What is a news organization's responsibility over content such as discussion comments, citizen-generated news coverage, and Twitter stream comments? Who has ultimate responsibility, and who is or should be in control of the information in this new "journalism as process" environment and ecosystem? There is little settled on these questions.

At the same time that news organizations are asking their editorial staffs to take on additional responsibilities for monitoring and participating in social media on behalf of the organization, they are issuing rules for social media use on private time. For examples of approaches to providing this guidance, see Reuters's policy guidelines at http://handbook.reuters.com/index.php?title=Reporting_From_the_Internet_And_Using_Social_Media and National Public Radio's at http://ethics.npr.org/tag/social-media/. Even a casual reading of both identifies several issues that organizations should discuss to prevent problems caused by employees using social media, problems that are often exacerbated by social media's wide reach and un-erasable memory or cache. These issues can be summed up as accuracy, honesty and transparency, accountability, civility (or respect), and legal questions about defamation and privacy. NPR's introduction acknowledges the "new and unfamiliar challenges" posed by social media use, and that this use tends "to amplify the effects of any ethical misjudgments you might make. So tread carefully." Here's an excerpt from NPR's policy:

> Conduct yourself online just as you would in any other public circumstances as an NPR journalist. Treat those you encounter online with fairness, honesty and respect, just as you would offline. Verify information before passing it along. Be honest about your intent when reporting. Avoid actions that might discredit your professional impartiality. And always remember, you represent NPR.

This is good advice for any organization's employees and representatives. Even, and perhaps especially, in social media, employees should be transparent about what they are doing and why. As the policy asks its readers to think, employees should ask themselves, "Am I about to spread a thinly sourced rumor or am I passing on valuable and credible (even if unverified) information in a transparent manner with appropriate caveats?"

NPR's policy also recognizes that National Public Radio employees do have private lives, or lives outside of work, lives that exist, in part, in social media. In those cases, the guidance is to follow the conventions of those platforms, but to recognize that "nothing on the Web is truly private." What is shared, even when completely personal and not identified as coming from someone at NPR or having to do with NPR in any way, could reflect on NPR. This makes it of concern to the organization. Thus, even in their personal lives, employees shouldn't write or do anything that could undermine the organization's credibility with the public or harm its standing as an impartial source of news. "In other words, we don't behave any differently than we would in any public setting or on an NPR broadcast," the policy reads.

To dramatize the risks, the policy includes this hypothetical:

> Imagine, if you will, an NPR legal correspondent named Sue Zemencourt. She's a huge fan of Enormous University's basketball team and loves to chat online about EU. She posts comments on blogs under the screen name "enormous1." One day, an equally rabid fan of Gigormous State ("gigormous1") posts obnoxious comments about EU.
>
> Sue snaps. Expletives and insults fly from her fingers on to the webpage. They're so out-of-line that the blog blocks her from submitting any more comments—and discovers that her i.p. address leads back to NPR. The blog's host posts that "someone at NPR is using language that the FCC definitely would not approve of" and describes what was said. Things go viral.
>
> The basically good person that she is, Sue publicly acknowledges and apologizes for her mistake. But that doesn't stop The Daily Show from satirizing about the "NPRNormous Explosion."
>
> Damage done.

A recurring question for news organizations, especially in the digital age, is when or even whether employees can take political positions, even in their personal lives, for the reasons alluded to above. The safest policy is, of course, to prohibit it, including using an individual Facebook page to express personal views on controversial issues. As the NPR policy states, "In reality, anything you post online reflects both on you and on NPR." Even participation in an online group might be perceived as endorsement. This might seem draconian, but in a business in which impartiality and, more generally, reputation are critical differentiators, such caution is wise.

As the Reuters policy acknowledges, "The tension is clear: Social networks encourage fast, constant, brief communications; journalism calls for communication preceded by fact-finding and thoughtful consideration." These very different priorities are in some ways mutually exclusive: speed, on the one hand; caution and a discipline of verification, on the other. Or as Reuters puts it, "Journalism has many 'unsend' buttons, including editors. Social networks have none." Everything Reuters employees write, say, or post online could be used against it in a court of law, in the perceptions of its audiences and sources, and, perhaps most dangerously, by people who want to harm Reuters.

Also worthy of note is the NPR policy's acknowledgement that it is a work in progress and that it will likely change over time. Employees are encouraged to send in questions of interpretation and suggestions for changes or improvements. An editor of standards and practices and an ethics advisory group at NPR have been charged with considering these suggestions for revisions of the policy. The stakes are too high not to routinize this important function.

▶ THE BENEFITS OF SOCIAL MEDIA

Social media adoption for organizations, whether in news or not, is complex. For most organizations, however, it should not be optional. The benefits are too great, and the expectations of readers, customers, and clients demand this adoption and that these organizations and companies join the conversation. Social media are timely, even immediate, and they are easily and readily accessible. In terms of distribution costs, they are almost always low cost or free. And they are powerful in helping organizations get their messages out and in bringing traffic in. Media sites using Facebook's "Like" buttons and other social plug-ins report, on average, a threefold increase in referral traffic, according to Facebook's own data. Readership among people who sign in at *The Huffington Post* with Facebook leads to an average of 22 percent more site pages and eight more minutes spent than for an average reader coming into *HuffPo* another way. ABCNews.com, *The Washington Post*, and *The Huffington Post* each report a doubling of referrals since adding social plug-ins, according to Facebook.

Thus, news websites have an opportunity to convert the bumps in traffic that result from big news events into more meaningful, longer-lasting reader relationships. Page views and unique visitor counts are important metrics, but so are Twitter followers and Facebook fans. During the Casey Anthony trial in 2011, for example, traffic to the *Orlando Sentinel's* website jumped to around 40,000 visitors per day from 3,000. Giving readers the ability to convert their episodic interest into regular contact with the website via either a Facebook page or a Twitter stream, or both, can help a news site to keep many of those new visitors.

With each and every story, but especially with big breaking news, news sites should include click options for a Facebook "Like," a Twitter "follow," an email newsletter "subscribe" button, a mobile app download, and even a print subscription. While deploying some of these social media tools, a news site might also want to track readers' loyalty using a tool such as Quantcast, which helps to determine the level of interest among visitors, or the "Visitor Loyalty" feature at Google Analytics, which shows the percentage of visitors who came to the site during a given period and the number of times they visited.

Regardless, the site should make it easy to follow the news on Twitter and Facebook and perhaps other social media tools and platforms, as well. Readers should be able to easily tweet and re-tweet articles. For larger news topics, news sites should consider setting up specific Twitter accounts for those topics and including a line somewhere on the page inviting readers to "follow us on Twitter for more updates on this story," or the like. The same is true with Facebook. When interactors download an organization's app, they are, in effect, signaling that they want to continue getting that organization's content. It's up to the organization, however, to make that app worth the trouble by providing *unique* content that they cannot get anywhere else and to make it easy to access and to use.

▶ HOW TO USE TWITTER

Twitter co-founders Jack Dorsey and Evan Williams have said that the microblog's appeal is due to its ease of use and its near-instant accessibility. In addition, the learning curve for using Twitter is relatively low for anyone familiar with texting compared to other platforms and networks. Twitter combines the attributes of radio with those of the telegraph. Like radio listeners, Twitter users can "tune in" to specific feeds, individual tweeters, and trending topics. Like radio broadcasters, tweeters can send out messages one-to-many. And like telegraph operators, tweeters can send out short messages quickly and over any distance.

Both Twitter and the telegraph have been blamed for an erosion of language. Email, texting, Facebooking, and chat, too, are likely having a corrosive effect on writing. The informality of writing for these online environments is "seeping into . . . schoolwork," according to a study by the Pew Internet and American Life Project, in partnership with the College Board's National Commission on Writing. Nearly two-thirds of 700 students surveyed acknowledged that their electronic communication style, which primarily is an informal, interpersonal style, found its way into school assignments. About half said they sometimes omitted proper punctuation and capitalization in their schoolwork, while one quarter said they used emoticons. These are alarming trends, calling for more education on the different styles that should be employed for different forms or kinds of communication, and for vigilance against interpersonal communication encroachments. These new forms are here to stay, however.

Twitter calls itself a microblog. (Other microblogs include Jaiku, Tumblr, Plurk, and Squeelr.) This is significant. It is not a social network in the way that Facebook or Myspace are, creating spaces for primarily interpersonal, social interaction, spaces in which users network together on the basis of weak ties. Twitter can, of course, be used socially, but it isn't inherently social, or designed to be primarily a social network. Tweeters are typically individuals, which leads to a great deal of, in Dorsey's and Williams's words, "incessant chatter." This capacity has led many to discount Twitter as simply another gathering place for nattering nabobs and self-involved online diarists. Such dismissal is a mistake.

As if to counter the myths about Twitter's capacities, Pulitzer Prize-winning writer Jennifer Egan (@egangoonsquad) used the microblog in 2012 to write her short story "Black Box." Serializing her narrative on Twitter through the *New Yorker* magazine's fiction account (@NYerFiction), Egan's story centers on a futuristic female spy and her mission as recorded in her mission log.

Ready to Tweet?

You know you have only 140 characters, so you know that whatever you tweet, it will need to be short and ever so sweet. A character can be a letter, number, punctuation mark or symbol, so employ all of these to make the space count. Use as few words as possible, and substitute words with easily intuited symbols whenever possible. This means editing, pruning, revising, and shortening. It does not mean incorrect punctuation. No one is offended when something is punctuated correctly, regardless of character counts; many are offended when you get it wrong, particularly if it is a first impression you are making. So use full stop periods and commas; put apostrophes in the right place; and use quotation marks and parentheses. Studies have actually shown that re-tweets contain *more* punctuation than original tweets. The steps you take to be clear and concise on Twitter will inform and help you in other media and formats, as well. And all that time you spent earlier becoming an expert headline writer will pay off on Twitter, where headlines can make all the difference.

Twitter is easy to use. Write a short message, click "Tweet," and you're done. To build a following, however, you must demonstrate your value and perhaps a discernible role. Some Twitter users focus on re-tweeting "found" articles and information on a topic or range of subjects. Others provide witty commentary. Still others prod and provoke. So find or decide your role, but be yourself. Twitter is powerful in removing or preventing noise, in connecting you fairly directly with your audience. In other words, if you're having fun, that sense of engagement will rub off on others.

A user's profile page, known on Twitter as a timeline, includes all tweets, whether or not they are directed to a specific user. This makes it easy to lurk, or to simply read and watch, rather than tweeting, as well. Twitter users typically follow friends and popular Twitter users, including celebrities, as well as organizations and news media.

Using Twitter means using hashtags, which are strings of characters immediately following the "#" character in a tweet. Any words preceded by this hash sign are used in Twitter to note a subject, event, association or group, or trending topic, and these hashtags make it possible for Twitter to thematically link conversations together. It is this "structure" of hashtags that facilitates impromptu interactions of individuals and brings them into these conversations, and it is this dynamic that perhaps explains why Twitter has been viewed as useful, even critical in social movements like Occupy Wall Street. Hashtags are an attempt to aggregate tweets in such a way as to develop or facilitate conversations in a natural, or seemingly natural, way. Because Twitter encourages association, users often think about what hashtags to include in their messages while writing their posts, and perhaps who should be "@-sign" mentioned in the post.

Twitter recognizes the # hashtag and automatically turns the character string into a search query link. In the long run, these hashtagged conversations become *de facto* Twitter groups, but unlike groups on Facebook, there is no registration process and, therefore, no actual group ownership. All it takes to create a hashtag and, therefore, the potential for a group or community organized around a subject or event is adding the # to a string of characters. Hashtags also make a topic easily searchable, like naming a tributary, however small, that flows into the larger Twitter river in such a way that it can be tracked to its source.

A question for editors, depending upon the event or subject, is whether or when to set up a separate Twitter account or to create a hashtag (or set of hashtags) on an existing account. Of course, existing hashtags should also be used to tap into the interest that's already out there. For big events, such as sporting events, conferences, and conventions, as well as developing stories, like hurricane coverage or political campaign coverage, it might make sense to use both a new Twitter account to communicate event information and assistance and a hashtag that can be used for conversations about the event or ongoing story. The next question for the editor responsible for the account is how long to keep the account going once conversation has died down or the event has ended.

Here are a few tips on creating and using hashtags:

▶ Determine whether to create your own hashtag(s) or simply to use those people are already using, or both.

▶ Search Twitter for keywords related to your topic when creating your own hashtags.

▶ Be careful with hashtags that already are widely in use. It's more difficult to break through the clutter.

▶ Encourage re-tweets (or tweets shared by Twitter users) by using both a hyperlink and a hashtag. The link should point to your content; the hashtag will keep the conversation about that content going.

▶ Keep your hashtags short (#reallylongtagsreallydonotworkwell); make them fairly obvious and direct (#occupywallstreet).

If you tweet, you will inevitably re-tweet and share hyperlinks. Given the 140-character limit, this means you will want to use a link shortener, such as TinyURL, bit.ly, or Twitter's own shortener linked at the bottom of any Twitter post. Another implication of re-tweeting and sharing is the need to credit others with their full Twitter handle, such as "from @newshound." A re-tweet, commonly abbreviated as "RT," allows people to forward tweets to followers, and they provide a way to facilitate the distribution and redistribution of tweets outside one's immediate network to broader audiences.

When starting out with Twitter, journalists (and public relations practitioners and marketers) should remember a few key facts about Twitter and its users. First, it is built on reciprocity. Approximately 70 percent of those you follow will follow you back, so begin by following a lot of people. But be discriminate. Don't follow anyone, but only those who will genuinely add to your nascent online community and who share your mission, interests, activities, or affiliations. Second, interact and engage. Many journalists mistakenly use Twitter as just another distribution platform. You should reply to posts, engage in conversation, and recognize your own responsibility to the community you are trying to build (or join). Third, make a good first impression. Your headshot should be accurate (a friendly face boosts followership), your bio should be accurate (transparency!), and your first tweets should be meaningful. An accurate biography rich in key words also facilitates you being found in searches. Fourth, tweet often. In the tributary-and-river analogy, your contributions should stream in on a regular and frequent basis. Finally, resist the erosion of language to which Twitter and social media platforms seem to be contributing. Use proper grammar, syntax, and punctuation. Mistakes will cost you followers.

To these "do's", Scot Hacker and Ashwin Seshagiri add a few "do not's", including:

▶ Tweeting just headlines. This isn't engagement.

▶ When a story breaks, wait until you have the whole story. No: post immediately as soon as you can, as soon as you have something accurate to run with.

▶ Go it alone. Twitter connects thousands; turn to your followers for help doing your job.

▶ Auto-pump your tweets to Facebook. The grammar of Twitter does not work on Facebook and vice versa. And it might confuse your Facebook "friends."

▶ Overdo your hashtags.

▶ Make it all, or even mostly, about you.

It's important to see that a person doesn't have to tweet to reap many of the software's benefits. For example, simply monitoring how Twitter's vast information network is being used can open a window on news and events and what they might mean to millions of people. Think of Twitter as a searchable human index updated in real time, much like GoogleTrends's reporting of what (and how) its users are searching. This alone should interest digital journalists. By simply having an account, doing some basic research via Twitter, and subscribing to some relevant feeds, journalists and public relations practitioners can use Twitter to:

▶ Generate story ideas.

▶ Do background research on a story.

▶ Identify sources.

▶ Track news and events, and their coverage, in real time and throughout the world.

Of course, there are advantages to using Twitter to publish, as well. Journalists with a Twitter account can:

▶ Conduct interviews with sources (or set up face-to-face interviews).

▶ Promote a story or series by tweeting headlines and hyperlinks.

▶ Collect feedback from readers and continue the conversation.

▶ Cover a live event.

▶ Network with other news organizations and journalists.

▶ Network with "citizen journalists."

▶ Provide the news organization with a human face and a personal touch.

And they can do all of this on the move, via a smartphone or tablet. It is no accident or coincidence that the demographic identified by one study as the fastest-growing group of Twitter users also is the fastest-growing group of users of smartphones—Millennials aged 18 to 24. Twitter has recognized its own utility to journalists and, in response, has published a suite of search tools to help journalists find what they're looking for. These search tools include:

▶ Twitter Search: a query-driven tool to quickly identify information on a certain topic or about a specific person (http://twitter.com/search).

▶ TweetDeck and Twitter for Mac: applications that automatically stream breaking news by topic into a person's Twitter feed and a good tool for monitoring an event, story, specific subject area, or person. These applications can also be used to monitor readership and the re-tweeting of a reporter's own tweets (https://dev.twitter.com/media/newsrooms/report#apps1).

▶ Archive Search: a tool for finding older tweets (https://dev.twitter.com/media/newsrooms/report#archive2).

▶ Twitscoop.com: a tool to track the most popular topics on Twitter (Twitscoop.com).

▶ TweetLater: this app schedules your tweets, posting them when you wish. You can also automate responses to new followers (tweetlater.net).

Another very powerful tool for journalists for making the most of Twitter is Twitterfall (twitterfall.com), a powerful interface that can turn Twitter's simple feed into a sophisticated source of specific, granular information. Twitterfall enables:

▶ Geopositioned customization: by entering your location, tweets can be filtered for those from that location using the key words you specify.

▶ Key word and topic tracking: enter the key words and/or hashtags you wish to follow and Twitterfall will filter tweets accordingly.

▶ Monitoring: using the Twitterfall interface, you can adjust the speed at which tweets scroll and select a user or group of users to track.

▶ Filtering: screen out re-tweets, filter by language, save your frequently used searches, and mark individual tweets as favorites.

▶ LIVE TWEETING

Twitter's immediacy, ease of use, and reach via both the web and mobile devices make it a powerful tool for live coverage of breaking news, conferences or meetings, concerts, sporting events, court trials, fairs, and festivals. Longer-term benefits of live tweeting from an event include building the reporter's or news organization's following on Twitter and building community among readers and visitors. Another capacity is delivering followers an immediate, visceral connection to the event or subject. But good live tweeting, like most everything else, requires planning and preparation, which is where editors come in. Before heading out, some key considerations include:

▶ identifying the audience(s);

▶ promoting the Twitter feed, perhaps with a preview story and by letting existing followers know of the live feed that is coming;

▶ researching the event or subject;

▶ contacting the event organizer or contact person to learn more of what to expect in the field;

▶ beta testing with the equipment or devices to be used in the field to troubleshoot, to get used to the tools, and to become comfortable with the 140-character limit;

▶ making sure that batteries are charged and that Wi-Fi or cell connectivity is available on site;

▶ thinking through whether to set up a separate Twitter account and deciding on hashtags so people can easily follow the coverage during and after.

Once the live tweet feed has begun, writers should:

▶ Set the scene and provide followers with a sense of place.

▶ Identify key players and preview readers on what to expect.

▶ Identify the lead of the "story," or the most important 140 characters of the day.

▶ Write tight and develop a rhythm and pace for tweets.

▶ Pass along what is seen, heard, perhaps even smelled, because good reporting depends on all five senses. Good reporters are good observers.

▶ Answer the basic reporting questions of who, what, when, where, and why.

▶ Track trends, surprises, critical moments, and emerging themes.

▶ Quote key actors or subjects, which, of course, requires interviewing and conversation.

▶ Interact with followers who begin replying to the tweets by answering questions and acknowledging comments.

▶ Perhaps include photos, some video.

▶ Identify others who are live tweeting or live blogging the event with whom to link.

As with any form of writing, it requires some practice and experience to figure out how active to be and to discover or determine voice and style. The 140-character limit takes some getting used to, though for some it is almost immediately a good fit.

Tactical Considerations

When cross-linking Twitter content with a website or mobile app, several tactical questions have to be considered, including:

▶ Which Twitter button style you should use. For sites in which pages receive a lot of tweets, the vertical option puts the most emphasis on the tweet count.

Celebrate the high number and draw attention to it. For sites with little traffic, or for pages for which traffic isn't relevant or important, however, a button without a tweet count makes more sense.

▶ Where the button should be positioned. The top of the page? Bottom? Both? Other places? For long pages, such as those for in-depth articles, bottom placement (or top-and-bottom placement) is preferred; readers may not return to the top of the page to click on a tweet button from which they've long ago scrolled away. For a page where all or most of the content is above the fold (or second screen), however, such as a video or photo slideshow, multiple buttons could clutter up the page.

▶ Whether to show or include a Twitter stream. Although such a stream might encourage interactors to click on the tweet button to join in on the conversation, it will take work to include Twitter reactions.

Isn't Twitter in Some Ways the Competition?

Of course, by using or incorporating Twitter into a communication strategy, an individual and/or an organization is sending interactors to someone else's platform. The risks, rewards, and return on investment should therefore merit this redirection of attention and traffic. It would seem logical, then, that whatever is given "for free" to Twitter (or Facebook or Instagram or whatever social media platform is being considered) should include a fairly easy, intentional way to get back to the organization's website and further coverage and content. The style, space, structure, and speed of most social media, especially Twitter, preclude most narrative storytelling. Entire novels have been written via Twitter, but those are the few exceptions that prove the rule (see the *Guardian*, "Twitter Fiction: 21 Authors Try Their Hand at 140-Character Novels," October 12, 2012, www.theguardian.com/books/2012/oct/12/twitter-fiction-140-character-novels). The medium is in important ways part of the message, an unavoidable fact explored in depth by the communication theorist Marshall McLuhan. Thus, Twitter is not a medium built to carry the freight of complex issues and coverage across a protracted period of time.

For example, the Charlotte, North Carolina, *Business Journal* newspaper has a reporter, Susan Stabley, who, when covering city council meetings and zoning commission meetings, prepares in advance links to background stories on zoning or council issues. She then tweets during the meetings with those links to increase traffic to *Business Journal*'s website (www.bizjournals.com/charlotte/). These links, used with a URL shortener, enable immediate feedback and analytics on how effective they are, so those using the social media can modify their headlines and content to see what drives more clicks. In addition, Stabley is building a network and an audience, something newspapers have historically called "circulation." Thus, Twitter and Facebook can compound "circulation," especially during big news events and crises, times when news organizations have an opportunity to build loyalty and trust by standing above the noise and misinformation. Whether any of this translates into money in the form of advertising dollars and paying subscribers or customers is difficult to measure, but then measuring the return on investment of print advertising has historically been difficult, as well.

Another downside to this otherwise compelling argument for integrating links is the fact that, increasingly, fewer people are clicking anything. Because "reading" and accessing information is taking place more on smartphones and, therefore, less on desktops and laptops, fewer interactors are bothering to click for more, to click to go to a website, any website. The return on investment therefore stops with the tweet. In addition, still fewer interactors use Twitter relative to either print news media or Facebook. Fortunately, to access Twitter content a person doesn't need a Twitter account and can see it by going to Twitter.com. Metrics show that Twitter adoption is growing, and in significant numbers. A longer-term question is whether using Twitter in these ways leads organizations to "train" interactors and clients and customers to get their information this other way, as opposed to directly from the organization. Maybe, but even recent history has shown that withholding content and disavowing the growing interest in social media won't deter people from using them. Isn't it preferable to keep trying to figure out how to work with the new gatekeepers than to totally ignore them?

The exception to this scenario is the niche information provider whose interactors are willing to pay for the content, such as Bloomberg News or *The Wall Street Journal*. Bloomberg sells expensive subscriptions; the *Journal* puts its content behind a paywall. Both provide information that gives its users a competitive edge—information that is hoarded. The *Journal* has had a paywall since it launched its website in the mid-1990s, and it has been a profitable website since the late 1990s. But few providers have been able to make paywalls work.

Approaches to Engagement

Tweeting, liking, following, and becoming a fan are not the only social engagement conversions organizations can encourage, but given the reach of Twitter and Facebook, they are arguably the most important. Fortunately, many if not most of the optimization techniques used to encourage Twitter and Facebook engagement can be applied to other social networks and bookmarking sites, as well. When combined with or integrated into page and site structures that encourage user-generated content and subscribing to syndicated content, these social media platforms can be powerful in generating traffic and building community. To systematically convert casual visitors into active participants, consider these first steps:

▶ **Keep share options manageable.** There are dozens of sharing mechanisms available, but that doesn't mean all or even most need to be utilized. The more options that are presented, the less likely an interactor will be to click on any one, so include only those networks and services you think interactors will actually use. As usage statistics become available, you can drop those that see little use.

▶ **Let history be your guide.** Take some of the lessons learned from email campaigns, landing page testing, and page optimization to guide in the crafting of new messages that can maximize social conversions. Specifically:
  ▷ What wording has resonated with your interactors?
  ▷ What calls to action have proven the most effective?
  ▷ What mistakes can help you avoid similar ones going forward?

▶ **Be truthful and transparent.** As in everything, be transparent in the presentation and use of social media. It should be obvious whether clicking will share the content or lead the interactor to a Twitter profile or Facebook page. This is especially true for Facebook, where identically styled "Like" buttons may reference either the resource the interactor is viewing or the site's Facebook page. Interactors are less likely to click where there is uncertainty about what will happen next.

▶ **Adjust and adapt.** Give more visual weight to the network that is most commonly used by your interactors. *The Huffington Post*, for example, places the "Like" button above its Tweet icon. Mashable, on the other hand, puts Twitter on top. The result? *HuffPo* gets more "Likes," while Mashable gets more tweets. This isn't an accident.

▶ **Practice run.** Even a little testing is better than no testing. Without some testing, you are just guessing.

Tools, Tactics, and Tips

With some context for strategic use of social media, think about some **concrete ideas** for leveraging social media with an emphasis on news-you-can-use and delivering a tangible benefit. The importance of providing something tangible might be one of the more important lessons of the success of apps. To begin brainstorming, consider the following:

1   Sponsor a competition, game, or contest.

2   Ask questions, such as "Would you . . . ?"

3   Respond to user questions and posts quickly and meaningfully.

4   Offer a "top 10" list or a "5 ways to . . . " list (or link to one that is online).

5   Interview experts and provide their answers to compelling questions.

6   Introduce your leadership team to a broader audience.

7   Promote events and new features and content.

These ideas facilitate engagement by audiences with products, brands, and organizations. Though measuring the effectiveness of engagement in terms of profits at the bottom line is difficult (one marketer called it the equivalent of measuring air conditioning), most marketers agree that it is essential to long-term growth. They are turning to Twitter, Facebook, Instagram, Tumblr, and other platforms to join in and begin these conversations, all with the hope of this intangible quality called "engagement."

Some of the inspiration has come from seeing what damage can be done when a brand or product isn't involved in a conversation that, at least for the brand, goes horribly wrong. Examples of this include the "Motrin Mom Disaster" of 2008, when pain relief brand Motrin ran a commercial empathizing with moms who carry their babies in a sling. Moms with blogs quickly organized to boycott the brand. Since then, a series of public relations disasters have arrested the attention of companies now turning to social media marketing experts for help. One such example is Percolate, which charges upwards of US$10,000 per month to monitor 6 million sources on the web for mentions relevant to the brand. These mentions are invitations to start a conversation.

Paul Adams, former head of social research at Google and Facebook's global director of brand design, told *Fast Company* magazine that brands err when seeking engagement by thinking of "heavy things," like developing media-rich experiences that people will want to share with their friends, when they should be thinking of "lightweight interactions" like those most people have with most other people most of the time. "You meet the first time, chitchat. You're not suddenly best friends," Adams said. This type of interpersonal conversation is what drives social media use. A corollary of this is that brands can't use social media primarily to pitch or sell, which will trigger "unfriend" actions and people tuning out.

Some brands have learned that their products simply aren't conducive to conversation, online or anywhere else. Examples include toilet paper, gasoline, and paper. Makers of these commodities can still participate in social and mobile media, but not in the ways that, say, clothing or electronics brands can. Charmin, for example, realized that few people wish to have a conversation about toilet paper, but that a mobile app that helps people find a public toilet can lead to a positive brand relationship. SitOrSquat is Charmin's response to the question of how to add something to the digital conversations consumers are having. Thus, providing something tangible, or serving a public with an amenity not unlike a public park, free concert series, or nature trail, can bring good results and build loyalty.

▶ ENGAGEMENT WITH FACEBOOK

With more than 1 billion people "Liking" and commenting an average of 3.2 billion times each and every day, Facebook is a communication force to be reckoned with, one that depends upon weak and strong ties among "friends." By using Facebook's unprecedented reach and through it building engagement, news organizations, brands, and companies can use Facebook interactions to influence behavior, including buying and reading decisions. Word of mouth, after all, is still the strongest form of advertising, and Facebook interactions are the virtual equivalent.

Using "Like" in Facebook is quite simple, and users do not have to visit Facebook to use "Like" or to become a fan or follower of a site, page, Facebook group, or area of

FIGURE 9.1

interest. The alternate method of attracting "fans" is to link to a page on Facebook, where the user can click a "Like" button displayed at the top. The obvious benefit of a direct "Like" is that the user is connected in one step, without the danger of failing to click on the Facebook page "Like" button. The biggest drawback is not being able to control the call to action or its appearance. Linking to a Facebook page, therefore, is similar to linking to a Twitter profile, and it provides the opportunity to closely associate following on Twitter and becoming a fan on Facebook.

What optimization methods can be performed at the page level depends upon which method is used, though, of course, both a direct "Like" button and a linked call to action can be used on the same page. Their performance, then, can be compared for future planning. When using the "Like" button directly, it is important to separate this from any other "Like" buttons on the page, and to identify for the user what it is they are about to "Like." When linking to a Facebook page, the same positioning considerations apply as with a Twitter-linked call to action.

For page "Like" buttons, "Like" seems the most natural label. For linked Facebook pages, however, perhaps invitations such as "become a fan on Facebook" or even "follow us on Facebook" might be more useful. "Like" buttons can help to promote sharing. Content gets three to five times more clicks if:

▶ thumbnail photos of people are included;

▶ people can add comments;

▶ "Like" appears at both the top and bottom of articles;

▶ "Like" appears near visual content, such as videos or graphics.

The "Like" box is a sort of extended version of a "Like" button for pages, and it displays a "Find us on Facebook header," the number of users who "Like" the page, recent posts from the page, pictures of profile photos, and, of course, a "Like" button.

The "Like" box takes up a fair of amount of real estate with all of its functions enabled, but it can be pared down and employed as a beefier call to action than the "Like" button. For active sites with large numbers of users and good content, the "Like" box may serve as an enticement by showcasing the page's usefulness and popularity.

During spring 2013, Facebook rolled out its page Insights tool to help users measure any one page's performance and to track interaction. By organizing anonymized demographic data about any page's visitors, Insights has taken some of the mystery

FIGURE 9.2 Facebook's own 'Like' box.

out of the question of knowing when and what to post to attract the most attention. Among the types of demographic information Insights provides on even an hour-by-hour basis going back two weeks are gender, age, and geographic location of "fans." So if, for example, you are targeting males 18 to 25 on the East Coast, the data will show over time how you are doing with that demographic post by post over time. Average reach, "Likes," comments, and shares are tracked, making it relatively easy to experiment with different types of posts at different times on different days. Compare this data with when your fans are on Facebook, which Insights also tracks, and you have at least a snapshot of your potential in terms of attention. One national healthcare association, for example, found that ideal times to reach its "fan" base are between 5 p.m. and 9 p.m. on weeknights and about noon during the day, or at lunchtime and just after work. Prior to knowing this, the association's social media team regularly posted in the morning.

Another lesson the healthcare association learned: Post most judiciously. Amidst a debate among its social media team about how many times to post, Insights gave evidence that "fans" hid, reported as spam, or "unliked" the association's page most often when the association posted more than twice per day. Insights generates "scorecard" data on these metrics as part of a section Facebook calls "People Talking About This" (PTAT). Data include:

- ▶ number of "Likes," including new "Likes";

- ▶ number of "unlikes";

- ▶ number of friends of fans;

- ▶ number of people "actively talking" about and commenting to your page;

- ▶ total weekly reach.

In addition, you can sort posts by type to compare which is reaching your fans more effectively, effectiveness that Facebook calls "virality." Insights post types include:

- ▶ photos,

- ▶ links,

- ▶ videos,

- ▶ platform posts,

- ▶ questions.

The data so far described are accessed fairly easily using the Insights dashboard. Selecting Page Level Data and exporting it as a Microsoft Excel file will provide a great deal more, perhaps even an overwhelming amount. But analysis at this tabulated data level can go beyond the graphs and charts the dashboard generates.

This chapter has focused on Twitter and Facebook, but there is a seemingly endless parade of social media platforms and services, from Instagram, Snapchat, and Pinterest for photography, to Vine and YouTube for video, to Tumblr and Reddit for amalgams of socially and non-socially mediated content. Because this book is about writing and editing, the more textually based platforms are the focus, rather than those dedicated to the sharing of images.

A Case Study: "End the 'R Word'"

When the R-Word.org website failed to catch on as the centerpiece of a campaign to excise "retarded" from common vernacular, 1/0 and Perfect Sense Digital teamed with Special Olympics International for a dynamic website thoroughly integrated into social media networks and driven by—no surprise—compelling content. The revamp and strategic approach to social media fueled a 30 percent jump in pledges in the first year and boosted page views by nearly double. Importantly, the Special Olympics took ownership of the campaign, housing it with its content management system (www.specialolympics.org/03–31–09_Spread_the_Word.aspx), and developed articles, images, events, videos, and slideshows.

For the year March 2009 to March 2010, it is estimated that the site reached nearly 4 million people through social media, including 55,000 Facebook users, more than 100 blogs, more than 1,200 tweets, and more than 16,000 video views. These numbers mean little in and of themselves, but collectively they demonstrate the impressions a campaign can generate by taking a multipronged approach and strategically integrating social media. Blogs such as "Girls Can't What" (www.girlscantwhat.com/weekly-challenge-spread-the-word-to-end-the-word/), Feministe (www.feministe.us/blog/), and Momlogic (www.momlogic.com/2009/03/spread_word_to_end_word.php) picked up on the campaign, as did mainstream media and online aggregators. On Twitter, celebrity tweeters such as musician John Mayer helped to drive pledgers to the website, while a "Tweetchat" hosted by @EndTheWord and @FanCommunity also led to pledges. Over on Facebook, 55,000 participated in a campaign drive "event" that took place across 16 Facebook groups.

The overall effect pushed consciousness and media attention of the campaign higher on the public's agenda and raised consciousness of the damaging effects of using the word "retarded." Some of the campaign's online homes:

▶ the Special Olympics website (www.r-word.org/);

▶ Twitter hashtag #rword;

▶ Facebook Cause Page;

▶ YouTube channel (www.youtube.com/EndtheRword).

▶ LISTENING

Thus far, the discussion has centered on sending out information and building community. The other side of the social media coin, however, is listening and engaging. Companies that aren't at least listening to what people are saying about them via social media, much less moderating and participating in those media, are taking a huge gamble. To cite one example of the potential rewards, Dr Pepper built an

8.5 million-strong fan base on Facebook that the soft drink company carefully tracks and tests. Sending out two messages daily via its Facebook fan page, the company also listens to its "fan" reactions, and software tools help the company to measure, among other things, how many times a message is viewed, how many times it is shared with other Facebook users, and what fan responses are. Using these tracking tools, Dr Pepper learned, for example, that diehard fans like edgy one-liners ("If liking you is wrong, we don't want to be right"); but that they do not like messages that focus on prices and special offers. Social media, therefore, offer platforms for targeted, niche, or specialized experiences.

In fact, a cottage industry has sprung up in the area of social media management and customer experience management. A company called RightNow, for example, monitors social media for corporate clients, searching for a company-relevant list of key words. RightNow software 'listens" to online chatter and alerts the client of negative comments, as well as positive.

At Delta Airlines, in a headquarters control room outfitted with monitors on the wall streaming social media mentions of airlines, Delta customer service agents hunt for traveler complaints and try to solve problems. Their objective is to prevent problems from going viral and turning into public relations crises. These agents use a computer program to search for terms such as "Delta sucks." The monitors show Delta mentions on Twitter and other sites, and when bad weather creates delays and missed connections, agents can monitor the tweets. Agents then respond with information about the causes of delays. "You are there with their emotions, good or bad," Allison Ausband, vice president of reservation sales and customer care for Delta, told *The Wall Street Journal*. Delta hopes to avoid the kind of backlash United Airlines faced in 2009 when musician Dave Carroll funneled his rage over his guitar having been broken by United Airlines staff into a viral YouTube video viewed more than 13 million times as of mid-2013 (available www.youtube.com/watch?v=5YGc4zOqozo); United's stock fell 10 percent as a result.

The lesson for the airlines, and everyone else, is clear: Disgruntled customers are turning to social media with complaints once handled in relative privacy with a desk agent. Millions are posting their experiences, both good and bad. Delta told the *Journal* that it sees social media as a chance to offer better customer service, creating a channel on Twitter called @DeltaAssist and telling workers in its social media lab to offer customers quick fixes. If one person is complaining, it's likely another hundred or so are facing the same troubles.

Some Questions To Think About

With these considerations in mind, an organization or company should think about:

▶ To what extent should we monitor chatter on or through social media?

▶ Is there any point to such monitoring if we aren't willing to do anything about the complaints that this monitoring will reveal?

▶ How far or to what extent should we go to address customer complaints as expressed through social media?

At IBM, as part of its "MobileFirst Digital Strategy," social media campaigns and programs must be what the company labels "SMART," or "specific, measurable, actionable, realistic, and time bound". In other words, each campaign must identify specific, measurable objectives, and they begin and end at predetermined times in order to be measured for effectiveness. They must also be accountable in terms of delivering the results "business leaders" determined were desirable before the campaign was executed. While not every organization should seek to mimic IBM, the company's MobileFirst focus on clearly defined goals, a strategy to reach them, and ways to measure success are instructive.

CHAPTER ASSIGNMENTS

1 Live tweet an event, a trip, a conference, or a meeting. Create a hashtag for your coverage or take advantage of hashtags already being used. Hyperlink where appropriate. Use either a laptop or a smartphone, and experiment with a live tweeting app, such as CoverItLive. There is no minimum or maximum for the number of tweets.

2 Partner up to work as co-writers of an entry to Triangle Wiki (https://trianglewiki.org), a regional version of Wikipedia. Select a person, place, or organization to write about. Research your subject. Collaborate. Write and post an entry of four to six paragraphs. Include links, and consider adding an image from Flickr or Creative Commons. Triangle Wiki also has a simple way to make maps, which can be helpful. Here's an example written by an undergraduate student at the University of North Carolina: https://trianglewiki.org/Sutton's_Drug_Store.

3 The website Reddit, which gets its name by adapting "read it," advertises itself as the "Front page of the Internet." (A case study on Reddit's role in the coverage of the Boston Marathon bombings is in Chapter 8.) Registered users can add links and opinions in more than 60,000 categories (or "subReddits") and make comments about what others have added. Comments determine whether a post gets a high ranking on Reddit's main page.

Your assignment: Post your reporting project done for the previous chapter to Reddit:

- Register for an account at reddit.com.

- Decide on a page title and select a "subReddit" category for your reporting. You will want to browse the subReddit categories. SubReddits you might choose from include Advertising, Journalism, Public Relations, News, or Photojournalism. Subscribing to some subReddit categories will order or organize your homepage and cut down on the clutter.

- Add your story.

- Click the "subReddit" you selected to see your article. (Be patient: It can take several minutes.)

Once posted, you can use Reddit to monitor opinions about your work and see it move forward in the content. You could also integrate Reddit into a blog, website, or press release to show the number of comments received from other Reddit users. This takes time, of course, so the purpose of this assignment is simply to become acquainted with the Reddit interface and ecosystem. You might also generate attention by tweeting out a link to your article.

▶ REFERENCE

Aaron Bradley, "How to Convert Website Visitors into Facebook Fans," Search Engine Land, March 20 (2011a), http://searchengineland.com/how-to-convert-website-visitors-into-facebook-fans-70557.

Aaron Bradley, "How to Convert Website Visitors into Tweeters," Search Engine Land, March 20 (2011b), http://searchengineland.com/how-to-convert-website-visitors-to-tweeters-70516.

Aaron Bradley, "7 Approaches to Engagement Conversion, 5 Explicit Tactics for Twitter & Facebook," Search Engine Land, March 30 (2011), http://searchengineland.com/7-approaches-to-engagement-conversion-5-explicit-tactics-for-twitter-facebook-70030.

Geoffrey A. Fowler, "Are You Talking to Me? Yes, Thanks to Social Media. And the Best Companies are Listening," *The Wall Street Journal*, June 18 (2012), http://online.wsj.com/article/SB10001424052748704116404576263083970961862.html.

Scot Hacker and Ashwin Seshagiri, "Twitter for Journalists," kdmcBerkeley blog, June 23 (2011), http://multimedia.journalism.berkeley.edu/tutorials/twitter/.

C. J. Hutto, Sarita Yardi, and Eric Gilbert, "A Longitudinal Study of Follow Predictors on Twitter," CHI 2013 conference paper, July 2013, http://comp.social.gatech.edu/papers/follow_chi13_final.pdf.

Scott McCartney, "The Airlines' Squeaky Wheels Turn to Twitter," *The Wall Street Journal*, October 26 (2010), http://online.wsj.com/article/SB10001424052702304173704575578321161564104.html.

Dhiraj Murthy, *Twitter* (Cambridge, UK: Polity Press, 2013).

Danielle Sacks, "Can You Hear Me Now?" *Fastcompany*, February (2013): 37–43.

Danny Sullivan, "By the Numbers: How Facebook Says Likes and Social Plugins Help Websites," Search Engine Land, May 22 (2011), http://searchengineland.com/by-the-numbers-how-facebook-says-likes-social-plugins-help-websites-76061.

"Twitter Use 2012," Pew Internet and American Life Project, May (2012), http://pewinternet.org/Reports/2012/Twitter-Use-2012/Findings.aspx.

Stephanie Yamkovenko, "5 Ways to Increase Engagement with Facebook's New Page Insights," Poynter, September 2 (2013), www.poynter.org/how-tos/digital-strategies/222045/5-ways-to-increase-engagement-with-facebooks-new-page-insights/.

10

Digital Media and the Law

He who receives an idea from me, receives instruction himself without lessening mine; as he who lights his taper at mine, receives light without darkening me.
        Thomas Jefferson, in a letter to Isaac McPherson,
                                    August 8, 1813

Monsieur l'abbé, I detest what you write, but I would give my life to make it possible for you to continue to write.
            Voltaire, in a letter to Monsieur le Riche,
                                    February 6, 1770

If all mankind were of the same opinion, minus one, mankind would be no more justified in silencing that one person, than he, if he had the power, would be justified in silencing mankind.
                                    John Stuart Mill, 1947

▶ INTRODUCTION

Digital publishing has introduced new questions for the law. Every day, court decisions and policies from both government and corporate America are reshaping and redefining our rights

---

CHAPTER OBJECTIVES

After studying this chapter, you will be able to:

▼

understand the legal contexts in which digital writers gather and publish information, with an emphasis on the freedoms and protections offered by the First Amendment to the United States Constitution;

▼

know the basics of libel law as it applies to publishing in general and, more specifically, to publishing in digital spaces;

▼

understand the basics of intellectual property law, including copyright, as it relates to digital content.

of expression, often in tension with some other imperative, such as right of reputation, commercial interests, and national security. This chapter focuses on digital media law as it relates to writing, editing, and publishing in digital media, but in no way is it meant to be a comprehensive survey; it is an introduction. After exploring the rights of access to information, the chapter looks at two of the more complex legal areas for digital media: libel and copyright. Finally, the chapter addresses the implications of digital publishing with global reach and, therefore, the often conflicting jurisdictions and laws of 190 countries.

▶ GATHERING INFORMATION

Congress shall make no law respecting an establishment of religion or prohibiting the free exercise thereof; or abridging the freedom of speech, or the press; or the right of the people peaceably to assemble, and to petition the Government for a redress of grievances.

First Amendment to the U.S. Constitution

The First Amendment guarantees the right to publish information about government and public issues, but it doesn't help much with access to that information. After the attacks of September 11, 2001 and subsequently the Iraq and Afghanistan wars, access to U.S. government information and records became yet more problematic. The government began removing information from the Internet, and it became less responsive to Freedom of Information Act requests for information. At the same time, the U.S. government's willingness to surveil even its own people by tracking electronic media, including telephone, Internet search, and email data, has inspired comparisons to authoritarian regimes. The government's aggressive secrecy and surveillance efforts have raised profound constitutional questions at a time when print news media have been in decline and have therefore been increasingly unable to hold that government accountable.

Constitutional law scholar Thomas Emerson said, "a democracy without an informed public is a contradiction." Democracy implies a significant level of transparency in government. When print periodicals first emerged in Europe in the 17th century, they saw their role as investigatory. During the English Civil War, when press freedom in England began to emerge, these periodicals promised that they would investigate what was going on and tell their readers. *The Parliament Scout*, a publication that began in 1643, stated it would "search out and discover the news." The next year, in 1644, a publication calling itself *The Spie* promised readers that it "planned on discovering the usuall cheats in the great game of the Kingdome. For that we would have to go undercover."

Thomas Jefferson famously said that he would rather live in a nation with newspapers and no government than in a country with government but no newspapers. But there are tensions, or competitions of interests and priorities, when the Fourth Estate seeks to watchdog government. Like most bureaucracies and institutions, government seeks to do its business behind closed doors and out of the public eye. Sometimes the secrecy is warranted. National security often demands secrecy, to name one instance. Individuals want their health, personnel or employment information kept secure and private. With a raft of federal laws promising information privacy, we arguably have more privacy than any generation before us. But we also have more surveillance than any generation before us, both by government and by corporations. And with the development and diminishing cost of ever-smaller video cameras and wearable but invasive technology such as Google Glass, we face surveillance by each other, as well. Facebook's facial recognition software is but the beginning.

Two landmark Supreme Court cases that established a constitutional right to access to information for all citizens, including but not especially journalists, are *Richmond Newspapers v. Virginia* and *Branzburg v. Hayes*. The case of *Richmond Newspapers v. Virginia* (1980) gave U.S. citizens "a right to know" how their government administrates justice. The U.S. Supreme Court ruled that the First Amendment, in fact, does establish the right to attend criminal trials. This constitutional right is for everyone, not just or especially news media. This decision could have been extended to cover legislatures, council meetings, and review boards, but it wasn't. For access at those levels, in most cases we must turn instead to statutory law, the product of legislatures, rather than constitutional law. Statutes that provide some guarantees of access include the Freedom of Information Act, state open meetings, and state-level open government laws.

Whether reporters should be allowed to protect confidential sources is a recurring question for the law, a question addressed in *Branzburg v. Hayes* (1972). Paul Branzburg, a reporter for the *Louisville Courier-Journal* newspaper, had cultivated sources within a drug ring; a grand jury not surprisingly wanted access to those sources. To protect the identities of those sources and to fulfill his promise of confidentiality, Branzburg argued that the First Amendment's protections of a free press should shield him from government requests for his privileged information.

In a very close, contentious 5–4 decision, the Court ruled that it has generally been held that the First Amendment does not guarantee the press a constitutional right of special access to information not available to the general public. Complicating *Branzburg*, however, was the majority opinion by Justice Byron White that stated that "without some protection for seeking out news, freedom of the press could be eviscerated." Despite the logic of White's opinion, journalists historically have had no more right or access to information than the general public, as the *Richmond Newspapers* case demonstrated, and therefore no special right to gather information from within government or about government.

To put it another way, the information buffet is open, so grab a plate and help yourself, media, but do not expect the government to come to you to wait on your table. Can you get exactly what you want? No, the buffet has what it has—meat loaf and baked potatoes. There is a public prison tour at 8 a.m. There are slideshow photos in the gift shop. These are available to anyone, including media, but no one will be coming to your table, saying, "Hello, my name is Eric Holder. I'll be your Attorney General today. I'd like to tell you about a few specials on the information menu." As mentioned earlier, since 9/11 the buffet has been shrinking. More and more information entrées, especially information on national infrastructure, transportation, and law enforcement records, are being taken off the table.

Without a constitutional imperative for government to open its doors, its records and files, meetings and dealings, we have to litigate. We have to lobby. We have to plead for legislative relief. One attempt at providing this relief is the Freedom of Information Act (FOIA), initially passed in 1966 and amended for the Internet in 1996. FOIA provides the disclosure of previously unreleased information and documents possessed by the federal government, but its effectiveness depends upon cooperation from government. FOIA covers agency records and information collected, maintained, used, retained, and disseminated by the federal government, and it is available to anyone, public or private, media and non-media. The 1996 amendment expanded FOIA to cover electronic information, including email correspondence. In addition, the Electronic Freedom of Information Act established priorities or rankings for agencies to use when petitioned for information:

► Top priority: requests in situations in which life or safety is at risk.

► Middle: information requested by news media for the public's interest.

► Low: everything else.

Often, using FOIA becomes a cat-and-mouse game. A request is made. Government agencies drag their feet, claiming national security interests or a prohibition in the

Health Information Privacy Protection Act (HIPPA) or some other statute to block access to information. The Bush and Obama administrations have exercised what could be called reflexive secrecy. Bush's attorney general, John Ashcroft, for example, ordered a more intensive review of requests by agencies already willing to stall requests. And after campaigning on promises of transparency in government, Obama became perhaps the most secretive president in U.S. history. In 2012, for example, the secret Foreign Intelligence Surveillance Court established in 1978 to authorize surveillance warrants for the National Security Administration and the FBI granted all 1,800 requests from U.S. intelligence agencies. This court has effectively created a secret body of law, regularly assessing broad constitutional questions and establishing important judicial precedents, with almost no public scrutiny. Absent from any of this is any adversarial process, which is a cornerstone of the rule of law.

In addition to a bureaucratic culture predisposed against helping media or private citizens obtain information, agency personnel called on to fulfill the requests typically have other job duties and roles, forcing a difficult choice: Either do their jobs or spend time fulfilling FOIA requests. Overburdened both by their own jobs and a large number of FOIA requests, many not surprisingly choose their jobs.

Good news came in 2007 when Bush signed into law the Openness Promotes Effectiveness in our National Government Act of 2007, also known as the OPEN Government Act. This law amended FOIA by establishing a definition of "news media," prohibiting an agency from assessing certain fees if it fails to comply with FOIA deadlines, and establishing an Office of Government Information Services in the National Archives and Records Administration to review agency compliance with FOIA (read the law in full at www.justice.gov/oip/amendment-s2488.pdf). The new definitions are liberal, meaning that most bloggers and digital publishers are eligible for reduced processing and duplication fees available to "representatives of the news media." The law also broadens the scope of information that can be requested.

The OPEN Government Act was the first makeover of the FOIA in a decade, or since it was first amended to account for the web. The act also brings non-proprietary information held by government contractors under the law, which effectively reverses an order by Ashcroft in the wake of 9/11 to resist releasing information when there was uncertainty about how doing so would affect national security. The legislation also creates a system for the media and public to track the status of their FOIA requests, as well as a hotline service for all federal agencies to deal with problems and an ombudsman to provide an alternative to litigation in disclosure disputes.

How To Use FOIA

Using FOIA to get information is relatively simple:

1 First, informally ask an agency's public information officer for the information you want, a method that is quicker, cheaper, and nicer than making a formal request. And it is surprisingly effective. In 2013, for example, Drew Hendricks, a peace activist in Washington State, blew the lid on a massive, secret U.S. law enforcement surveillance program in conjunction with AT&T by simply asking West Coast police agencies for the information.

2 If working with an information officer in person is either not feasible or unsuccessful, you can file a formal, written request under FOIA. Each agency must identify the person to whom to submit requests, as well as its FOIA procedures and electronic indices of those popular records it releases as a matter of course.

3 Once a request is made, the agency must release the documents or provide a reason for exemption. Exemptions must cover only the information to which it is applicable, not the entire record.

4 FOIA gives agencies 20 business days to determine whether to grant or deny a request, except for "unusual circumstances," such as sudden popular demand for a particular record.

5 If a compelling need is demonstrated, such as danger to human life, agencies are required to expedite requests.

6 Agencies can charge for information, including electronic information, to cover the actual costs of getting the information and duplicating it.

7 If 20 days expire, the person requesting the information can file a complaint in federal district court.

But FOIA has several exceptions or exemptions that agencies can cite in denying information, such as:

1 National security, the broadest category, and the only category that allows the executive branch to determine the criteria for release of documents rather than Congress. This exemption covers military plans, weapons and operations, and intelligence activities; programs for safeguarding nuclear facilities; and U.S. foreign relations, among other categories.

2   Agency housekeeping practices or rules that relate to internal personnel rules and parking and sick-leave policies. This exemption is meant to avoid swamping agencies with trivial requests.

3   Statutory exemptions, which include documents that Congress has declared in other statutes to be confidential. Examples are personal tax records, census bureau records, patent applications, and Central Intelligence Agency records.

4   Confidential business information, including trade secrets, private commercial information, contracts or information related to seeking a contract.

5   Agency memoranda, including working papers, studies, opinions, policy drafts, staff proposals and reports used to make a final report, agency policy or agency decision of some kind. This exemption is similar, in practice, to the attorney–client privilege.

6   Personnel and medical files in which the release would warrant an invasion of someone's privacy.

7   Law enforcement investigations where the information released would interfere with law enforcement proceedings or investigations, invade personal privacy, disclose the identity of a confidential source, endanger someone's life, deprive a defendant of a fair trial, or reveal protected enforcement techniques.

8   Financial records and bank reports.

9   Geological data and maps concerning oil, gas, and water.

In addition to the FOIA exemptions, other federal statutes can deny disclosure of information, and some of these laws are complementary to or redundant with FOIA exemptions. A few examples:

▶   The Homeland Security Act, section 214, states that the government cannot disclose critical infrastructure information provided by agencies and private businesses, including information about the national electrical power grid, nuclear power plants, or air transportation.

▶   The Privacy Act of 1974 states that the government can only use "personally identifiable records" for the purpose for which they were created and for which the information was gathered.

▶   The Family Educational Rights and Privacy Act (FERPA) protects student records, including student disciplinary records of nonviolent crime and violations of institutional rules.

▶ The Driver's Privacy Protection Act of 1994 prohibits the release of driver's license information without a driver's consent.

All 50 states also have public records laws, though they vary state by state. Several state courts have held that federal judicial interpretations of FOIA are at least helpful in interpreting similar language in state public record laws, and many of these laws are similar to FOIA. An excellent resource for identifying and accessing state-level FOI laws is FOIAdvocates, available at www.foiadvocates.com/records.html.

Open Records and Open Meetings: Sunshine Laws

The Government in the Sunshine Act was passed into federal law in 1976 to open most federal government meetings to the public. In addition, all 50 states have their own "sunshine laws" on their books, laws aimed at increasing openness in government. These state laws offer different degrees of access along a wide spectrum of openness, making it difficult to generalize, but the purpose of these laws is to hold government accountable. The general purpose was succinctly stated by Georgia Supreme Court Chief Justice Charles Weltner in a 1992 opinion: "Because public men and women are amenable 'at all times' to the people, they must conduct the public's business out in the open" (*Davis v. Macon*).

As was stated in a 1980 Georgia Supreme Court case, *Athens Observer v. Anderson* (1980), the purpose of open government and open meetings laws is threefold. Quoting from the decision, state government should provide access so that:

▶ "The public can evaluate the expenditure of public funds."

▶ The public can evaluate "the efficient and proper functioning of its institutions."

▶ Accountability can "foster confidence in government."

Open records acts typically apply to documents, papers, letters, books, tapes, maps, photos, and computer-generated information and files, and they cover every state department, agency, board, bureau, commission, and authority; every county and municipal corporation, school district, and political subdivision; and non-profits receiving funding from tax dollars. Similarly, open meetings acts generally cover meetings of any state, county and regional authority, municipality, school district and political subdivision, whether appointed or elected. The laws apply to non-profits receiving tax monies, but not to advisory groups and quasi-governmental bodies that collect information, make recommendations and advise government.

▶ LIBEL AND DEFAMATION

There are two major forms of "malpractice" possible in the "practice" of journalism: invasion of privacy and libel. Libel and defamation are the most common legal claims that drag journalists into the courts, and it is an area of the law that has heated up because of the often vitriolic anonymous expression enabled by discussion boards, comments sections, and other public forums online. Even the fear of libel litigation can silence journalists into self-censorship. And while most digital writers aren't typically worth suing from a financial point of view, being poor is not a great legal defense when faced with a libel action. Digital writers should therefore be aware of the law and how to stay out of the courts.

Libel has three essential ingredients: the questionable material must be printed or published (written), erroneous or false, and defamatory. Spoken defamation is termed slander, and it is handled differently by the law. Just like medical malpractice, libel is almost always a tort, or civil wrong, and not criminal. Although about half of the 50 states still have criminal libel laws on the books, criminal libel cases are extremely rare. Since 1910 there have been no cases in this area of the law in Georgia, to cite just one state as an example. And libel is primarily state law, though the states' approaches are guided and shaped by U.S. Supreme Court precedent.

The premise in libel law is that a reputation has been damaged and that it can be repaired through the awarding of monetary damages. This reasoning is, of course, flawed, but it is the law's attempt at justice and, though not perfect, it beats dueling, which was the way these kinds of disputes were handled in the past. Libel can appear in headlines, in a news story or editorial, in a press release or company newsletter, in a blog post, in advertising copy, on a Facebook wall, in a letter to the editor, in a chat room, or in statements made orally at a public gathering. Since 1997, the courts have viewed communication online in much the same way as they have historically regarded or treated material in print.

Allegations of libel are included in about three-fourths of all the lawsuits filed against mass media, but most libel suits are dismissed before they ever get to a jury. When a suit does make it to trial, media are likely to lose. Juries are unpredictable, and ordinary citizens often think the media are unfair, manipulative, and exploitative. Robert Lichter of the Center for Media and Public Affairs told the *American Journalism Review* that he thinks there's a feeling that journalists have overstepped their boundaries. "People don't look on [journalists] the way journalists like to view themselves—as the public's tribune, speaking truth to power, standing up for the little guy. They don't look like the little guy anymore," Lichter said.

Libel cases take an average four years to litigate, and lawyers typically take home 50 percent or more of the winnings. Litigating is no fun, except, of course, for the lawyers, but people get mad at how they are reported in the news and want to sue. They can't win, typically, but they're hurt and angry and want someone to pay. They should probably write a letter to the editor, or call an editor to talk about what happened. But lawyers will take their money.

You protect yourself from a libel suit by knowing the law and by doing a good, professional job reporting, writing, and publishing. Sometimes doing additional reporting or gathering more information or sources can prevent the problem. Good journalistic and communication practices are the best defense. Good, careful, accurate reporting generally prevents successful libel suits, so know the law, have a solid story and follow the records or documentation. Libel occurs only where or when what has been published is untrue, so stay away from things that are not true. Do enough reporting to discern truth from untruth. Be fair and honest. If you are writing negatively about a person, give that person an opportunity to respond.

Michael Hiltzik, a Pulitzer Prize-winning investigative business reporter for the *Los Angeles Times*, said the single most important technique in his career has been "getting the documents." The whole point of dealing with sources is to get them to point to things you can get in black and white, he said. Hiltzik and Chuck Phillips teamed to win a Pulitzer for a story exposing that the Grammy Awards, an event held supposedly for charity, generated huge income but, in fact, scant little for charity. Grammy organizers threatened legal action, including a libel suit, but "couldn't lay a hand on us because everything was written down in documents," Hiltzik told the Committee of Concerned Journalists.

Criminal libel cases are of little concern. They occur when an individual is charged under criminal statutory law. Some statutes, for example, make it criminal to disturb the peace by criticizing public officials. The person's speech is protected under the First Amendment, but the disturbance caused by the speech could land the person in jail for criminal libel. When these arrests or charges are challenged, the criminal libel law in question is almost always found to be in violation of the U.S. Constitution's First Amendment.

Dead people are also of little concern, at least concerning libel claims. Only the living can sue for libel, and a living person can't sue on behalf of a dead person. Someone can sue, die, and have that suit continued by survivors, but this is rare. Businesses can sue, as can non-profits, churches, and charities. Companies (and the people who work for the companies) can also sue, an area of the law known as trade libel. The government cannot sue, at least not successfully. Individual staff members, however, can sue, but whether they can win depends upon a host of factors, including whether they are public officials (a governor or mayor) or private citizens (such as a secretary or administrator).

In the United States, unlike most areas of the world, when someone sues, the burden of proof is on the plaintiff, who has to prove at least six things. There are therefore six elements of any successful libel suit, or six hurdles that a plaintiff must clear in order to win the case. The plaintiff must clear all six, though some are relatively low and others higher. If a plaintiff trips up or fails to clear any one hurdle, the media win. The six hurdles are:

- ▶ defamation;
- ▶ identification;
- ▶ publication (and republication);
- ▶ fault;
- ▶ falsity;
- ▶ injury.

Defamation

A plaintiff has to prove that the published or printed material is, in fact, derogatory, or something that holds him or her up to hatred, ridicule, or contempt. Accusing someone of a crime qualifies, as do accusations of serious moral failings or incompetence in business or professional life. Juries decide what is defamatory, which means that interpretations can vary with the times and even with geography. Tom Cruise once sued for libel after being described as gay. The case was dropped, but it is difficult to imagine that such a description would be seen by a jury in southern California as, in fact, defamatory, though in southern Mississippi it might.

A community would not think less of a doctor or businessperson who makes a single error, and this reasoning explains the **single mistake rule**. Stories that suggest a pattern of incompetence, that go beyond asserting a single error, can be found to be defamatory, though not necessarily libelous. (Remember that libel has three ingredients, with defamation being only one of those three.)

There are three kinds of defamation, according to the courts: libel *per se*, libel by interpretation, and libel *per quod*:

▶ Libel *per se*, or **libel on its face**, occurs with accusations that are obviously defamatory. A published statement such as, "Smith killed the postal worker" is libel *per se* if, in fact, Smith did not kill the postal worker (and Smith can demonstrate the article can be interpreted to refer to him or her and not another Smith). It does not cover merely embarrassing information, like stating a person's age as ten years older than they actually are or having them earn a PhD from the wrong school.

▶ **Libel by interpretation** concerns something published that is or could be libelous depending upon at least one of a number of competing interpretations. One of the competing interpretations must be defamatory. The plaintiff must prove that the defamatory interpretation is the interpretation that was intended and that this interpretation is the one readers would be expected to hold.

▶ Libel *per quod* concerns something that has been published that becomes defamatory when readers add something commonly known that does not appear in the story. Not surprisingly, this form of libel is very rare. The writer may or may not have knowledge of the added fact or element, and usually it is the plaintiff who provides this missing piece of information. For example, a Jewish runner well known for sitting out of competitions held on the Sabbath is reported by a newspaper to have won a race incorrectly described as taking place on a Saturday. The story isn't libelous on its face, but when the public adds the fact that the runner previously has never run on the Sabbath, that public might hold the runner in contempt for sacrificing or surrendering his standards or values. (The bizarreness of the example hints at the reasons this is not a busy area of the law.)

Identification

If you write that someone embezzled, you have defamed that person and he or she will be able to easily clear the first hurdle. To prove identification, a plaintiff has to prove that at least one other person could read the story and identify the plaintiff as the person referred to or described in the story. Publish the plaintiff's full name and usually this hurdle has been cleared. Identification can also result from publication of a nickname, description, title, or affiliation.

Publication

If the actionable material was published or broadcast, the plaintiff clears this hurdle, as well. Did the accusation reach a third party? Sending a note to a second party doesn't count, but add just one intermediary and a plaintiff has met the minimum contacts requirement. Listservs, Facebook walls, tweets, press releases, blog entries, and email can all be found to have been "published." An interoffice memo, faxed or emailed press release, tombstone, Post-it note on a cash register, or bounced check thumbtacked to a restaurant wall can all qualify as having been "published." Under what is called **the republication rule**, the person reporting and/or writing the story is fully and legally responsible for the libel. That person's source can be sued for slander, but it is the reporter who is responsible for the published libel. Thus, "I just repeated what they said" is not a successful defense in a libel case. Repeating a rumor is not necessarily libelous, but publishing it could be, and anyone who participates in publication can be named in a suit: copyeditors, publishers, editors, press release writers, owners and publishers, Internet service providers. Plaintiffs, not surprisingly, go after the money, however, which typically puts the owner in the most jeopardy.

Fault

The most complicated area in libel law is fault. Briefly, different types or classifications of plaintiffs have to prove different standards or levels of libel, specifically fault, a hurdle added in 1964 with the landmark U.S. Supreme Court case, *Times v. Sullivan*. Prior to this case, civil libel law had been governed by the doctrine of strict liability. In other words, reporters strictly and legally were responsible for what was published. "Did you write it? Then you are responsible." Libel is much more complicated today. In *Times v. Sullivan*, the Court ruled that plaintiffs must prove what is known as fault or, specifically, that public or government officials must prove a standard of fault called "actual malice." By distinguishing public officials and assigning a higher level of fault, the Court ruled by implication that private citizens need prove only negligence. All plaintiffs have to clear the hurdle, but different classifications of plaintiffs must clear varying fault levels. Thus, *Times v. Sullivan* put an end to strict liability.

The highest fault level is known as "actual malice," defined as showing a reckless disregard for the truth and/or knowledge of falsity. To clear this high level of fault, a plaintiff has to prove that the reporter or writer knew the published material was false or that the reporter or writer demonstrated a reckless disregard for truth. The term's definition underlines how good, honest, professional reporting and writing can prevent successful libel claims. If you have three reliable sources, you cannot be guilty of actual malice-level libel. If you have no reliable sources, just the word of an unemployed former insurance salesman with a grudge, as was the case in a libelous *Saturday Evening Post* story on supposed game-fixing in college football, and you could be guilty of actual malice-level libel. Relying on only one discredited source can be interpreted as reckless reporting.

It is important to note from *Times v. Sullivan* that the majority opinion supported an aggressive, free press. Justice Brennan wrote that at issue was "a profound national commitment to the principle that debate on public issues should be uninhibited, robust, and wide-open, and that it may well include vehement, caustic and sometimes unpleasantly sharp attacks on government and public officials." Brennan's opinion established the actual malice defense. It is also important to note that in this case advertising (also called commercial speech) was ruled protected by the First Amendment for the first time, though at a level lower than that for political speech. (Note: Political speech in this context has nothing to do with politics, at least not necessarily; it refers to noncommercial speech. The term uses the Greek root *polis*, meaning "the people." Political speech, therefore, is the people's speech.)

In rulings after *Sullivan*, the Court made it clear that it wants more people to have to prove actual malice before successfully suing for libel. Public officials were joined by public figures, a category that includes celebrities and the well-known, as well as people with power and influence in society who therefore are worthy of media scrutiny. The Court had serious people in mind, but it is this strand of legal reasoning that ultimately evolved to include celebrities, who now must prove actual malice, as well.

All plaintiffs must fall into one of the four plaintiff categories, a classification that determines the fault level that must be proven. The four are:

▶ all-purpose public figures;

▶ limited or vortex public figures;

▶ public officials;

▶ private citizens.

Public figures make themselves public by seeking fame or notoriety (media attention), and public people have access to media to refute things said or written about them. They can call a press conference, for example, and media will show up to report what is said. The same media that are allegedly libeling them can be used as a remedy to the libel. Since *Times v. Sullivan*, the courts have subdivided the public figure category:

▶ **All-purpose public figures**, or people with widespread fame or notoriety such as LeBron James or Beyoncé Knowles. These figures typically are household names or people with special prominence in society. They are considered to have pervasive power and influence and are therefore continually newsworthy. Consider celebrities who sell their "exclusive" wedding or baby photos to periodicals for millions of dollars. Public figures have virtually no private aspects to their lives, at least in a legal sense, so their lives are fair game, as the TV shows *Entertainment Tonight*, *TMZ*, and *Access Hollywood* demonstrate. Once a person has been classified in this category, that public figure never falls out or lapses back to the lesser fault level category, regardless of how obscure he or she might become.

▶ **Vortex or limited public figures** are once-private figures who have been pulled into the public sphere, like an object swirled into a vortex. The key court case for this category is *Firestone v. Time* (1972), which involved the wife and heir to the Firestone tire fortune finding herself listed in *Time* magazine as getting a divorce for cruelty and adultery. The magazine column was in error, however, and Mrs. Firestone sued. The question for the Court: Given her fortune and profile in philanthropy, was Firestone a public figure who therefore must prove actual malice? Or, because the reason for the publicity was a divorce, a private matter, was she a private citizen? The Court noted that she was a socialite, and that she had hired a publicity clipping service. Nonetheless, for the purposes of the lawsuit she was classified as a private person because her divorce was deemed by the Court to be an essentially private matter. Had *Time* written about Firestone's role as head of a cotillion or charity, she likely would have been classified as a public figure.

Since the *Firestone* case, a test of sorts has emerged from case law to help courts determine a plaintiff's classification for the purposes of establishing a fault level. Courts should ask:

1   Is the published material about a *public controversy or real dispute*, the outcome of which affects a substantial number of people? Firestone's divorce was a real dispute, but its outcome did not affect a substantial number of people. (The Court has not defined "substantial number of people.")

2   Did the plaintiff *voluntarily participate* in the public controversy?

3   Did the plaintiff voluntarily participate to *affect the outcome* of the issue, question or controversy?

Case law suggests that a person cannot lose vortex public figure status, at least in connection with the issue or event that led to the status in the first place. This principle holds true for former public officials, as well; they don't lose their public status once they retire or lose a re-election.

In contrast to actual malice, **negligence** is simply failure to exercise ordinary or reasonable care. Plaintiffs who are deemed to be private citizens need only prove this relatively low level of fault. Some courts rely on professional standards, calling in editors and academics to testify to standard practices. The Court is interested in the number and credibility of sources used, in red flags raised about the story's veracity, and in the newspaper's or website's policy for sourcing and verifying accuracy. Some courts follow what is known as the "reasonable person standard," which asks how a reasonable person might respond in similar circumstances. This so-called "reasonable person" is a fiction, of course; there is no such person. The notion is applied in the abstract.

A lack of thorough investigation, lack of verification of information from official and reliable sources, and a lack of contact with the subject of the story have all been found to be negligent. What is deemed negligent, therefore, fails to measure up to what is considered good reporting practice. The Court is looking for substandard reporting, for malpractice, and not merely the absence of professionalism or good practices.

Falsity

Libel is, by definition, false, whereas defamation has nothing to do with truth or falsity. To win a libel claim, a plaintiff is going to have to prove that the published story is false, an element of libel law unique to the United States. Until only very recently, truth (or falsity) has not been a factor in England, and it is not a defense in Australia, New Zealand, or Canada. In the United States, the courts require only substantial truth, at least for private citizens, not that every word be true. Remember, public figures and public officials will have to prove actual malice; media need only prove *the absence* of actual malice, not absolute truth. Careless errors are not enough to lose a libel suit. If a published report states that a person embezzled US$75,000 and the actual amount was $70,000, the error will not likely qualify as substantially false.

Injury

Another relatively easy hurdle to clear is demonstration of injury. A plaintiff needs only one psychologist to testify to the need for medication. In this category are types or classifications of damages:

▶ **Compensatory (or actual) damages** compensate for harm done or harm proven, and they include damage to reputation and personal suffering. They are also called actual damages.

▶ **Special damages** are those one might think are actual damages. Examples include losing a job and therefore income, having to move and sell his or her house, and requiring three years of psychotherapy.

▶ **Punitive damages** are meant to punish the defendant. The jury decides these, and no plaintiff eligible to sue for these fails to because it is this classification that promises the big money awards. Juries look at the financial status of the defendant and will seek to punish that individual or organization. The results typically are huge awards, though almost all judgments are reduced on appeal.

Not all libel cases systematically proceed through the six hurdles. A judge might be motioned to dismiss a case, a ruling called summary judgment. If a defendant can persuade a judge that the plaintiff cannot possibly win, summary judgment is a possibility. Second, there is a **statute of limitations** for libel actions. In most states it is one year. If the actionable material was published or aired more than a year prior to filing the claim, that claim typically can be summarily dismissed. If the material was published online, the clock begins on upload, or when the site publishes, tweets, or posts it, as opposed to when someone downloads, reads, or accesses it.

Sometimes a person or organization will try to use the courts to intimidate, never intending to win a libel action and recover for injury but rather to scare or pressure a defendant. When so recognized by the court, these actions are known as **strategic lawsuits against public participation** (**SLAPP suits**). More than 20 states explicitly bar or severely limit such lawsuits, and the high cost of defending a SLAPP suit is one of the concerns spurring states to act. In one example of an anti-SLAPP suit action, in 2008, the Maine Supreme Judicial Court struck down a defamation lawsuit filed against a former legislator who claimed that the plaintiff was using the court system to try to stifle free speech in a political debate. The defendant successfully gained dismissal of the lawsuit on the grounds that it violated Maine's anti-SLAPP law, which is intended to protect a citizen's right to directly or indirectly petition the government through public discourse, a right found to be protected by the First Amendment.

Thus, asking a court to recognize a lawsuit as a SLAPP is a defense against a libel claim over and above tripping a plaintiff up on any one of the six hurdles. There are other additional defenses, as well, including the following:

▶ **Absolute privilege** covers what is published in documents coming out of or as a part of senate deliberations, judicial proceedings, and other official government business. No matter what is said or printed as part of these deliberations, this defense covers the speaker. So this defense is not intended to specifically or even primarily shield media.

▶ **Qualified privilege (or fair report) defense** shields media when they report on or with official government reports and meetings. The courts recognize the importance of scrutiny of government proceedings, meetings, and activities as part of news media's watchdog role. Acting as a sort of video camera, media can claim this defense and not necessarily be responsible for the truth or falsity of what occurs in those meetings and proceedings, provided the reporting is fair and accurate. If, for example, a local citizen at a city council meeting charges that an official took a bribe, accurate reporting of the accusation is protected by this defense. The qualified privilege defense is especially valuable in political campaign coverage, when it is particularly difficult to parse fact from fiction.

▶ **First Amendment opinion defense** covers rhetorical hyperbole, fair comment, and criticism. This defense varies from state to state, and it is based on common law. The defense covers opinions, arts and music criticism, and parody and satire. Generally, hyperbole, parody, and exaggerated statements that a "reasonable person" would not believe as literally true are therefore protected. Because political cartoons, parody, and satire are strong vehicles for expressing public opinion, they are generally protected even if they offend or inflict emotional injury. In addition, statements incapable of being proved true or false also are typically protected. The 1984 *Ollman v. Evans* case produced the **Ollman Test**, which is used by lower courts to guide use of the defense. The test asks courts to consider these questions:

  ▷ Can the contested statement be proved true or false?

  ▷ What is the common or ordinary meaning of the words?

  ▷   What is the journalistic context of the remark?
  ▷   What is the social context of the remark?

In a 2003 case, *Batzel v. Smith*, the Ninth Circuit Court interpreted into libel law many of the same protections for bloggers that have been traditionally recognized for journalists. The Court ruled that bloggers, website operators, and email list operators cannot be held responsible for libel in information that they republish. The decision is based on Section 230 of the Communications Decency Act of 1996 (CDA), which states that "no provider or user of an interactive computer service shall be treated as the publisher or speaker of any information provided by another information content provider."

▶ ANONYMOUS SPEECH AND SECTION 230

The fantastic growth of the web and of digital discursive spaces, including those offered in and by social media, has exacerbated a problem long wrestled with by the courts even in the analog pre-web era—anonymous defamation. The courts are faced with the difficult, sometimes seemingly impossible task of balancing a person's, company's, or organization's right to a good name, on the one hand, against a speaker's First Amendment right to anonymous expression, even that which defames, on the other, in and with a medium that enables and encourages cheaply—even freely—published, globally distributed, cached and searchable expression. A legitimate state interest exists in the compensation of individuals for the harm done to them by defamatory and false statements, but in making it too easy for plaintiffs to force the discovery of anonymous speakers' identities, the state could unnecessarily, perhaps even unconstitutionally, chill online expression. In John Doe defamation suits, therefore, courts are asked to weigh plaintiffs' rights to seek redress for damaging, false expression against defendants' rights to anonymously speak or publish.

Typically, the first step in a defamation action against an anonymous speaker for expression posted or published online is to seek a subpoena on the defendant's Internet service provider (ISP) in order to obtain that speaker's identity. It is difficult for a plaintiff to sue, after all, unless he or she knows who made the actionable statements. By most of the standards issued by district courts and intermediate state courts, once issued the subpoena an ISP then notifies the accused that his or her identity is being sought in order to give that defendant an opportunity to contest the subpoena. Different ISPs deal with subpoenas for the identity of anonymous speakers in different ways, usually in conformity to their own user agreements and privacy policies. Of course, if the speaker is anonymous or pseudonymous, notifying that person of the action can prove difficult. Conversely, it is impossible to defend against a subpoena to force disclosure if you have not been notified of the subpoena in the first place.

Anonymity in expression is regulated by a multitude of federal and state constitutional provisions, state and federal statutes, and state and federal court decisions. Just how broad a right one has to be anonymous in digital spaces in the United States is unclear and unstable. Most courts faced with questions that involve a speaker's claimed right to anonymity cite the majority opinion in *McIntyre v. Ohio Elections Commission*, an opinion that interprets into the First Amendment the right to anonymous expression by finding the state of Ohio's interests in "preventing fraudulent and libelous statements" and in "providing the electorate with relevant information" insufficient to justify a ban on anonymous speech that was not narrowly tailored, according to the decision. Lower courts have applied the precedent set in *McIntyre* to online expression by recognizing that speech on the Internet is entitled to full First Amendment protection, as the Supreme Court declared in *Reno v. A.C.L.U.* in 1997. These courts have, therefore, generally sought to protect the identity of online speakers.

This constitutional freedom protects even speech that is crass, offensive, insulting, or objectionable; in fact, it protects speech that is especially these things. "One man's vulgarity is another's lyric," wrote Justice John Marshall Harlan, in *Cohen v. California*. The Court in *Times v. Sullivan* has made clear that through the First Amendment the United States has a "profound national commitment to the principle that debate on public issues should be uninhibited, robust, and wide open," and that because that debate is sometimes messy, some false speech must be protected in order to ensure that uninhibited debate.

Section 230 of the Communications Decency Act (the full text of the section is found at www4.law.cornell.edu/uscode/47/230.html) protects third-party publishers, and as federal law it pre-empts state laws. The courts have rejected attempts to limit Section 230 to "traditional" Internet service providers, instead expanding its protections to news websites and blogs, including them in a more expansive "interactive computer service provider" category. Practically, Section 230 protects websites and digital spaces when and where users are allowed to post or comment, even where those sites edit or delete entire posts. Sites run into legal jeopardy or liability when they contribute commentary or substantively change posts in editing, and the courts have yet to clarify what is and is not an acceptable amount or degree of editing. As Karen Alexander Horowitz has found, however, decisions interpreting or otherwise relying on Section 230 have been wildly inconsistent, from offering blanket immunity to depriving immunity when and where an ISP engaged in even minor editing.

▶ COPYRIGHT AND INTELLECTUAL PROPERTY ISSUES

Copyright as a concept was not necessary until the printing press, which provides an early example of how the law lags behind technological development and innovation. The Internet has put an unprecedented strain on copyright law as a result of the ease with which intellectual property can be copied, downloaded, uploaded, altered, mass emailed and mass duplicated, hacked and stolen. Complicating legal questions further, unlike analog copies, a digital copy typically has 100 percent fidelity to the original; the copies look or sound every bit as good as the original. This is unprecedented.

During the 16th century, English law protected printers only, not authors or painters, or those we would think of as the originators of the intellectual property. This changed in 1710 with "An Act for the Encouragement of Learning, by Vesting the Copies of Printed Books in the Authors or Purchasers of Such Copies, during the Time Therein Mentioned." This awkwardly named law gave a legal claim of intellectual property ownership to the creator, or to someone who bought the creative rights from the creator, and it is this law that is (or, more accurately, once was) the basis for U.S. copyright law. The U.S. Constitution's copyright and patent clause empowers Congress to "promote the Progress of Science and useful Arts, by securing for limited Times to Authors and Inventors the exclusive Right to their respective Writings and Discoveries." Implied in this verbiage is that people will innovate and create if they are guaranteed protection for their work for a limited time. How Congress has defined "limited," however, has changed over time.

In the nation's beginnings, U.S. law gave the copyright owner the right to protect his or her creation for up to 28 years, or for two 14-year terms. Registering provided the first 14 years; one renewal provided the next 14. In 1831, the timeline lengthened to cover the original 28 years plus an automatic 28-year renewal *and* an additional 14-year renewal, or the potential of 70 years in total. Musical compositions were added in 1831 and photography gained protection in 1865, largely because of the commercial value of photography of the Civil War. Translation rights followed in 1870.

Before 1978, copyright law was an opt-in system, granting protection only to those who registered and renewed their copyrights, and only if they marked their creative works with the © symbol. In 1978, Congress created an opt-out system, meaning that copyright protection no longer need be solicited. Protection is granted automatically to a created work once it is in fixed form, and this protection now extends for nearly a century, whether or not the author or creator needs it or even knows he or she has it. The law once offered protection only to those who wanted it, and for a "limited time."

Current copyright law universally grants it, regardless of need, even though according to the government's own study only about 2 percent of copyrighted works 55 to 75 years old have any commercial value, and it protects that copyright for longer than the creator's lifetime. U.S. copyright law makes little sense, and it has strayed far from its authors' intent more than 200 years ago.

Another way to think about the current intellectual property law regime is to consider a few famous authors of the past. William Shakespeare wrote *As You Like It* between 1598 and 1600, basing his plot and his play's general outline on Thomas Lodge's 1590 play, *Rosalynde, Euphues Golden Legacie*. Lodge "borrowed" his play from Chaucer's *The Cokes Tale of Gamelyn*, a 14th-century poem. It is unlikely that under contemporary U.S. copyright law either Shakespeare or Lodge could write or, more accurately, publish their plays without risking a lawsuit. Intellectual property law in the United States has changed almost completely since Thomas Jefferson first articulated it for U.S. law in 1790. Copyright law has, in fact, taken a 180-degree turn, which may help to explain how Fox News could plausibly sue humorist Al Franken and his publisher for naming Franken's book *Lies and the Lying Liars Who Tell Them: A Fair and Balanced Look at the Right* in 2003. Fox sued specifically for Franken's use of Fox's trademarked "Fair and Balanced." Fox's lawyers argued that use of the slogan would "blur and tarnish" the network's reputation. Franken was described in the lawsuit as being "unfunny," inspiring Franken to consider counter-suing for use of the word "funny," which Franken said he had trademarked. Fox lost its case, but that the question had to be answered in a court of law points to fundamental problems with intellectual property law as it is practiced in the United States.

For most works, there are two pieces of property: first, the physical or material content and the words (and/or visuals) in the physical document; second, the organization of facts in that printed or published work. Consider the textbook you are now reading. Whose is it? You own your physical copy of the book, which is why you can sell it to a second-hand bookstore or back to the student bookstore and keep the money. But the publisher and/or the author of the book own the copyright, protecting the expression of its ideas. The tricky part, then, is how to treat the two very different properties, and not to treat them in the same ways. Intellectual property is largely intangible, but it is mistakenly, tragically treated by U.S. law more like tangible property, like a piece of land or a lawn mower.

According to U.S. copyright law, "All works of authorship fixed in a tangible medium of expression" receive copyright protection. This definition applies to writings and online postings, paintings and animated gifs, music, drama, Flash movies and recordings. It does not protect the ideas themselves, only their fixed expression. How can you know the idea without its expression? You can't, so the two are in some ways indivisible. The fixed expression can be a printed book, an email, even a scribbling on a napkin.

Generally, the copyright owner is the author of the created work. Exceptions are works made for hire, such as those routinely published in newspapers and magazines and on the web. Copyrights may also be sold or given away, such as in publication contracts that transfer copyright from an author to the publisher of the work. Reassigning copyright requires a written statement of transference. Acquiring a previously unpublished creation, such as a manuscript, does not mean that one has acquired its copyright.

In the last 40 years, Congress has extended copyright terms 11 times, each time favoring private incentive versus the enrichment of the public domain. When the Sonny Bono Copyright Term Extension Act (CTEA) added 20 years to existing and future copyrights in 1998, Eric Eldred and other commercial and non-commercial users of public domain works sued. On October 9, 2002, the U.S. Supreme Court heard oral arguments that the CTEA is unconstitutional. However, in January 2003, the Supreme Court ruled by a vote of 7 to 2 that the CTEA does *not* violate the constitutional commandment that copyrights be granted for a limited time. The Bono extension, therefore, locks up or excludes a vast majority of creative works in order to protect the 2 percent with any commercial value. This means, as Kembrew McLeod noted, that we are "allowing much of our cultural history to be locked up and decay only to benefit the very few." The song "Happy Birthday to You," for example, will not enter the public domain because of the *Eldred* ruling until 2030. Copyrighted in 1935 by the Hill sisters, the song was sold in 1988 by Birch Tree Group to Time Warner. That the song is protected explains why restaurants have their own versions of "Happy Birthday"; singing "Happy Birthday to You" in a public place would be regarded as a public performance of a copyrighted song and would therefore require Time Warner's consent.

Websites, software, and apps typically include in their user agreements an articulation of copyright rights covering content produced for or on or with those sites, software, and apps. Myspace's user agreement, for example, states that once you have logged on, you "grant Myspace.com the nonexclusive, fully paid, worldwide license to use, publicly perform and display such content on the Web site." This means that essentially all photos and blog entries, video and music clips are the property of Myspace. Thomas Jefferson, conversely, was not primarily concerned with protecting the commercial interests of the last known user of the property, but rather with fostering innovation, development, knowledge, and progress. "He who receives an idea from me, receives instruction himself without lessening mine; as he who lights his taper at mine receives light without darkening me," Jefferson wrote. Justice Sandra Day O'Connor wrote in her *Rural Telephone Service v. Feist Publications* decision in 1991 that "the primary objective of copyright law is not to reward the labor of authors, but to promote the process of science and the arts." The founding ethos of the Internet was consistent with Jefferson's philosophy and with O'Connor's jurisprudence, but not with the current intellectual property regime.

The danger, as McLeod wrote in his 2005 book *Freedom of Expression*°, is in corporate interests wielding intellectual property laws like a weapon and in overzealous owners eroding the expressive freedoms of ordinary Americans. McLeod posits that we self-censor because we might get sued, even where there is no threat; we censor ourselves in backing down from a lawsuit even when that suit is frivolous, often because of the expense of even winning the case; and we are losing freedoms because everything from human genes and business methods to slogans, gestures, and scents are being privatized and commercialized. We should not be required to hire an expert to determine whether a symphonic orchestra can perform a work composed in 1945, or whether a library can display documentary photographs of the Japanese internment.

Having spelled out copyright's protections, we next should look at what it means practically to own a copyright. There are six permutations protecting a copyright owner's right to granting, limiting, or prohibiting:

- ▶ reproductions (such as prints of paintings or limited edition versions);
- ▶ derivative works (like a videogame version or website or online encyclopedia);
- ▶ public distribution;
- ▶ public performance;
- ▶ public display;
- ▶ public digital performance of a sound recording.

The above list means that there are several works that are not covered, including:

- ▶ trivial materials;
- ▶ ideas (remember, it protects only their expression);
- ▶ utilitarian goods (like a toilet or, more specifically, how the toilet works);
- ▶ book or movie titles and names;

▶ lists of ingredients;

▶ standard calendars and rulers;

▶ methods, systems, procedures, math principles, formulae, equations, and the periodic chart of elements;

▶ anything that does not offer its origin to the author (non-original works).

Copyright holders, then, have five distinct rights to a given creation. The holder can copy, distribute, display, perform, and create derivative works from the original creation. These derivations include translations, abridgments, and adaptations, such as making a movie from a novel. Another right, called a *moral right*, entails that one cannot change or mutilate a creation, such as removing an artist's name from a painting. Moral rights were originally recognized by European countries and now are recognized in the United States, as well.

The *Rural Telephone v. Feist* case proved important for databases, CD-ROMs, and digital anthologies. Feist Publications combined Rural's telephone directory with others to create a regional phone directory that it then printed and sold for profit. Rural Telephone sued and lost, with the Supreme Court allowing Feist's alphabetical listing of residents with a telephone, arguing that such public information cannot be copyrighted because there is no "idea" there. The listing is not novel or unique, and copyright does not cover purely "sweat of the brow" labor, in Justice O'Connor's words. Since 1991, *Feist* as valid precedent has been expanded, even though it was a relatively narrow ruling when issued.

A related qualification is that facts cannot be copyrighted, only the way in which those facts are expressed. The naked truth cannot be copyrighted. URLs, for example, cannot be copyright protected, meaning a copyright holder cannot prevent or control their publication, including in hyperlinks. Unique expressions of truth, including facts, however, often can be copyright protected. The copyright protections we normally associate with print also govern the use of audio, video, images, and text on the Internet and the web.

In the United States, copyright terms are a bit complicated because of a series of extensions granted by Congress and upheld by the Courts. Generally, however, works published:

▶ before January 1, 1923 are protected for 75 years from the date the copyright was first secured;

- ▶ from January 1, 1923 to January 1964 were required to have copyright renewed during the 28th year of their first term of copyright, which then covered them for 95 years from first publication;

- ▶ on or after January 1, 1964 to December 31, 1977 are protected for 95 years with no need of renewal;

- ▶ from January 1978 in their second term of protection automatically have the full 95-year term without requiring renewal;

- ▶ prior to 1906 or published by the U.S. government are in the public domain and require no permission to quote.

These terms and limits are spelled out on this webpage from Cornell University Copyright Information Center: http://copyright.cornell.edu/resources/publicdomain.cfm.

In the United Kingdom and the European Union, copyright terms generally are shorter, and they depend upon who owns the copyright. For a copyright held by an author, the work is protected for 70 years from the end of the year in which the author died. For a copyright held by the publisher, works are protected for 70 years from the end of the year in which the work was first published. If the author is not known, the work still is protected for 70 years, but from the end of the year in which the work was first published. Works published by the British government generally can be reproduced free of charge for uses such as analysis and commentary, provided that use is credited and non-commercial. More information on these provisions is available at the National Archives (www.nationalarchives.gov.uk/information-management/our-services/click-use-faqs.htm). More general copyright information governing use in the UK, also hosted by the National Archives, is available at www.nationalarchives.gov.uk/legal/copyright.htm.

Fair Use

Much of what digital writers and editors wish to do is potentially protected by a provision of copyright law known as "fair use." This provision is the right to use copyrighted material without permission or payment under some circumstances, especially when the cultural or social benefits of the use are clear. Fair use is a generally applicable right, meaning that the law does not have to provide an explicit authorization for the specific use.

We can avoid infringement and legally use copyrighted materials if we understand and comply with fair use guidelines, or by obtaining permission for use from a copyright's owner. Fair use is the most significant limitation on a copyright holder's exclusive rights, but determining whether the use of a work is fair or illegal is not a science. There are no clear, stable guidelines that are universally accepted. It is, however, generally understood that copyright owners' rights are exclusive and monopolistic except in four sets of circumstances. These are:

▶ where the work is not eligible for copyright protection (government information, for example, is generally not eligible, as it is the people's information);

▶ where the work is not an original—copyright does not cover copies, like a print of Van Gogh's "Sunflowers," for example, but only the original "Sunflowers" painting;

▶ where the copyright has expired;

▶ where the work's copying is covered by fair use.

The doctrine of fair use is meant to provide "a rule . . . to balance the author's right to compensation for his work . . . against the public's interest in the widespread dissemination of ideas and information on the other," according to a district court opinion. Fair use generally covers:

▶ small amounts of copying, generally understood in print to be around 150 words or less;

▶ the advancement of ideas, education, information, and knowledge, such as copies of a journal article distributed to students in a classroom;

▶ all intellectual property.

Since the U.S. Copyright Act was enacted in 1976, federal judges typically ask four questions in determining whether the use is, in fact, covered by "fair use." The individual who wants to use a copyrighted work must weigh these four factors:

1   Is the use transformative? In other words, what is the purpose and character of the use?

2   What is the nature of the copyrighted work?

3   How much of the original work was changed? What amount and how much substantiality does that amount represent when viewed as a part of the whole?

4   What is the effect on the market or the potential market for the copyrighted work?

These questions are implicit in the U.S. Code, Title 17, Chapter 1, Section 107, which reads, in part, "The fair use of a copyrighted work, including such use by reproduction in copies or phonorecords or by any other means specified by that section, for purposes such as criticism, comment, news reporting, teaching (including multiple copies for classroom use), scholarship, or research, is not an infringement of copyright." To better understand this dense language, let's unpack these four factors.

1   **What is the purpose and character of the copying?** What is the copyrighted material being used for? Teaching? Comment and criticism? Scholarship and research? If so, it is probably covered. This factor permits a professor photocopying an article, even in full, and passing it out to students in a classroom. In digital terms, the professor can store a .PDF of the entire article behind a password-protected firewall, for his or her students to access using their passwords. If the professor copies an article in full, then charges students $15 per copy, it would likely be viewed as an infringement. In general, educational copying must be:

▶ brief (usually less than 1,000 words);

▶ spontaneous (where there is no time to get permissions from publishers);

▶ labelled with a copyright notice somewhere on the copied material(s), crediting or otherwise identifying the copyright owner(s);

▶ equal to or less than the cost to the student of obtaining the original; if it cost the professor $1, he/she can sell it for no more than $1.

Finally, ask whether the new work offers something above and beyond the original. Does it transform the original work in some way? If the work is altered significantly, used for another purpose or to appeal to a different audience, it is more likely to be considered fair use.

2   **What is the nature of the copyrighted work?**

▶ Is it a workbook intended to be used only once? If that's the case, copying the workbook probably is an unprotected use.

▶ Is the work out of print? If it is, copying it is more likely to be considered fair use.

▶ Is it informational or creative? If it is a newspaper, your right to copy is probably protected because it is informational. A poem, however, is more likely to be protected. The more a work tends toward artistic expression, the less likely it will be considered fair use to copy it.

▶ Has the work been published? Copyright is meant to protect in order to encourage people to publish. If you are not the author and it has not been published, be very careful. The courts want to protect the author's right of first publication. Generally, however, unpublished works are less likely to be considered fair use.

3   **How much is used and, just as importantly, what does the use represent in terms of the "essence" or substantiality of the original work?** Using only 150 words typically is a fair use, unless those 150 words are the heart and soul or essence of the original work. The more you use, the less likely it will be considered fair use. If the amount approaches 50 percent of the entire work, it is likely not to be considered a fair use of the copyrighted work. If the very small portion used is the essence of the work but it is used in a wholly different way, as in a parody or satire, it is likely permissible. To help us understand this last distinction, consider the Supreme Court case *Campbell v. Acuff-Rose Music* (1994), which concerned 2 Live Crew's reworked parody of Roy Orbison's "Pretty Woman." The 2 Live Crew version used the lyrics: "Big hairy woman, all that hair ain't legit; Big hairy woman, Cause you look like Cousin It," mimicking Orbison's, "Pretty woman, walking down the street; Pretty woman, the kind I'd like to meet."

The plaintiff's argument was based on two claims:

▶   The parody is a commercial use. 2 Live Crew is making money.

▶   2 Live Crew is using the "heart of the original," or the essence of the song, so the amount appropriated should not be a factor.

The Court disagreed, recognizing that it is the "heart of the original" that makes the parody most likely to "conjure up the [original] song for parody." In other words, what was copied had to be recognizable to be heard as a parody. In ruling, the Court also suggested that the four provisions or criteria for fair use are not binary. If you fail one or more, you still might not be infringing. Rather, the four exist on a sort of continuum, where an overall balance of fairness is struck between the old work and the new.

4   **What is the effect on the market?** This factor is often the most important, at least in the courts. It covers direct impact, such as lost sales, and indirect impact, like that on derivative rights. For example, *Castle Rock Entertainment v. Carol Publishing* in 1997 centered on a book entitled *The Seinfeld Aptitude Test*. Seinfeld's distributor, Castle Rock, won the case because of the claimed effect on the market of the book in preventing Castle Rock from profiting from a similar work, a "Seinfeld"-based trivia test.

Generally, the more the new work differs from the original, the less likely it will be considered an infringement. If the audience for the new work is the same as that for the original, as was the case for *The Seinfeld Aptitude Test*, it will likely be considered an infringement. If a new work contains anything original, it is more likely the use of the copyrighted material will be seen as fair use.

This summary of fair use and its provisions isn't comprehensive, and it omits other permissions to use copyrighted material, such as those covered by Creative Commons (http://creativecommons.org/) licenses. A copyright holder can elect to share his or her work, and a Creative Commons license provides the mechanism to allow specified uses. Some musicians, for example, license others to reproduce, remix, and/or distribute their works at no cost, provided they are credited for the original. Flickr was one of the first major online communities to incorporate Creative Commons (CC) licensing options into its user interface, giving photographers the ability to share photos on terms of their choosing. As the Flickr community has grown, so has the number of CC-licensed images. As of late 2013, there were more than 200 million on the site, establishing Flickr as the web's single largest source of CC-licensed content. CC licenses, like those offered by Flickr, stipulate the ways in which copyrighted materials can be used. Creative Commons was established as a response to the U.S. Supreme Court upholding of Congress's extension of copyright terms by 20 years in 2001 with the *Eldred v. Ashcroft* decision.

The Internet and Copyright

As we have discussed, digital content—0s and 1s—is easy and inexpensive to copy and distribute, and digital copies have all the integrity of their digital originals. Furthermore, the prevailing culture on the Internet is that content should be free and freely obtained, even where copyright protected. We live in a cut-and-paste culture. Google, YouTube, and the blogosphere are cut-and-paste, record-and-stream worlds. They bump up against U.S. law, including and perhaps especially the Digital Millennium Copyright Act (DMCA).

During the mid-1990s, the World Intellectual Property Organization framed digital copyright rules in negotiating two treaties, and from those treaties came the DMCA of 1998. Among its provisions: You cannot circumvent copyright protection-using devices or their technologies. You cannot, for instance, use a file-sharing software program to circumvent copyright and copy and distribute content. You cannot alter the code in DVDs that prevents copying, or use a descrambler to pick up satellite broadcasts.

The DMCA has been at the center of a storm of litigation, including *MGM v. Grokster* in 2005, a case that echoed the famous 1984 Sony Betamax case (*Sony Corp. v. Universal City Studios*). In the Sony case, it was acknowledged that the VCR can be used to play home movies, and it can be used to illegally copy TV programming. Should VCRs, then, be illegal? The Supreme Court ruled that they should not. The manufacturer of the machine should not be held liable for the use to which it is put by the consumer. VCRs do not violate copyright, in other words; people do.

In *MGM v. Grokster* (and Streamcast), Grokster argued the Betamax defense from the previous Sony case: "Don't hold us responsible for miscreants." The Supreme Court ruled, in sending it back to the lower court for decision, that Grokster (and Streamcast) could be sued because there was evidence that the companies knew their software was being used primarily for illegal uses and did nothing about it. As a result, Grokster shut down on November 7, 2005, agreeing to pay a US$50 million fine. Grokster's website was changed to say that its existing file-sharing service was illegal and no longer available. "There are legal services for downloading music and movies," the message said. "This service is not one of them."

The *Grokster* decision significantly weakened lawsuit protections for companies that had blamed illegal behavior on their customers rather than the technology that made such behavior possible, which since 1984 had been an effective defense. This weakening has helped the recording and film industries in their campaigns against file sharing, campaigns simultaneously being waged on several fronts.

"Hollywood could be brought to its knees by the digital anarchy perpetuated by 12-year-olds . . . If the value of what [movie studios] labored over and brought forth to entertain the American public cannot be protected by copyright, then the victim is going to be the American public." Jack Valenti, formerly chief executive officer of the Motion Picture Association of America, said this more than 20 years ago. He was referring to the VCR.

In June 2009, a 32-year-old woman from Brainerd, Minnesota, lost her copyright infringement case over downloaded music and was assessed US$1.92 million in damages, or $80,000 per song for the 24 songs she was accused of downloading. Of the more than 30,000 suits brought by the Recording Industry Association of America (RIAA) against alleged file-sharers, the Minnesota woman's is one of only a handful to go to a jury. The damage amount underlines the high stakes in downloading and sharing copyrighted digital content, and the lengths to which the RIAA is willing to go to protect its control regime.

Who, then, can best manage the commons, or the shared public resources, culture, its icons and slogans, and intellectual property? The people or private industry? Although it belongs to the people, as a matter of free speech, it is most often litigated as private, commercial property. Corporate interests are most often the winners; the commons and the public good, then, are the losers.

The DMCA has another troubling aspect: a takedown notice. The act subjects online service providers to distributor liability if that provider fails to remove from its service *potentially* copyright-infringing content posted by a third party if that provider knows or has been notified that the content could infringe another's copyright. The DMCA's takedown policy has, in effect, criminalized legitimate research, stunted software development, and chilled expression. Merely by threatening ISPs with litigation under the DMCA, intellectual property owners can silence speakers simply because they do not like what the online speakers have to say. This intimidation has, on occasion, censored First Amendment-protected parody and satire. The Church of Scientology invoked the DMCA in calling for Google to block links to websites critical of the church, claiming that those sites were reprinting copyright-protected content owned by the church. Google blocked the sites, stating that, "Had we not removed these URLs, we would be subject to a claim of copyright infringement, regardless of its merits." It did not matter that the republishing was almost certainly protected by fair use provisions of U.S. copyright law.

▶ THE WORLD'S BIGGEST PUBLISHER: THE U.S. GOVERNMENT

An important exception to copyright, as described in U.S. Code 17, Section 105, is that almost any work of the U.S. government is prohibited from being copyrighted. This includes works by governmental agencies and works commissioned by the government specifically for a governmental agency, and it means that virtually everything published by the Government Printing Office, the world's largest publisher in terms of the sheer amount of information it disseminates, typically is fair game.

All webpages, email messages, and newsgroup messages are copyrighted, however, unless clearly stated otherwise. Copyright holders thus retain all rights to copy, distribute, display, perform, and create derivative works from their Internet publications. For example, a user cannot distribute someone's email message without expressed permission; the private email correspondence is itself copyrighted and the user simply has one copy of its contents.

Copyright law generally allows hyperlinking without permission, and historically sites have welcomed links from others since this practice can boost traffic, advertising rates, and revenues. In the high-profile *Ticketmaster v. Microsoft* case in 1997, Ticketmaster sued Microsoft for linking to its site without permission. Ticketmaster objected specifically to Microsoft's practice of deep linking, or linking deep within Ticketmaster's site rather than to the event ticket seller's homepage. Ticketmaster claimed, among other things, that Microsoft diverted advertising dollars by avoiding its homepage. Although the complaint was based primarily on trademark law rather than copyright, in arguing deep linking the case has copyright implications for digital writers and publishers. Linking, including deep linking, generally is not considered a copyright or trademark infringement as long as there is no implication of an association with the linked site. Ticketmaster and Microsoft settled out of court.

▶ INTERNATIONAL LAW AND A GLOBAL MEDIUM

Internet communication transcends geographic boundaries, and normally that is a good thing. For journalists who publish online, however, the transborder nature of the media format, in particular, and Internet communication, in general, could mean that local laws everywhere, from Australia to Zimbabwe, apply to them. Where an article is downloaded and read can be more important than where it is published or uploaded, which makes digital writers and publishers potentially subject to the laws of 190 countries. Not surprisingly, the result is dizzying jurisdictional complexity. With no international consensus to guide how or even where jurisdictional disputes should be resolved, online writers should beware.

The nature and popularity of digital communication make international legal questions all the more important. Technological innovation means digital communication exists in a permanent state of flux, with new ways of doing things perpetually posing legal questions without precedent. The sheer number of people using digital spaces puts a premium on finding solutions to what is a growing number of transnational disputes and international jurisdictional questions.

For journalists who write and publish digitally for large media organizations, awareness of potential legal challenges internationally could prevent legal actions that threaten to hale the employer organization into a foreign court. For lone, untethered writers who do not have the benefit (or bane) of large constituent legal departments, the lack of significant material assets abroad and relative anonymity likely provide ample protection against lawsuits in most cases.

▶ CONCLUSION

Good, thorough, professional information gathering and writing and publishing practices should keep you out of court. Corroborate a claim with three credible sources and you should be fine. Avoid intruding on a person's privacy by publishing what is protected by statute and you should be fine. Obtain copyright permission to republish digital content and you should be fine. But stay up on the news as it relates to digital content and the law. The fast pace of technological innovation and, in contrast, the slow pace of change in the law guarantees that lawyers will have plenty to do for a long, long time.

CHAPTER ASSIGNMENTS

1 You are an editor with a news blog and aggregator website. Many of your writers include with their submissions graphics and images simply found and "borrowed" from the open web. You are charged with drafting a policy that will guide contributors as to what they can and cannot appropriate, basing your policy on the notion of fair use. Write that policy.

Length: about 750 words.

2 In this hypothetical, you are legal counsel to The PuffingtonHost.com, a news aggregator that faces a libel action. Advise the site as to how to avoid or win the libel action based on the following facts. On September 2, 2014, The PuffHo publishes a story with the following headline: "Six Killed in Pair of Wrecks." The published story includes this paragraph:

> Six people were killed Saturday night in a horrifying pair of alcohol-related crashes near Yankee Stadium after a sold-out baseball game. Five of the six victims had stopped to help after the first accident.

The accidents occurred on a congested street near the Stadium at about 11:45 p.m., roughly two hours after the Yankees' victory over the Red Sox. The identities of the victims had not been released by early September 3. New York Police Sergeant Rocco T. Ruggiero said that a white Ford Explorer ran a stop sign and pulled onto East 161st Street. The Explorer was likely coming from the stadium and alcohol was a factor, Ruggiero said.

The Explorer struck a silver Toyota Prius in the intersection. The driver of the Explorer that ran the stop sign was killed. Other motorists and one person riding a bicycle stopped to help.

A green Chevy van heading east then slammed into the good Samaritans and into both the Explorer and the Prius. Ruggiero said that the third motorist was arrested on suspicion of drunken driving and faces "more very serious charges."

The driver was not seriously injured, and he was taken to a local hospital to be treated. Ruggiero identified that motorist as David Simmons, a 19-year-old Brooklyn College student from Queens, New York, whose address is a campus dormitory. Brooklyn College officials confirmed that Simmons is enrolled there as a student. They said he is a soccer player and the vice president of the campus chapter of SADD—Students Against Drunk Driving.

Five victims were pronounced dead at the scene; the sixth died *en route* to the hospital. Five of the six were males. Their ages were not released.

As authorities blocked off streets in the area, bodies lay on 161st Street covered with sheets. Robin Hubier was leaving her apartment on a bicycle when she saw the green van pass her. "I heard a sound and saw something, but that's about all," she said. As she pedaled closer, she saw that the van had hit people. "It's a tragedy," Hubier said. "All I can say is that it's a damn tragedy. Whoever was driving the van was too much in a rush. I think people like that guy are just too stupid to know when it's unsafe to drive."

Simmons sues The PuffHo for libel *per se*, seeking US$5 million in damages. Simmons said the story was libelous because it falsely reported that he was guilty of drunk driving and that it falsely portrayed him as stupid. Simmons said he was not drunk and that he's not stupid. He said he majors in interdisciplinary studies at Brooklyn College.

In your advice to the site, provide counsel on the following concerns:

▶ What type of libel plaintiff is the court likely to make Simmons?

▶ What, then, will be the requisite standard of fault in this case?

▶ Will Simmons be able to prove the requisite standard fault?

▶ Are there other defenses PuffHo might consider?

In the second part of this assignment, rather than being published to PuffHo.com, the coverage is tweeted by a reporter at the scene, the police station, and the hospital. Ruggiero now is suing for libel because of the reporter's live tweets. How might your counsel change?

This assignment is entirely fictitious; the names, places and events were invented to create the above hypothetical.

Online Resources

ADLAW (www.adlawbyrequest.com/)
A good source of legal information for advertising and marketing researchers.

Art of Public Records Searches (www.virtualchase.com/articles/public_records_research.html)
How-to site with help in finding and searching public records repositories.

Digital Media Law (www.dmlp.org/)
Legal resources for citizen media from the Berkman Center for Internet and Society.

Electronic Frontier Foundation (EFF) (www.eff.org/)
The EFF is a donor-supported membership organization that works to protect citizens' rights regardless of technology and to educate the press, policymakers, and the general public about civil liberties issues related to technology.

EFF Legal Guide for Bloggers (www.eff.org/bloggers/lg/)
A guide developed especially to inform bloggers of their legal rights in publishing online.

Electronic Privacy Information Center (EPIC) (www.epic.org/)
Established in 1994, EPIC is a public interest research center in Washington, DC, that tries to focus public attention on emerging civil liberties issues and to protect privacy, the First Amendment, and constitutional values.

Federal Communications Commission (FCC) (www.fcc.gov/)
The FCC is charged with regulating interstate and international communications by radio, television, wire, satellite, and cable. This site offers links to regulations, news, complaint forms, bureaus within the FCC, and licensing information.

Federal Communications Law Journal (www.repository.law.indiana.edu/fclj/)
Published by the Indiana University Maurer School of Law.

Federal Trade Commission's Privacy Page (www.ftc.gov/privacy/index.html)
Protecting consumers' personal privacy is a duty of the FTC. This page outlines how the agency attempts to do this.

First Amendment Center (www.firstamendmentcenter.org/)
A non-partisan foundation dedicated to free press, free speech, and free spirit for all people founded by the Freedom Forum.

Freedom of Information Act (FOIA) (www.state.gov/m/a/ips/)
Site explaining the FOIA and how to use it, at the U.S. Department of State.

Free Expression Policy Project (FEPP) (www.fepproject.org/)
Founded in 2000, FEPP provides research and advocacy on free speech, copyright, and media democracy issues.

How to File a FOIA Request (www.fcc.gov/guides/how-file-foia-request)

IPTA blog (www.iptablog.org/)
Blogger Andrew Raff's thoughts about the relationships between law, communication, technology, and the creative arts.

JDSupra (www.jdsupra.com/)
Source for all sorts of legal documentation, cases, briefs and the like, a sort of WebMD of the legal profession.

***Journal of Information, Law and Technology* (www2.warwick.ac.uk/fac/soc/law/elj/jilt/)**
Electronic law journal covering a range of topics relating to information technology law and applications.

***Jurist Legal News and Research* (http://jurist.law.pitt.edu/)**
Published by the University of Pittsburgh School of Law.

Landmark Supreme Court Cases (www.streetlaw.org/en/landmark/home)
Site developed to provide teachers with resources and activities to support the teaching of landmark Supreme Court cases.

Law.com (www.law.com/)
A daily news website for practicing lawyers, with search.

Media Law Resource Center (www.medialaw.org/)
A non-profit information clearinghouse originally organized by a number of media organizations to monitor developments and promote First Amendment rights in the libel, privacy, and related legal fields. The "Hot Topics" section is especially useful.

Politech (www.politechbot.com/)
A blog by Declan McCullagh, an investigative journalist with *Wired* magazine. Topics include privacy, free speech, the role of government and corporations, antitrust, and more.

Privacy.org (www.privacy.org/)
A site for news and policy developments in the area of privacy. The page is a joint project of the Electronic Privacy Information Center and Privacy International.

The Privacy Place (http://theprivacyplace.org/)
Site for news on privacy-related policy developments.

***Privacy Times* (www.privacytimes.com/)**
A subscription-only newsletter covering privacy and freedom of information law and policy; it is primarily for attorneys and professionals.

Reporters Committee for Freedom of the Press (www.rcfp.org/)
A nonprofit organization dedicated to providing free legal assistance to journalists since 1970. Excellent source of news on free speech issues.

University of Iowa Library's Communication and Media Law Resources (http://bailiwick.lib.uiowa.edu/journalism/mediaLaw/index.html)
The content here is precisely what the name suggests. Excellent search functionality by topic.

U.S. Copyright Office (www.copyright.gov/)
The Copyright Office advises Congress on anticipated changes in U.S. copyright law; analyzes and assists in the drafting of copyright legislation and legislative reports, and provides and undertakes studies for Congress; offers advice to Congress on compliance with international agreements and is where claims to copyright are registered. This site has links to copyright law, international copyright treaties, general information, and copyright studies.

U.S. Supreme Court Blog (www.scotusblog.com/)
A surprisingly lively, very current blog and website, richly sourced with links to primary source documents such as briefs and precedent cases.

▶ **REFERENCES**

Andre Bacard, *The Computer Privacy Handbook* (Berkeley, CA: Peachpit Press, 1995).

David Banisar and Simon Davies, *Privacy and Human Rights 2000: An International Survey of Privacy Laws and Developments* (Washington, DC: EPIC, 1999).

Michael Barbaro, "Target Tells a Blogger to Go Away," *The New York Times*, January 28 (2008), www.nytimes.com/2008/01/28/business/media/28target.html.

Committee of Concerned Journalists, "Reporting Tips from Pulitzer Winners," *Project for Excellence in Journalism*, July 29 (2006), www.concernedjournalists.org/reporting-tips-pulitzer-winners1.

Samuel Dash, *Unreasonable Searches and Seizures from King John to John Ashcroft* (Piscataway, NJ: Rutgers University Press, 2004).

Paul Farhi, "In the Tank?," *American Journalism Review*, May/June (2008), www.ajr.org/Article.asp?id=4516.

Samuel Friedman, *Guarding Life's Dark Secrets: Legal and Social Controls over Reputation, Propriety, and Privacy* (Palo Alto, CA: Stanford University Press, 2007).

Anita B. Frohlich, "Copyright Infringement in the Internet Age: Primetime for Harmonized Conflict of Law Rules?," *Berkeley Technology Law Journal* 24, no. 51 (2009).

Simson Garfinkel, *Database Nation: The Death of Privacy in the 21st Century* (Boston, MA: O'Reilly & Associates, 2000).

Nathaniel Gleicher, "John Doe Subpoenas: Toward a Consistent Legal Standard," *Yale Law Journal* 118 (2008): 320, 330.

Karen Alexander Horowitz, "When is § 230 Immunity Lost? The Transformation from Website Owner to Information Content Provider," *Shidler Journal of Law, Communication and Technology* 3, no. 14 (April 6, 2007), www.lctjournal.washington.edu/Vol3/a014Horowitz.html.

Charles Jennings, Lori Fena, and Esther Dyson, *The Hundredth Window: Protecting Your Privacy and Security in the Age of the Internet* (New York, NY: Free Press, 2000).

Lawrence Lessig, *Code and Other Laws of Cyberspace* (New York, NY: Basic Books, 1999).

Kembrew McLeod, *Freedom of Expression®: Overzealous Copyright Bozos and Other Enemies of Creativity* (New York, NY: Doubleday, 2005).

Steven Nock, *The Costs of Privacy* (Hawthorne, NY: Aldine de Gruyter, 1993).

Ashley Packard, "Wired But Mired: Legal System Inconsistencies Puzzle International Internet Publishers," *Journal of International Media and Entertainment Law* 57 (2007).

Jeffrey Rosen, *The Naked Crowd: Reclaiming Security and Freedom in an Anxious Age* (New York, NY: Random House, 2004).

Daniel J. Solove, *The Digital Person: Technology and Privacy in the Information Age* (New York, NY: New York University Press, 2004).

Peter P. Swire, "Elephants and Mice Revisited: Law and Choice of Law on the Internet," *University of Pennsylvania Law Review* 153 (2005): 175.

Ben Worthen, "Best of the Business Tech Blog," *The Wall Street Journal*, June 3 (2008): B6.

Appendix A
The Core Values of Digital Journalism

Free press can, of course, be good or bad, but, most certainly without freedom, the press will never be anything but bad.

Albert Camus, French novelist, essayist, and dramatist

Were it left to me to decide whether we should have a government without newspapers, or newspapers without a government, I should not hesitate a moment to prefer the latter.

Thomas Jefferson

Presented here are definitions and descriptions of the core values of journalism, values that are essential regardless of medium. These values include **accuracy**, **reasonableness**, **transparency**, **fairness**, and **independence**.

▶ JOURNALISM VALUE 1: ACCURACY

Without accuracy, what would be the point of journalism? The Society of Professional Journalists' Code of Ethics instructs journalists to maximize truth and minimize harm, making accuracy the starting point for good journalism. Get the facts, check and double-check them, then report with enough contextualization that the collection of facts can tell a truth, if not the truth. Here is an accuracy tip sheet abstracted from the Knight Citizen News Network, an initiative of J-Lab: the Institute for Interactive Journalism.

Before Writing

1. Routinize your work. The best way to maintain accuracy is to develop a system and stick to it.

2. Take time to read back to an interviewee the spelling of his or her name. If you need an age, ask for a birth date and year.

3. Avoid using secondary sources to verify facts.

4. If you have to use secondary sources, find at least two and make sure they agree independently; don't simply ask one to confirm what the other said.

5. Verify phone/fax numbers, web and email addresses. Plug the URL (web address) into a browser to make sure it works. Call the phone number.

While Writing

1. Identify sources. Readers need to know where the information came from so they can judge for themselves its credibility. Online has put an even higher premium on this kind of transparency.

2. Do not confuse opinions with facts. Opinions make personal journalism lively, but make it clear to readers. It is easy to jump to conclusions when you are predisposed to believe something.

After Writing

1. Leave fact-checking and editing for last. For a thorough copyedit, print out the content. spell-check your work. Read it backwards. Read the copy out loud. Try to see both the forest and the trees, so always read (at least) once for content and effect. Read (at least) once for the mechanical errors, including those of grammar, punctuation, and keystroke errors. And remember, errors often come with friends. Find one? Keep looking. There may be others.

2. Proof-read corrections for readability because error can be introduced even when correcting copy.

3. Assemble all source materials—notebooks, interview transcripts, tapes, books, studies, photos, everything used to report and write the story. Go over the story and compare it to the original sources. On projects and even on daily stories, some reporters make one printout for names and titles, another for quotes, a third for other details.

4. Fact-check. Many magazines use professional fact-checkers, and they still manage to make mistakes.

5. Call sources back and double-check key facts. When describing a financial transaction, a medical procedure, or how a sewer bond works, there's nothing wrong with calling the source and asking him or her to listen to what you've written. Editors at *The Oregonian* in Portland concluded that the three most frequent sources of error are working from memory, making assumptions, and dealing with second-hand sources. Avoid these whenever possible.

We should not rely on another person's figures. Do the math. If challenged by the complexity of the math or statistics or, say, how a survey was conducted (confidence level, margin of error, sample size, etc.), get some help. Do not pass along information you do not understand yourself, words of advice valid for much more than simply math.

Word processing has created great efficiencies. It has also made it a lot easier to leave off identifying information on first reference. Moving paragraphs around often results in a second or third reference becoming the first, so make sure you have full name and title on that first reference.

Check maps when providing geographic information, including routes and locations. Be careful with city and county names. The city of New York is in the county of New York, which is, in turn, in the state of New York.

Check for balance. Are the major perspectives or voices or points of view represented in the story? This is the Rule of Fair Comment, and it is aimed at avoiding one-sided or one-source stories, which are incomplete and, therefore, inaccurate. Talk to as many people as possible, even circling back and speaking again with previous sources after learning more from subsequent ones. Try not to allow the first source you speak with to frame the entire story.

Do your research. Read archived material on the topic. This important background material can provide corroboration for names and titles, and it can help you to avoid misassumptions. It can also help spot inconsistencies and contradictions. With Lexis Nexis Academic and other online databases, checking the archives has never been easier.

▶ JOURNALISM VALUE 2: REASONABLENESS

Web content that exhibits reasonableness will be even handed and will incorporate as many perspectives as is possible. In other words, the information will have no obvious conflicts of interest, or it will clearly acknowledge where potential conflicts might exist. The information will be consistent in presenting the facts and will clearly identify opinion when and where it is such. Here are a few questions to check a story's reasonableness: Is the article offering a balanced, reasoned presentation that incorporates the many sides of an issue or question or topic rather than one that is selective or slanted? Is the tone calm and reasonable? "Everyone in City Hall is a thief," for example, clearly lacks reasonableness, as well as plausibility. Check also for severe language ("Anyone who believes otherwise has no basic human decency") and sweeping generalizations ("This is the most important idea ever conceived!").

▶ JOURNALISM VALUE 3: TRANSPARENCY

Chapter 2 described disclosure and transparency, which are crucial to establishing and maintaining credibility online. Blog readers, especially, want to know our motives, our experience and expertise, our background, and, especially, any financial interest we have in the publication or dissemination of the story or article. So reporters and writers should be up front with this information. In addition, linking to source materials, providing brief biographical information somewhere on the page or site, and triangulating facts, figures, and data can communicate thoroughness and transparency. Make it easy to be contacted, document your source material, and include however parenthetically any tie to or interest in these sources you might have. Readers will wonder:

- ▶ Where did the information come from?

- ▶ What sources did the creator use?

- ▶ How well is the information supported? Even if it is opinion, a sound argument will probably have other people who agree with it.

Corroboration uses information to test information. It is most important in cases where information is surprising or counterintuitive.

Transparency is needed in disclosing motives and potential conflicts of interest, and biases and subjective approaches should likewise be acknowledged. Transparency of process also contributes to credibility, which has to do with linking to documents, sources, and supporting evidence. This transparency of process also serves to place the individual post or article in the collective, connective tissue of the online information space.

Transparency should also be the goal when things go wrong. When mistakes are made, publish an apology, take responsibility, and correct the mistake. In addition to correcting the record, this kind of transparency shows that we all are human and that we are interdependent. We demand transparency in the institutions and organizations we cover; it only makes sense to offer that same transparency of process and product to readers.

▶ JOURNALISM VALUE 4: FAIRNESS

How many sides to an issue are there? Two? Think again. There are likely hundreds. Are your accounts providing as many of these perspectives as possible? What does balance look like in your story? Have you slanted the facts, or selectively, disingenuously included only certain ones to make a point? If you are attacking someone or a perspective, are you including different viewpoints? Are you giving the subject an opportunity to respond?

Balance and fairness are not about giving "equal weight to two sides." They have more to do with incorporating several different perspectives and giving relative weight to those different perspectives. An exposé on the toxic waste dumping practices of an industrial manufacturer should not strive to give the company's public relations officers equal time or space to tout the wonderful things the company is doing in the community. Balance and fairness are a bit more complicated than that. While giving the polluter an opportunity to respond, the story should maximize truth and minimize harm.

"Take readers to the margins and extremes, but do not dwell there at the exclusion of the 'middle'—report on ambiguity, consensus and ambivalence," the American Society of Newspaper Editors (ASNE) states. Understand that communities have many different layers and dimensions, and that we need to move between and within them to capture the mosaic of voices, viewpoints, events, problems, and solutions that exist.

Balance and fairness also strive to reflect a community's diversity and wholeness, which will include, according to the ASNE, "the good, the bad and the profoundly ordinary." The ASNE also recommends that writers and reporters:

▶ Look beyond conflicts to explore underlying issues and perspectives—this will help to engage people and create a greater sense of possibility.

▶ Avoid falsely creating or over-presenting "sides" or points of view where they don't exist.

▶ Step back and reflect on the patterns within news coverage and communities— provide balance over time, not just on a day-to-day basis.

▶ JOURNALISM VALUE 5: INDEPENDENCE

Ideally, we have no conflicts of interest when reporting, writing, and publishing, because the "watchdog" responsibility of journalists requires independence. To hold the powerful accountable and cast the first stone requires an independence and purity of motive that only independence can produce. Independence is at the heart of journalism's essential role in a self-governing democracy, and it sets a standard for professionalism and ethical behavior. This value calls for us to guard and defend the role of a free press and to give a voice to as many perspectives as possible without favor and without being unduly influenced by anyone. Independence means avoiding membership in, and associations with, any group or individual who could compromise our integrity or credibility before our readers.

The Society of Professional Journalists (SPJ) built upon this language when it revised its code of ethics in the mid-1990s. The SPJ's "Act Independently" principle includes the following: "Journalists should be free of obligation to any interest other than the public's right to know." The code also states that journalists should:

▶ Avoid conflicts of interest, real or perceived.

▶ Remain free of associations and activities that may compromise integrity or damage credibility.

▶ Refuse gifts, favors, fees, free travel, and special treatment, and shun secondary employment, political involvement, public office, and service in community organizations if they compromise journalistic integrity.

▶ Disclose unavoidable conflicts.

▶ Be vigilant and courageous about holding those with power accountable.

▶ Deny favored treatment to advertisers and special interests and resist their pressure to influence news coverage.

▶ Be wary of sources offering information for favors or money; avoid bidding for news.

These are guidelines, not absolute rules. They do not preclude tough calls, particularly when one or more of these imperatives are in tension with one another. In those situations, it helps to have a collaborative decision-making environment and a process of ethical decision-making already in place.

▶ ONLINE NEWS ASSOCIATION

These core journalism values are reflected in the mission and vision statement of the Online News Association (ONA), which is composed largely of professional online journalists. The sssociation has more than 1,200 professional members whose principal livelihood involves gathering or producing news for digital presentation. Here is the association's vision statement, reprinted with permission:

> ONA is a leader in the rapidly changing world of journalism; a catalyst for innovation in story-telling across all platforms; a resource for journalists seeking guidance and growth, and a champion of best practices through training, awards and community outreach.

> OUR VALUES:

> We believe that the Internet is the most powerful communications medium to arise since the dawn of television. As digital delivery systems become the primary source of news for a growing segment of the world's population, it presents complex challenges and opportunities for journalists as well as the news audience.

> Editorial Integrity: The unique permeability of digital publications allows for the linking and joining of information resources of all kinds as intimately as if they were published by a single organization. Responsible journalism through this medium means that the distinction between news and other information must always be clear, so that individuals can readily distinguish independent editorial information from paid promotional information and other non-news.

> Editorial Independence: Online journalists should maintain the highest principles of fairness, accuracy, objectivity and responsible independent reporting.

> Journalistic Excellence: Online journalists should uphold traditional high principles in reporting original news for the Internet and in reviewing and corroborating information from other sources.

> Freedom of Expression: The ubiquity and global reach of information published on the Internet offers new information and educational resources to a worldwide audience, access to which must be unrestricted.

> Freedom of Access: News organizations reporting on the Internet must be afforded access to information and events equal to that enjoyed by other news organizations in order to further freedom of information.

▶ REFERENCES

John Bender, Lucinda Davenport, Michael Drager, and Fred Fedler, *Reporting for the Media* (Oxford, UK: Oxford University Press, 2001).

Bonnie Bressers, "Getting a Fix on Online Corrections" (Columbia, MO: ASNE, 2001), www.asne.org/kiosk/editor/01.march/bressers1.htm.

Mark Briggs, *Journalism 2.0* (Washington, DC: Knight Citizen Journalism Network, 2007), www.kcnn.org/resources/journalism_20/.

Brian Carroll, "Culture Clash: Journalism and the Communal Ethos of the Blogosphere," *Into the Blogosphere* (Minneapolis, MN: University of Minnesota, 2003), http://blog.lib.umn.edu/blogosphere/culture_clash_journalism_and_the_communal_ethos_of_the_blogosphere.html.

Bob Haiman, "Best Practices for Newspaper Journalists" (Arlington, VA: Freedom Forum, 2000), www.freedomforum.org/publications/diversity/bestpractices/bestpractices.pdf.

Knight Community News Network, "Principals of Citizen Journalism" (Washington, DC: J-Lab), www.kcnn.org/principals.

C. Max Magee, *The Roles of Online Journalists* (Chicago, IL: Medill School of Journalism, 2006).

The New York Times Ethical Journalism Handbook (September 2004), www.nytco.com/pdf/NYT_Ethical_Journalism_0904.pdf.

Poynter Guide to Accuracy, www.poynter.org/content/content_view.asp?id=36518.

Tom Rosenstiel and Bill Kovach, *The Elements of Journalism* (New York, NY: Three Rivers Press, 2007).

Appendix B
Freelance Writer Pay Rates

One of, if not *the* most frequently asked questions about freelancing, is how much to charge or expect to be paid. What follows are some estimates and best guesses, but it's important to remember that there is little uniformity. It will depend upon, among other variables, the circulation or reach of the publication, the sophistication or specialization of the subject, the experience of the writer, and often simply the needs and whims of the publication. That said, here are some guidelines for pay:

- ▶ Hourly rates: US$55 to $85.

- ▶ Per word: 5 cents to US$1.50.

- ▶ Flat fee per article:
  - ▷ 250–300 words: US$250;
  - ▷ 500–600 words: US$400;
  - ▷ 600–900 words: US$800;
  - ▷ 1,000–1,500 words: US$900;
  - ▷ 2,000–3,000 words: US$1,200–1,500.

Another schematic for pay, for feature stories:

- ▶ Simple, single-dimension stories that require a few phone calls, emails, or interviews: around US$100.

- ▶ Medium-complexity feature stories, requiring a number of telephone calls, emails, or interviews: around US$150.

- ▶ Complex feature stories, requiring special research and knowledge, and a number of telephone calls, emails, or interviews: US$150–$200.

- ▶ Sidebars of approximately 250 words written in story form and accompanying a larger feature: US$50–$100.

Index